a voice
in the
wilderness

a voice in the wilderness

Edited By David Porter

OM
publishing

ESWICK
MINISTRY

First published 1997 by OM Publishing

02 01 00 99 98 97 7 6 5 4 3 2 1

OM Publishing is an imprint of Paternoster Publishing,
P.O. Box 300, Carlisle, Cumbria, CA3 0QS, UK.

British Library Cataloguing in Publication Data

A catalogue record for this book is available from
the British Library

ISBN 1-85078-285-7

Typeset by David Porter Text & Editorial
Greatham, Hampshire
and printed in the UK by Mackays of Chatham PLC, Kent

CONTENTS

THE ADDRESSES

'A Voice in the Wilderness'

Introduction by Jonathan Lamb, Chairman of the 1997 Keswick Convention

We Christians naturally think of the Holy Spirit's ministry as comforting. He is the one called alongside to encourage us. But frequently the work of the Comforter is to disturb. His ministry will make us uncomfortable.

No-one listening with an open heart and mind to expositions of Malachi, Jeremiah, James and the Beatitudes can avoid the Spirit's disturbing ministry, challenging one's assumptions and values. Prophets like these are usually unwelcome guests at religious gatherings. They upset the status quo. They have an unnerving tendency to expose hypocrisy. For an audience at the end of the twentieth century these prophets will go for the jugular and have no patience with religious fakes.

The overwhelming impression I had in Keswick in the summer of 1997 was of a congregation of thousands hungry for God's word, ready to face the uncomfortable truth that the Scriptures brought to us. The theme of the Convention pointed to the demanding challenge of being God's people in God's world—to be a voice in the wilderness—and this message is reflected in the pages that follow. The penetrating teaching of James and Jeremiah, the directness of Malachi, and the radical teaching of Jesus Himself all point to the importance of standing up for truth against prevailing cultural trends, and living a life of consistency and integrity whatever the cost.

There is no doubt that we experienced the encouragement and comfort of the Spirit's ministry too, and hearing God's word in fellowship with thousands of other believers from around the world was one aspect of that. But the real danger for any Christian Conference is when it becomes an end in itself, cosy and insular, reinforcing prejudices and affirming complacency. That was not the purpose of the two weeks of the Convention—its real impact needs to be measured in terms of changed lives and changed churches, and in the impact we hearers make on the society in which we live. James is famous for stressing the importance of doing, not simply hearing. This book is therefore a further contribution to that end, and I hope that in its pages you will capture something of the disturbing as well as the comforting ministry of God's Spirit through His word.

On behalf of the Convention I would want to express our thanks to all of the speakers, who were faithful to demanding sections of Scripture and relevant and contemporary in their application; and also to David Porter who has once again provided the careful editing of this selection of the summer's preaching, and to his wife Tricia who transcribed some 115,000 words of spoken ministry.

I hope you will enjoy the read, with all of its demanding provocation, and that it will help you in some way to be God's voice in the wilderness of our secular society.

Jonathan Lamb
Chairman of the Keswick Convention Council

Editor's Introduction

Readers familiar with the annual Keswick volume will find that the method is the same as always; I have attempted to retain the flavour of the spoken occasion, and as usual the speakers have graciously waived the right to scrutinise the edited and abridged text, though a member of the Keswick Council has read the book before publication on their behalf. This means that we are able to get the book to you in time for Christmas.

Reluctantly, much is omitted. Many excellent and provocative illustrations did not make it to the printed page, and some illuminating asides and very funny anecdotes had to be left behind. I have, however, included every reference to Scripture, even if some have had to be judiciously shortened. Consequently an open Bible will prove a valuable reading companion. For the parts I had to leave out, the inimitable sound of the preacher's voices and the addresses that could not be included, I recommend the excellent tape and video libraries (see p.255).

In the text, pronouns referring to the Persons of the Godhead are capitalised, but not in quotations from the Bible. This should be helpful in distinguishing between quotations and paraphrases: the latter are also usually identified by 'cf' in the reference.

I would like to thank my wife Tricia, who once again has typed brilliantly for much of the summer, transcribing Keswick tapes; and Nigel Halliday, who gave the final text a professional and thorough scrutiny. Those who over the years have watched the Porters' investment in technology play an increasingly prominent role in the annual volume will be interested to know that this year's volume was entirely produced by myself and Tricia, and typeset using PagePlus 5.0, Word 97 and a Hewlett-Packard 6MP Postscript laser printer.

David Porter

'Living What You Believe'
Studies in the Letter of James
by Bishop Michael Baughen

1 : 'Whenever You Face Trials' (James 1:1-8)

Introduction to the letter and its background

When you eat in the House of Lords and you haven't any guests, the rule is that you sit at a long table in the first available seat. You don't know who you'll be sitting next to and you can't choose. It's always a stimulating experience!

James is not someone I would choose to go and sit next to. He's uncomfortable. And yet, like a lot of those people at the dinner table, he is stimulating and challenging. He's not comfortable, he's very earnest, he's morally strong, he has a great concern for the poor and the oppressed, he has a straight preaching style, he doesn't pull his punches. And most of all he exposes our double standards. What he expects is consistent Christianity.

So who is James? Commentaries and Bible dictionaries discuss this at length. James son of Alphaeus? No, he disappeared without trace. James the brother of John? He was martyred in AD 44, so it's extremely unlikely it is him, because that's too early. Is it some other person, pretending to be James the Lord's brother? If it were, he'd have claimed, 'I'm James, the Lord's brother.' The fact is, he was able to introduce himself simply as 'James'. In the Acts of the Apostles there's only one James who really stands out: James the Lord's brother. I'm sure that he is the author.

He emerges in the Acts of the Apostles in the most extraordinary way. He was the leader of the Jerusalem church. When Peter got out of prison so remarkably (Acts 12) he

told those who had been praying to go and tell 'James and
the brothers'. At the Council of Jerusalem (Acts 15) it is of
course James who presides and sums up brilliantly. In Acts
21, when Paul goes to Jerusalem, he goes to see 'James and
the elders who were present'. Paul in Galatians 2 describes
this James, with Peter and John, as one of the pillars of the
church (Gal. 2:9). But have you ever thought, how did it
happen? This is James, the Lord's brother—part of the
family that didn't believe in Him: (John 7:5). Yet they lived
with Him. He was their oldest brother. They'd been
around in that home for years and years, they'd laughed,
teased each other, walked together and had family events
and did all the things families do. Then suddenly their
brother became a prophet claiming to be the Son of God. It
took some getting used to! Yet they were still around, because in John 7 at one point they asked, 'Are you coming
with us?' and He said, 'No, I'll come up later.' They still
expected to travel as a family even when He, our Lord, was
preaching. So what happened?

One of our sons is a listener. When we were at All Souls
Langham Place, you couldn't see him in church. He'd disappear up the back staircase somewhere, but he was there.
When in his later teens he came to a personal faith, with it
came a huge understanding of the Christian faith far in
advance of the rest of the family. He had absorbed it for
years, listening. Then suddenly, as a convert, wham! You
didn't need an Alpha Course or a Beta or a Gamma
Course—he was there. James, I think, was like that. He
was on the edge of the crowd, and he'd absorbed it, such
that his writing is intelligent Greek with Hellenic ideas. He
was the sort of person who reads encyclopaedias.

Our Lord didn't press him until the Resurrection; 1
Corinthians 15:7, 'He appeared to James.' He waited till
James was ready and appeared to him. That clinched it.
Before you knew where you were, James was the leader of
the Jerusalem church, with a huge influence through the
Acts of the Apostles, and I believe, this letter. He became a
giant overnight.

There's one particularly important thing to understand about James before we get into the letter. You probably know that Luther described it as 'an epistle of straw', because it didn't say very much about Jesus or about the cross. But while we're used to hearing Paul talking about Jesus, James actually stands alongside his brother. We have to understand that when we hear James, we are hearing the Sermon on the Mount in action. There are thirty-six direct references in James to our Lord's teaching, possibly more—some people find sixty. What did He say when He sent the seventy-two out? 'He who hears you hears Me.' In the same way James is not saying, 'There is Jesus,' but is standing alongside Him, speaking as Jesus. He did so out of an understanding of the back streets of Jerusalem, an understanding of poverty and need, and a great burning sense of justice, like many people today. And suddenly, it all comes into action. It's been said that words of Jesus drop out of James freely and spontaneously; he's so absorbed them that they are part of his very thinking. Is that true of you? Do you speak as Jesus would speak in a situation? James was soaked in Scripture, so he thought and acted the Scripture of his brother, his Lord.

All this is background to this letter written in the midst of the persecution that came all through the Acts and later. It came in Jerusalem, a city where the Zealots were rising up, encouraging the people to resort to violence in order to rid themselves of the Romans. Many people were fed up with living under oppression, and they began to listen to them. There was massive taxation, oppression of the poor by the rich (including the Jewish rich), much suffering, and people losing their lands because of the moneyed landowners. It all depended where you lived. If you lived in poverty, you lived on the downside of the sewers where the wind blew the stink over you, and if you were rich you lived the other side. James, as the leader of the church in Jerusalem, was implicated in these struggles. It's a matter of burning importance to him. He preaches restraint and the need for wisdom, faith, endurance and patience. Yet in no sense is he a wimp about his righteous concerns. So he's like a convert into our own churches who wasn't brought up with all the right language and experience. He comes in differently, freshly, powerfully challenging us. And if we are prepared to let him, he will comfort us this morning, but he'll discomfort us for the rest of the week.

The greeting and its significance

James describes himself as 'a servant of God'. That's a marvellous title. Would you accept that for yourself? 'But,' you might say, 'Jesus said, "I don't call you servants, I call you friends."' Exactly! We take on the role of servants as His friends. Someone got very angry after I preached on Paul as the slave of Christ one night at All Souls. He grabbed me by the lapels and said, 'I will never be called the slave of Christ, I'm the child of God by grace.' I said, 'Of course you are. And so am I. But if you know the epistle to the Romans, you'll know that in Romans 12:1, after all the exposition of grace, Paul says, "I urge you to offer your bodies as living sacrifices." You volunteer as a servant, because you are a child of grace.'

So he speaks of himself as a servant, like Moses did and Jacob (James is the Greek form of Jacob). Here was someone who had a great sense of being there to serve God. I hope you have that sense that by grace you've been saved and you live to serve Him. 'I am a servant of God.'

But look what he says next: 'and of the Lord Jesus Christ'. This is quite a leap from the brother in whom he didn't believe. He can now speak of Him in that supreme phrase, *kyrios*—'Jesus is Lord', the confession of Romans and of the New Testament. 'No-one can say "Jesus is Lord" except by the Holy Spirit' ... 'Come, Lord Jesus'. At St Ebbs in Oxford I was confirming a group of undergraduates. I asked each of them the question, 'What did Jesus mean to you before?' They all said, 'Nothing. He was irrelevant, just a human being.' Out there in the world, Jesus is nothing. It's only when the Spirit of God opens your eyes you see He is Lord. The Spirit of God had opened James's eyes. 'Jesus is Lord, my Lord, the Lord Jesus Christ.' This wonderful description comes later in other ways, to show how much he loves Him.

'To the twelve tribes scattered among the nations'—a strange phrase. It's resembles Peter's, 'To God's elect, strangers in the world, scattered through Pontus, Galatia ...' (1 Pet. 1:1). The chosen people of God have been scattered by persecution, and he comes to encourage, steady and lead them in this responsible position that he holds, as people of God under oppression.

And then comes 'Greetings'. The word means 'joy to you'. A lovely phrase! Try it on your neighbour afterwards, 'Joy to you'. And that aspect of the greeting is going to come out in the epistle itself.

The best for God

James is a preacher. I began to study him for the first time a year or so ago. I read this epistle a dozen times and still couldn't get to grips with it. It's partly like a preacher's notes, or a lot of sermons cobbled together. And yet, to a large extent, this makes it a vivid, challenging tract which keeps coming back to the same themes but from different angles, and punching the point home like any good preacher. Verse 4 speaks particularly about maturity—'that you may be mature and complete'—and that, I think, underlies all that he says right through the letter. He says it in different ways, and it's forged in the heat of trials and problems and under suffering, just as today he might write in Northern Ireland or in Rwanda, or persecuted in an Islamic country, or suffering personally in his own life.

James is not content with second-best for God. Are you? What does God get from us, first or second? Are we content with 'That'll do,' or are we the people who want to bring the best? Remember Cain and Abel. Do we just bring along an offering, or do we want the best for God? God only accepts the best. The rest is rejected. We might as well save our breath. How important it is that we apply those standards to what we do! When I watch athletes training, getting up morning after morning to improve, and then I think how many Christians couldn't be bothered even to open their Bible this morning, I say, 'Just a minute; do you want to be the best for God, or not?'

I read once that Paul Daniels, the TV conjuror, went when young on a six-week sea voyage to Singapore. He was having great difficulty in learning a new trick: making a half-crown coin vanish from his hand. For five weeks he struggled, then with just a week to go he decided to practise the trick over the side of the ship. It sharpened his mind wonderfully, because he didn't want to lose the half-crown! By the end of the trip he had mastered the trick for life. I thought, what about as a Christian striving—in music or in speaking, in pastoring or training, even in being trained oneself—to be the very best with the gifts God has given you? James was not content with second-best.

Eight ways to mature in trials and testing

Let us look at eight ways to become mature that James shows us in this passage.

Rejoice (verse 2)

What a start! Nothing stuns the unbeliever more than seeing a Christian able to have joy in the midst of suffering. It's different to happy-clappiness. It's not a matter of 'Hallelujah anyway'. It's something very deep within, that is there regardless of the circumstances.

There wasn't a lot of joy in the Jewish tradition. Bits came through in the Old Testament, like Habakkuk's 'Though the fig-tree does not bud .... and the fields produce no food ... yet I will rejoice in the Lord, I will be joyful in God my Saviour' (Hab. 3:17-18). And when we come to the New Testament, in particular we find James challenging us in the same way as his brother, his Lord, did. In John 16, for instance, when He says, 'No-one will take away your joy' (16:22)—come on, what's the context?

Suffering. They may hurt you, they may persecute you, they may kill you, but no-one can take away your joy. Is that true? Do you have that reservoir underneath, however much the storms rage above? It's a wonderful thing. 'Ask … and your joy will be complete,' He says (verse 24), but the context is that of suffering.

Now, my friends, let me suggest to you four sub-aspects of joy.

First, it is *an anchor*. In Luke 10, when the seventy-two were sent out on the mission, they came back and said, 'That was terrific! It was far better than You actually said it was going to be! This happened, that happened, the other happened.' Do you remember, our Lord said, 'Don't rejoice in this. Rejoice that your names are written in heaven.' That's a tremendous lesson for ministry. When I was first ordained in Nottingham I used to have a club on Saturday and Sunday nights. It was up and down, up and down. At the end of the year, I felt, 'I can't do this.' Until this text spoke to me. If you are geared to circumstances as success or failure, you're going to be zooming up and down in the Christian life. But if you are geared to the thing that can never ever change, your name is written in heaven; your joy will be full, underneath, all the time. So you can have joy in the midst of suffering. This is the anchor to the soul, which our Lord intended it to be.

Secondly, there's *assurance*. 'Blessed are you when people insult you, persecute you … Rejoice and be glad, because great is your reward in heaven,' said Jesus (Matt. 5:11-12). And how often that has had to be something deep within my own heart, particularly as a bishop. When I've been kicked and knocked and gone through all sorts of things, I've had to come back to the fact that the Lord knows the truth even if the newspapers don't. And it's the cause of joy, even though the newspapers are a cause of pain.

Thirdly, there's *'always'*. You know the text: Philippians 4:4. 'Rejoice in the Lord always'—and just in case you haven't got it firmly in your minds, 'I will say it again: Rejoice!' It's as if he is saying, 'You name anything that can happen, you still have a joy that no-one can take from you.' That's a wonderful thing. My wife Myrtle and I had that text in our early days of ministry; we made it our marriage text for all our life. We went through a lot. Myrtle was seven times in hospital in our first curacy. And as the ambulance bell got nearer, we got used to claiming that text as we prayed, 'Rejoice in the Lord always.' It's been a very precious text to us.

Fourthly, the *advance* of the gospel. Perseverance is the result of this joy (verse 3). But it does advance the gospel. 'In this,' says Peter, 'you greatly rejoice'—(1 Pet. 1:6), and that's the sufferings. 'You may have had to suffer grief in many kinds of trials ... so that your faith ... may be proved genuine.' So in many ways there is a joy; that even in this very testing which is very uncomfortable, I am growing. Thank you, Lord! Hallelujah.

So there are four things in the midst of—what sort of joy? Well, it says any joy: 'nothing but joy' is the underlying translation. Every kind of joy, and every kind of circumstance. It doesn't have to be restricted; you can have any joy, because it's all there whatever the circumstance is. And notice, James says, 'Consider it ...'. That means it's got to be (and the Greek confirms it) a settled conviction. In a sense you need that settled conviction before you hit the problems. If you've worked it out and thought it through, even though it's rough when you hit the problems or they hit you, and you are thrown amidships by circumstances, you are going to trust in the Lord to that degree. Regardless of circumstance, you are more able to meet it. If you haven't done that prior considering, you are knocked for six and it takes some time to get back to where you were.

So it's a conviction. And in trials of many kinds, the things that befall you, the troubles, the problems, the difficulties of the world—it's a wonderful text. 'You know,' James says in verse 3, 'you know ...'. There is a conviction that comes out of it all. You are absolutely convinced— when you've thought about it, you've seen and examined it,

you've got it between you and your God—you know that it
is going to produce results. Thank you, Lord! So rejoice.

Persevere (verses 3-4)

'You know that the testing of your faith develops perseverance. Perseverance must finish its work so that you may be
mature and complete, not lacking anything.' That's one of
the great things, isn't it, about such things as trials; they do
act as something that helps us to grow. Paul says, 'We also
rejoice in our sufferings, because we know that suffering
produces perseverance; perseverance, character; and character, hope. And hope does not disappoint us, because God
has poured out his love into our hearts by the Holy Spirit'
(Rom. 5:3-5). So it's the same for Paul and for James, this
great sense that perseverance is a productive arena in which
we grow. Trials test faith, as it indicates here in verse 3, 'the
testing of your faith'. Of course they do. If you're not ready
for it they can throw you to pieces. 'Why has this happened
to me?' How often have I heard that down through the
years? 'I've been going to church all my life. Why has this
happened to me?' Because you are a Christian, are you
never going to have any problems or illnesses? If so, becoming a Christian would save on health insurance!

That's not true of the world. We share in it. What matters is how we meet trials—God with us. But none the less
they do test us. They test us to grow. When I was a boy I
was taken to a steel mill and shown the testing of a steel
bar. The machine tested it until it broke, to find its breaking point under tension. But God does not test us to break
us; He tests us to strengthen us. Isn't that so? 'You may
have had to suffer grief in all kinds of trials,' says Peter.
'These have come so that your faith ... may be proved
genuine and may result in praise, glory and honour when
Jesus Christ is revealed' (1 Pet. 1:6-6). So what is perseverance? 'Oh, I'm not going to put up with this'? Oh no, no,
no. You are a Christian! Here's Paul again. 'I'm going to
boast in my troubles, if this is the way in which the power
of God is going to be upon me' (cf 2 Cor. 12:9). Persever-

ance isn't just putting up with things. It's an active, not a passive word. It's 'All right—let's go for it!' Someone said to me last night, 'I lost my husband and three children at the age of thirty-nine. And God said, "Well—for the rest of your life, enjoy the holiday till you go home." And,' she said, 'I've tried to think positively ever since.

What is perseverance? It's courage and robustness. But, if you understand this passage, it is co-operating with God. Very often, circumstances in the Bible are things that happen to us and mould us. But James says, 'Come on, let it finish its work' (verse 4). That is a deliberate word. Perseverance is actually working on you, rather like yeast. Co-operate with it! Don't say 'Oh, this is hurting!' Say, 'Come on, Lord; I understand that this is a way in which You are moulding me. Let me co-operate with You. Let me see this and consider it, so that I may grow through this experience and become (verse 4) "mature and complete".'

Pray (verse 4-5)

Next, pray. Pray particularly for wisdom, because if you are mature and complete you don't want to lack anything: 'If any of you lacks wisdom, he should ask God, who gives generously to all without finding fault, and it will be given to him' (verse 5).

Wisdom is important. What's the difference between wisdom and outstanding courage, or perseverance, or joy? You could be in command of the Charge of the Light Brigade. You could perhaps have joy on your horse, and perseverance to gain the objective; but there wasn't much wisdom behind the people who sent men into that slaughter, any more than there was at Gallipoli, or some other battles. Wisdom is something more than courage and perseverance. It is discerning the right thing to do; it's seeing as God intends you to see.

That was Solomon's request: he asked for wisdom from God 'to distinguish between right and wrong' (1 Kings 3:9). God gave him 'wisdom and very great insight' (1 Kings 4:29); it was a gift of God. I had to learn this early on in my ministry, in the back streets of Nottingham. Several people came to faith without any educational background at all. One of them couldn't read or write, but three weeks after his conversion was answering hard questions about Christianity from his workmates; his answers were brilliant. Where did he get them from? From God. He had real wisdom after three weeks, without any education.

Wisdom is something that rides above education. How do we seek and find this wisdom? We ask for it. If you lack it, ask for it. There have been many times when, as a bishop, I have thrown myself on the floor of my study, at the end of my tether over problems that I've been facing. I've said to God, 'I've prayed, thought, acted and done everything I possibly can. I cannot see any other way of acting; please, now I have to hand everything over to You.' And in every case He acted, within weeks, within days, sometimes within hours. Once I and members of my staff at Chester said to each other, 'There is no way through this problem. Come on! Let's put the brakes on. With God there is always a way through.' So we stopped and prayed for wisdom; and then we saw the way through. Ask, ask, ask. And it will not be given you stingily, it will be given you generously. You will be stunned, it will be more than you could ask or think.

It's true of our church prayer gatherings, our personal prayer gatherings and our personal lives. When you lack wisdom, ask for it: 'Lord, we don't know.' Be honest with Him. So often this is the prayer of the New Testament. In Ephesians 1 and Colossians 1 we are encouraged to pray for fellow Christians, that they may have wisdom—it's a wonderful gift of God.

Be single-minded (verses 6-8)

When I went to theological college, I believed in prayer. But one day I saw a fellow student, whom I knew quite well, looking at the mail boxes. I asked him what he was waiting for. He replied that he had prayed for an answer to something, and he now expected the letter to come. I

thought, 'Oh—I don't think I ever prayed like that!' But
the letter arrived, it was put in the box. And I had to start
looking at what my own prayer life was like. Did I actually
expect God to answer prayer? Did I really trust Him? Was
I was single-minded? Or was I like the rather nominal Jew
with whom I'd sometimes talked? He wasn't much of a
practising Jew but he did go to the synagogue on the Day
of Atonement. When I asked him why, he said, 'Just in case
it brings me luck next year—it's better to go than not to
go.' Many people pray like that, hedging their bets; they
don't really believe He's going to answer but they pray
anyway just in case. So they don't get anywhere.

But here is faith, not in prayer but in God as God.
Prayer is not some sort of monument we erect to make God
pay attention. We don't say, 'Look, I've been standing here
for three hours—do something!' We pray because we *trust*
in the great God, that's the essential thing.

To James, faith is very much (as one person put it) the
prow and stern of his whole experience. It is a single-
minded devotion to his Lord. Where does single-
mindedness come from? Remember the Sermon on the
Mount: 'You can't serve God and mammon ... The eye is
the lamp of the body ... You cannot store up treasure in
heaven and treasure on earth ... You can't be double-
minded.' James is bringing it out in a particular way here,
but he is echoing this. You cannot have double-
mindedness. Do you remember John Bunyan's character
Mr Facing-Both-Ways? Or Augustine's famous prayer:
'Oh Lord, grant me purity—but not yet'? You can't fool
with God. Either you mean it or you don't. If you don't
mean it, then save your breath, you needn't pray. But let's
address God in faith, and of course in trust, and His own
will, not to make Him do our will. When I confirm people
as a bishop, I have to say to them, 'Do you believe and
trust?' It's a very good question. It's not just belief, it's
trust. And do you actually trust God?

So this double-mindedness of doubt in verse 6 has no
anchor to the soul, it's exposed to the ocean. I have empa-

thy with that! Sea-sickness pills, here we come! I hate it
when you are tossed about on a rough sea. Well, here is
someone thrown around in a rough sea. The only other
place where this word is used is in Luke 8, of the storm on
Lake Gennesaret. Jesus, in the middle of the storm, said
'Peace! Where is your faith?' (cf Luke 8:25). And He says it
to us: 'Where is your faith?' You are in the middle of a
storm, but if you want an anchor to the soul it's no good
bouncing with the storm and being hit by every wave in
every direction, 'blown and tossed by the wind' (verse 6)—
the very thought of it makes me reach for the sea-sickness
pills.

Many Christians are like that. You never know where
they are. But underneath, in the real Christian, there is a
single-mindedness. The storm rages, and you weep with
them, and you share with them, and they are going
through pain and difficulty. But there is a foundation in
their soul because they are single-minded people who trust
God's wisdom, His grace, His love—even though He slays
them (cf Job 13:15). Is that true of you?

Know your value (verses 9-11)

Trials and problems can be exacerbated by believing that
there's greener grass on the other side of the fence. If I lived
there … if I'd been born here … if I looked like that … if I
were a preacher … if I weren't a preacher … if I were in
that parish, or in that area …. Oh, it's dead easy, isn't it!
But God has put you where you are. Cheer up, friends—
that's where He wants you to be. And if we reckon our
value in terms of location or position ('Why have I been
overlooked?'), family circumstances, riches or poverty, we
are always going to be in a mess. That's one of the troubles
in the world, in this awful age where there's such insecurity
for so many people, and redundancy is so prevalent; it is
extremely difficult for many, many people. So if your value
lies in being in employment, you are devastated as a human being when you lose it.

We know that as believers in God, our value is as children of God. That cannot alter, whatever the circumstances. That's where the anchor has to be. We need to know that deeply; this is what really matters. So James says to the poor, 'See your high position in Christ.' It's a wonderful state. We ought to take pride in this high position. What is that? Heirs of the kingdom? Grace lavished upon you? All that is Christ is yours? Citizens of heaven? A tremendous future ahead of you? His child for ever? Ah! You've got something to rejoice about, even though the circumstances are rotten.

And to 'the one who is rich' (it doesn't actually say 'brother', notice, but perhaps 'to the one' is the same thing)—is this the non-Christian rich, the Jewish rich, rich people who have become Christians? It's not just money, but power and exploitation of other people. He says to them, in effect, 'What are you? Your life is going to pass away like a wild flower. If your trust is in your high position, you are on a very rocky foundation.'

For example, in Hebrews 10 we read those wonderful words, 'You sympathised with those in prison and joyfully accepted the confiscation of your property, because you knew that you yourselves had better and lasting possessions' (Heb. 10:34). Frankly, it's more difficult for the rich to give. In some ways it's easier to be poor (though not in other ways!) Sometimes we need to be pulled back to that. A number of years ago we went to Venice for the first time. Venice was stunning, we loved it very much indeed. But the one thing that got to me was that most of the paintings are of people in authority—soldiers, bishops, rulers and more. Actually I was just nauseated by it. So we went on to Florence. Well, there's much the same there. Except for Michelangelo's sculpture of the naked David. The lack of clothes was such a refreshing contrast; because there were no robes of authority, no trappings of great dignity that separate us so easily, though we have to wear these things so often in life. I have to, for example, in my job.

Then we went on to Albi, in the South of France, to which we were linked in Chester. There on the arch of the cathedral there is a painting ostensibly of heaven—people before heaven are underneath, and then in heaven, above. And in heaven they are all the same, they've all got white robes on. Below they are in their other clothes. And there's a great sense in which in the end, this is what we are. We are either a child of God or we are not. These positions we have to hold—and very often have to fulfil them whether we like them or not—are not in themselves what gives us value. What gives us value is our relationship to God. That is why as a bishop I've always carried a piece of towelling in my pocket, to remind myself that I am a servant first of all; that lovely title that James adopts in verse 1.

So we're saved by grace, we're children of God by grace, we are heirs of heaven by grace—that is a wonderful truth.

Keep your eye on the tape (verse 12)

Many, *many* years ago, I used to go to the hairdressers'. (My wife clips the edges now and gives me a polish. When I do television items for the BBC or ITV, they always powder my head. Which is all right—unless you forget, and walk out in the rain afterwards.)

But when I used to go to the barber's, like kids of my age in the cheaper barbers in those days, I was always sat upon a plank placed across the arms of the barber's chair. I was forever looking at everything on his shelf, and he was forever clipping me under the chin—'Head up, head up, head up ...' And now, after forty years of ministry, I have to constantly say to myself and to other people, 'Head up, head up, head up. Realise who you are. Keep your eye on the tape. "I'm a child of God, I'm running the race set before me, looking to Jesus. I want to keep the faith and finish the course."' Many people think it's the end at forty: 'Oh, my life is over, I'm forty'—fifty, sixty, seventy, eighty, whatever it happens to be, oh dear, oh dear! But Christians are still running as long as we have the strength, and after that we are certainly running inside. So isn't it a wonderful thing that James says here? 'Blessed'—it's the same word as is used in the Beatitudes—'Blessed is the man who perseveres under trial, because when he has stood the test, he will receive the crown of life ...'—it's not a matter of the crown itself but of life. The crown of living here for Jesus is life, *life*, LIFE—life to the full, life eternal, life with our Lord for ever. Wow! Wow! My favourite word—Wow!

So Paul can say, 'Think of the glory that will be revealed in us, the glorious freedom of the children of God' (cf Rom. 8:21). The negro slaves singing their spirituals could look away, and say, 'Steal away to Jesus,' even though they were suffering. They could see this great wonderful sense of all that God has prepared for those who love Him. We need to teach more about heaven; we don't teach enough about it. And it's wonderful for us to realise this. Joy breaks through here: 'Blessed are you ...'

The day I was sixty-five, I happened to have a day off and we went to some function or other, and all through it my mind kept saying, 'I'm sixty-five! I'm sixty-five!' I wanted to go out into the street and say, 'I'm sixty-five'— not that anybody else was interested at all. But why don't you leap down the street in Keswick and say, 'I'm a child of God! I'm a child of God, hallelujah, wow!'

'Blessed, blessed is the person who perseveres and has the crown of life ahead.'

Watch out for evil bait (verses 13-16)

In contrast to the spiritual life in verse 12, trials can bring spiritual death.

Many people want God or their minister to be a cushion, something one can stick pins into and blame. Or they let rip at God. People say, 'The Psalmist lets rip at God; I should let rip at God.' Yes—but where in the New Testament does anybody let rip at God, except (you may want to suggest) our Lord upon the cross, in our name, when He quotes Psalm 22? Though even then, I think that suggestion is pushing it.

Yes, in the Old Testament; because you expected if you followed God to have your quiver full of children and your field full of corn. If you didn't, you said 'I haven't got it.'

And if that's your Christianity—'I'm a Christian, therefore I want this, want that, want this, want that, and expect this to be delivered'—then you are always going to be very angry. But if you are someone who can trust God even though He slays you, then you can have a joy that cannot be taken from you. If you feel you've got to be angry with God, do so. But He is like any parent with a child; you let them pummel you but you hope they'll grow up.

So this is the flip side of the coin. Suffering either tests us and strengthens us, or it throws us into doubting, despairing and blaming. There seems to be no central path. But read Deuteronomy 8:2; it's the testing of the people of God. 'Remember how the LORD your God led you all the way in the desert these forty years, to humble you and to test you in order to know what was in your heart, whether or not you would keep his commands.' This was a way of helping, testing you that you might grow.

Evil, in this passage, is perhaps evil conditions. I get very angry when people say that crime in many of our cities has nothing to do with poor conditions. You go and live or work there, and you will think very differently indeed. It's all very nice to say it in the comfort of the House of Commons, but not when you live there.

And there are other sorts of evil. The Garden of Eden wasn't rotten conditions. The temptation was a straight temptation: not to trust the goodness of God. And we so easily fall for it; that's the trouble. The danger is that we are hooked. The word in the Greek here is 'bait'; the devil puts bait out one way or the other. If we fall for it we are hooked. And it takes a lot to unhook us, because now we are landed and dragged away. We are 'enticed' by this bait. It is sometimes by evil impulse or desire that is not of itself sin; but if we let it hook us, if we give way to it—then, O Lord, forgive us! It's just like in Psalm 1, the person to whom the blessed man is compared: 'He *walks* in the council of the wicked'—that's all right—'and he *stands* in the way of sinners'—oh, oh—and then 'he *sits* in the seat of the scornful.' They hooked him.

'Don't be deceived,' says James (verse 16). O, teenagers of today, my dear friends, watch it.

Trust the goodness of God (verses 16-18)

It's the wisdom of God to discern what is evil and what is good. In the Garden of Eden there is distrust in the goodness of God: 'You will not surely die … For God knows that when you eat of it your eyes will be opened, and you will be like God, knowing good and evil' (Gen.3:4-5). They distrusted God's goodness. Don't be deceived.

But (verse 17) God is the giver of every good and perfect gift. The smorgasbord of God's grace! Do you believe it? This is our God. All the enticement of the world and its rottenness, its darkness, its evil, its tarnishing and all the wretched stuff that's all around us—stand outside it, and see the goodness of God! 'Every good and perfect gift'— know it and believe it! He is 'the Father of the heavenly lights'. Some people say James couldn't have said that, it's a Greek concept. Goodness me, this man was reading the encyclopaedias of those days! No problem. This is a lovely phrase, 'the Father of the heavenly lights'—that is, of all creation, in a world where people tended to look at the stars as we still do today, and say, 'Look …'

Of course it's ridiculous to talk about 'the stars' in the sense of planetary influences and horoscopes. Yet people reject God these days and believe that instead. We have had the wife of a past President of the United States, and here in Britain people in the aristocracy and royalty, who are pandering to this muck, this falsity, this blasphemy to the living God—who alone is the Father of heavenly lights. In Him is no darkness at all, not even in His testing and training of us. There is no shadowy side to God. Everything He does, even when He is testing us, is to help us grow. It is in the open, it is in love, it is in grace, it is in goodness. Because this is our God, the God of goodness and love.

And now this glorious verse to end with: 'He chose to give us birth through the word of truth, that we might be a kind of firstfruits of all he created' (verse 18). What a verse. Wow! We could spend the next fifty minutes on this alone! It is through the word that the world came into existence, and through the word we are reborn: as Peter says, 'For you have been born again, not of perishable seed, but of imperishable, through the living and enduring word of God' (1 Pet. 1:23). Oh, hallelujah! Isn't that true for you? You have been born again, born again; go down the street and say it: 'I've been born again, O Lord, thank You!'

And yes, there's something else, 'that we might be the firstfruits...'. Come on; let's see it. We are to live, and pray, and work, and weep, and grow, and mature, and be more like the person Jesus wants you to be: touching this world in its pain and agony, as Jesus did Himself, and as James did with his immense courage and joy for our Lord.

God is good. God is wonderful! But God wants you and me to be more like Jesus.

2 : 'Be Changed by the Word and Consistent' James 1:19-2:13

When he says, 'My dear brothers', James is always starting a new section, and he does so this morning. This is a very practical and demanding passage. In a church where my wife and I served a long time ago there was a group of people who thought they were wonderful do-gooders. They were the sort of people who went round making a lot of noise about what they were doing; collecting money and handing it over with great trumpeting, and regarding themselves as the best people around. In fact, what they did could have been done by most Christians in about five hours. But one of these people—they were so proud of themselves, some of them!—said to me, 'We've just come back from holiday, and the sun shone the whole time. That's what the Bible says, Rector, isn't it? "The sun shines on the righteous."' He wasn't being funny! It's the nearest I've ever got to kicking a member of my congregation on the shin. James would have done so! I was able however to remind him that the Scriptures say the sun shines on the righteous and unrighteous, and the rain also falls on the good and the evil; because the rain was the blessing (cf Matt. 5:45). However, he wasn't satisfied with that.

Three warnings and exhortations (1:19-27)

We come first to the section up to the end of chapter 1. It's a tremendously challenging passage, enough for three sermons and a whole week of Bible readings.

Do not react; be changed (1:19-21)

We sit in this tent in this glorious part of the world. But go and stand on the West Bank of Jerusalem now, or stand as a Christian in an Islamic fundamentalist country; try to be a Christian in Afghanistan at the moment, try to be a

Christian in some of the appalling parts of the world where to live as one is difficult—Cambodia, for example. When we think of any of the trouble spots of the world we are coming near to the situation in Jerusalem, where there was oppression, where the aristocracy oppressed the poor, where there was Roman rule, where if you were poor and downtrodden you felt you were powerless. You needed only someone who was a rabble-rouser, such as the Zealots, to come round and say, 'Now's the time to get up and fight. Join us! We are going to win by guerrilla warfare, by killing the aristocracy, by acting in this or that way.' That was the situation. And the whole business of James is to try to moderate it, to hold it back. And the message goes on, and on, and on. Here we are 2,000 years later, with similar situations all over the world.

The world doesn't change, because man is always a sinner. It's quite right, I think that governments should remind themselves of the great statements of earlier days, that the trouble with all our Utopian schemes, as one leading socialist philosopher said, is that man is a sinner and he wrecks everything we plan. We are in this situation, wherever we are and whoever we are. So there is a great tendency to be incited and to hear only those who would incite us, so that we become more and more bigoted. Think of the bigotry that there is in Northern Ireland, as well as the wonderful Christians who seek to cross the divide.

These situations are very real, into which James is speaking as someone who is there; the head of the church in the city where it's happening. I should remind you that in AD 70, because of the Zealots, Jerusalem was destroyed, the temple was destroyed and the Zealots themselves were forced to their last stand at Masada. It did end in the way in that James warned it would happen, because they didn't heed him. So he says, 'Do not react, be changed.' And this is a very large matter when you feel you are powerless.

Last year I read Nelson Mandela's book, *Long Walk to Freedom*, which some of you may have read. It's a very informative, moving and challenging book. But I found myself wrestling in my own mind—was he right to resort to terrorism in order to achieve the results he wanted in South Africa, terrorism for which of course he was put in prison? As I reflected on that question and on some passages of James where James seems to argue against such action, I talked with some of the sisters of the Community of the Holy Name who lived next door to us in Chester and had worked in Soweto. When I expressed my reservations they told me, 'You should have lived in Soweto. If you had, you wouldn't say that.' Of course; when you live in a situation like South Africa, or Rwanda or similar places, you tend to see things very differently. But I do know that in many parts of Britain, not least in the diocese in which I worked, in parts of Merseyside for example, there were places where people felt utterly powerless and frustrated. These were serious things to have to face as a Christian, and you can understand people who become angry.

We say, 'We're not in that situation.' Well, yes and no, because quite often we do find ourselves cornered by circumstances or problems. The more I meet and talk with people even here at the Convention, I find that there's a huge amount of pain here. There are people suffering, people just divorced who are hurt beyond measure by what's happened, people who've been left single, people who are in situations of poverty, and so on. There's a lot of pain. And very often in these difficult circumstances, we want to react; unless we keep, as this passage says here, with 'the word planted' in our hearts, time and time again accepting the word.

But verse 19 must surely speak to every one of us here. We should be 'quick to listen, slow to speak, and slow to become angry'. I need to hear that again and again. However much I've had it done to me, I know how easy it is for me to do it to other people; suddenly to see something in the newspaper, to not check it, to not attempt in any way to see what lies behind it. And then to say, 'Look at that!' instead of wanting to know what the truth is. As a Christian I should be concerned about the truth, and not be distracted by the way in which truth is so often twisted or facts taken out of context. And yet we go on doing it. We all do. I have to put the brakes on myself; journalists and reporters used to ring me up saying, 'So-and-so said this, what's your reaction?' I used to respond; it would be published. Then I would find out that what the person was reported to have said wasn't what was actually said.

So now I ask them to ring back after I've had a chance to check a transcript. Or I refuse to answer unless they give me a transcript themselves. But it isn't easy to learn that— to be quick to listen, slow to speak and slow to become angry. The founder of Stoicism says that human beings have two ears and one mouth so that they can hear twice as much as they speak. That's not a bad guide! The careless word—as King Herod found out in his promise to Salome, or as jewellery tycoon Gerald Ratner discovered after he made a thoughtless comment on the quality of his products—can (as we will find out tomorrow in relation to the tongue) set a whole fire going.

So verse 20 says, 'for man's anger does not bring about the righteous life that God desires.' The Zealots wanted to attack the Romans and their vassals, but James wants them to be 'peacemakers who sow in peace and raise a harvest of righteousness' (cf 3:18). It's one of those things that we find even in the fight for the faith: you can be very aggressive in the fight if you are not careful, you can get very strong about what people are doing. Then you read a passage like 2 Corinthians 10:1 that says, 'By the meekness and gentleness of Christ'. These are our weapons, not the weapons of the world. With the word and the Spirit and the gentleness of Christ—that is the way, it says, we demolish strongholds (cf 2 Cor. 10:3-4). And do you know what the word 'demolish' is? It's the same word as taking down the body of Jesus from the cross. They didn't do that aggressively, they did it gently. So often, you lose an argument if you are aggressive, rather than come with the strength of conviction but with the gentleness of Christ in the way in which you present your case.

Verse 21 warns us to 'get rid of all moral filth'. Well of course, we don't want vulgarity and foul words, but they are often associated with anger. What we need is the word implanted, but not just that; to accept the word implanted, to live under the word, to submit to the word, to let it grow in us and be watered by God and developed by God and blessed by the Spirit, till day after day after day after day after day the word of God is affecting us and moulding us and changing us.

If we are not changing as Christians, there's something radically wrong with us, isn't there? I think that elderly Christians (and I'm one of them) are like Chinese pork— either sweet or sour. If you are sour, you are an absolute menace to the church, because younger Christians say, 'If that's what they are like after being in the church for forty years ...' And if you are a sweet elderly Christian then people say, 'How wonderful! Look at that lovely person, always wanting to encourage the young, and wanting the best to go forward for the Lord Jesus.' Which are you?

You may say, 'He's always been like that. He's had a temper for the last forty years.' Well, he shouldn't have had. He shouldn't! Because if the word of God is implanted within us, we should be changing. Yes, slowly; yes, it's a fight; yes, the sinful nature is within us; but yes, the grace of God is within us, and this is the aim. So there is a great need for all of us here to hear the first part of this: to be people who have this word planted in us, affecting us.

Do not just listen; act on what you hear (1:22-25)

It's very easy to be a good listener and to leave it at that. You can listen to Bible expositions and addresses at Keswick, you can discuss sermons, you can roast the preacher, you can read Christian books, you can gain theological degrees—but nothing happens, and the change that we were thinking about just now does not happen; because you have to be someone who 'looks intently' (verse 25). It means 'gazes, meditates'.

It's not a matter of: 'Oh, I've done my Scripture Union

portion for today, off I go.' Not unless you stop and medi-
tate, unless at lunchtime you can think, 'That's what God
said to me this morning,' unless at teatime you can say, 'Oh
yes, now I'm beginning to see more of it.' Unless you've
done that, you haven't meditated, you haven't thought, you
haven't let the word get in. You've looked at it, and as verse
24 says, you've gone away as if you'd looked in a mirror
and immediately forgotten what you saw.

Now I know that sometimes one looks into the mirror,
and is glad to go away again and forget! But sometimes
that's what we do with the word. We look at it and it's too
convicting to take seriously. So we forget it and go away
again. Yet the word has to be challenging. It has to be
something that reaches us. So often today, in the case of
many young Christians, the word is a long way from their
daily lives. They are a long way from the discipline of
Scripture, on which many of us here were brought up. And
that's going to create a desperately dangerous situation in
the years to come. Be changed by the word; He will bless
you, it says, if you do this. You're more likely to be in tune
with God (cf verse 25).

In verse 25, too, James speaks of 'the perfect law'. The
perfect law reflects the perfection of God. C. S. Lewis
found it very difficult to speak of the law as 'sweeter than
honey' (Ps. 19:10), until he saw that the law of God, and
for us the whole word of God, is the outline of the perfect
way to live. When you come nearer and nearer to the perfection God wants—'Be perfect ... as your heavenly Father
is perfect,' as Jesus said in the Sermon on the Mount (Matt.
5:48)—the more you find the smoothness of the running of
the life that God has given you.

And so there is a very great sense in which you look into
the perfect law, which is of course the New Testament fulfilment of that psalm; and when you do, you are challenged by it. After all, in Matthew 5 (of course James is
quoting his brother, the Lord, time and time again) we are
told to love our enemies, and so to love them that we overcome evil with good. That is quite something! Some of us

can't even love our friends, let alone our enemies! The
Sermon on the Mount perhaps ought to be a constant
reading in our lives, because it speaks not just of murder
but of anger with your brother. There's so much of this
around in the Christian church, and even in some church
newspapers; in August I gave up church newspapers for a
year, because so many people in them were slanging each
other. I look back to Matthew 5, and say: this is so far from
the perfect law; this doesn't reflect Christ.

So, thirdly,

Do not have a worthless religion, act on it (1:26-27)

This is religion as James interprets it; either worthless or
worthwhile. He now touches on elements that he's going
to explore later on.

He mentions the tongue. In particular he's touching on
the Zealots, who whip people up and persuade them to
listen only to their voice, not to a balanced presentation.
And in this way they are twisted and turned. You see it
happening in all sorts of parts of the world.

But for many of us it is more the fact that we find it very
difficult to control our tongue. As you get older, you think
back on all the things you wish had never happened in
your life. Very often it's something that you wish you had
never, ever said. It may only be an off-the-cuff remark that
was misinterpreted—but you wish you hadn't said it. If you
can't control the tongue, says James ...

Of course we wrestle constantly with this. Some people
say, 'I can't.' There's no such word in the Bible! 'I can do
all things through Christ who strengthens me' (cf Phil.
4:13, AV). How many of you were brought up with that
text? It was the words for one of the choruses I wrote for in
Youth Praise. I called it the A10 chorus, because I banged it
out while I was driving, and rushed into High Leigh to
write it down!

You don't hear those verses so much today. We were
brought up on those words, they were the very centre of
Keswick and of conviction. Nowadays it's so much about

experience—what I should feel like. But 'I have been crucified with Christ, yet I live, because Christ lives in me'
(Gal. 2:20) ... 'I can do all things through Christ who
strengthens me.' Hallelujah! And so we cannot say, 'I
can't.' But we need to fight it—fight it—fight it! Knowing
that so often it is the words of our mouth, as well as our
lives, that let down the Lord Jesus. God forgive us.

And then, caring action. Of course we are going to come
back to this as well. It is discovering His will in our lives, it
is real action, not, as George Tyrell put it (and like the person I quoted when we began this morning), the kind of
'going out and doing good' which is chiefly 'going about'.
We all suffer from those people, do-gooders in the wrong
sense of the term. James speaks of goodness because the
heart is filled with love, and with the desire to reach people
and touch people.

He reaches out into examples. The force of verse 27 is
not that he is listing the sum of religious action, but that in
his time these were some of the staring problems that
needed to be faced. It's no good saying 'The Bible says
we've got to do these things, and that will be pure religion.'
They are an *example* of the way in which, there and then,
there was practical action in the midst of Jerusalem. And he
calls us to this practical action together.

Now both groups mentioned were people who bore
particular suffering at that time. You remember that in Acts
6 the widows were being overlooked in the daily distribu-
tion of food; and there was a great desire to care for those
who had no-one to care for them (cf 1 Timothy 5). It was
an important issue in the church. But for many of us the
issue is how to apply the Lord Jesus's love to the sections of
society in which we live, at home and abroad. There wasn't
much of it in my upbringing in the Christian church. We
needed the breakthrough with organisations like Tear
Fund to start blowing our minds, to make us face the needs
of the world. We reacted, because we said, 'That's a social
gospel, and we don't want anything to do with that, we just
want the true gospel'—yet the nineteenth-century evan-

gelicals led in both.

We restore it to some extent, when we go and touch the needs of society with the love of Christ. Myrtle and I were able to go out and see Operation Christmas Child in Bosnia, while the war was actually going on. The shelling was continuing, it was a dangerous mission—the notice boards in Chester said, 'Bishop goes on danger mission.' But none the less we were there, and bringing aid in the name of Christ to the Muslim community, a thrilling thing to do. One saw and felt what it was really like to be there, with no bank, no money, no post office, nothing. The people who remained there serving were doing it for nothing, and they could have got out. It was very moving to see what people would do.

We have to say to ourselves, what is the great need? William Booth said about money, 'We will wash it in the tears of the widows and orphans and lay it on the altar of humanity.' Just a few weeks ago I was at Harrow School to speak to the boys in the chapel. Before that I met up with the chaplain at 35 West Street. He told me, 'This is the place where the young Lord Ashley, who became who became the Earl of Shaftesbury, was at school at Harrow.' From that house in West Street he stepped out and saw a pauper's funeral going up that steep hill to the churchyard. And the young Lord Ashley was so horrified by the sight that, there and then, he dedicated his whole life to the cause of the poor and the friendless. And he did it with the passion of the Lord Jesus. Later when he became the Earl of Shaftesbury and entered Parliament he weighed in against the terrible conditions in mental asylums, and the fate of children in industrial towns where five-year-olds were being made to stand up all day at machines for fourteen hours a day. And it was people like Shaftesbury who, in the name of Christ, with a passion for the real gospel of the Lord Jesus, reached out and spoke out with great courage, about the terrible conditions in the mines and the chimney sweeps.

There have been many people in history who for the

cause of Christ have tackled slavery and other evils. Today
we say to ourselves, 'What is the issue where we live?'
When we worked at All Souls in London, we decided that
we couldn't meet every condition at that time; but the one
major social condition in the centre of London is loneliness, and we sought to address that first. Other things followed on. So ask yourselves; what is it in this area where,
in the name of Christ, we can move? There must be
something. Christians have been pioneers in hospitals and
hospices and so much else.

And then there's holiness here; 'keep oneself from being
polluted by the world' (verse 27). Again, of course, a real
Christian wants to avoid that pollution, which is so subtle
to all of us in the present day. When I was at All Souls, we
organised an event for the media, attended by the then
head of the BBC and the then head of ITV, at which
Malcolm Muggeridge gave a lecture. In that very large
gathering, with many people, including the top people,
from the media there, Malcolm Muggeridge turned on
them and said: 'Television is like the experiment of the frog
in the water: you gradually heat the water and the frog
doesn't know it's getting warmer until it expires.' He said
to the leaders of the media, 'That's exactly what you are
doing to this country. You're affecting morals and the way
in which people think and act, and this country doesn't
realise what you are doing to it—until it will be too late.'

That was eighteen years ago. How true he was—but did
the balloon go up after that! Yet I believe Muggeridge was
right. We are all affected by the media. And so is the world.

So we have this very great challenge to real religion
here. We haven't time to take it further, but it's a challenge
to be practical. A few years ago Mother Teresa spoke at the
National Prayer Breakfast in Washington. She was com-
mending love, and they were all nodding approvingly.
Then she spoke powerfully against abortion. It wasn't po-
litically correct in America to speak about that at a public
meeting or at a national prayer breakfast—you were supposed to avoid controversy. Some applauded, some sat in

stony silence. And then this little figure leaned forward
towards the microphone and said, 'If you don't want the
children, give them to me. I'll take them.' And she spread
her arms wide. The whole assembly stood and applauded
her—because she did not believe in worthless religion.

The loving insight of believers (2:1-13)

'My brothers' begins chapter 2, and that means it's a fresh
section, probably a totally fresh sermon. These are all little
sermons, which is why we keep coming back to the same
themes.

Glorious Lord! (verse 1a)

Religion isn't actually mentioned again from now on. We
start this passage with this title as '...believers in our glorious Lord Jesus Christ'. Now we say, 'Of course that's what
I sing, "The glorious Lord Jesus, Hallelujah!"' Yes, it's a
wonderful phrase, but it isn't just an enthusiastic phrase. In
the Greek it's literally 'the Lord Jesus Christ of glory'. So
we might think of passages like the Transfiguration, where
they saw His glory; or Hebrews 1:3, 'the radiance of God's
glory'; or John 1:14, 'We have seen his glory, the glory...'.
We could quote a lot of passages like that, but just remember you are standing alongside James, who's standing
alongside Jesus, and that the passages I've just quoted are
what other people are talking about in their descriptions.

How did our Lord use the word 'glory'? Well, He used
it for instance in Matthew 24:30, 'They will see the Son of
Man coming on the clouds of the sky, with power and great
glory.' He used it in Matthew 25, of the sheep and the goats
before Him, 'when the Son of Man comes in his glory, and
all the angels with him, he will sit on his throne in heavenly glory. All the nations will be gathered before him'
(25:31).

In fact, when our Lord uses the word, primarily it's
about judgement. And what underlies this epistle (in fact
the more you read it, the more you see it) is His sense that

this life is also to be judged for the way that as His servants we have lived. Not that salvation depends on it—they were saved by grace—but it is part of the judgement at the end. And this therefore becomes a type of reminder, and a reminder also perhaps, by implication, of the way in which the Lord became the Lord of glory; that He came as a suffering servant, that He identified with those who are misunderstood; He identified with those in poverty, for He never possessed anything. He identified with those who suffer in the world in which we live. He identified with the situation of having powerful authorities like the Roman and Jewish authorities acting against you. Suddenly He identifies with so many sections of the society in which we are; and His pathway was not one of aggression, but of crucifixion, of self-giving, of supreme sacrificial love. And thus, underneath that title, 'the glorious Lord Jesus,' there is a tremendous significance.

Don't show favouritism (verse 1b)

This is a major aspect of double-think with many of us. The word is a three-part Greek word: it means, 'to the face receiving'. If I look into a camera you would get it: to the face receiving. If you glanced through the viewfinder you would see my face, the externals. And that's what James is saying. We so often only look at the outside.

Did you see that TV programme where they sent someone to buy a car wearing very old clothes and driving a clapped-out old banger? He turned up at a posh car showroom, and no salesman would even come out to see him. Well, eventually they did, reluctanctly. Then he went back and changed into an expensive suit and came in a Jaguar or suchlike—and they all rushed out to serve him. Similarly a lady reporter went to a market stall wearing old clothes and made up as an old lady; she was swept aside and told they hadn't got whatever it was she asked for. Then she went back dressed to kill—smart modern young dress—and they fawned over her and found what she wanted. We say, 'Yes, that's what the world's like.' Really?

Not you? Not me? I'm afraid there is that in all of us.

In 1 Samuel 16 Samuel had to choose from Jesse's sons one to be king. A tall impressive man—'Surely this must be him,' said Samuel. 'No,' said God. Then they brought a lad from the hills who was looking after the sheep. And God said, 'Man looks at the outward appearance, but the Lord looks on the heart.' And down through my history, dealing with youngsters in Bible classes and so on, I've thought, 'These are terrific ... those are not so good.' And often the 'not so good' ones now stand as men and women in Christ, and the others are nowhere. Lord, forgive me! Don't look on the outward appearance, see through the outside. I am always challenged by the story of the 'Elephant Man' John Merrick, that young fellow underneath that foul skin, whose doctor looked straight through to the inside and saw the man he really was.

Yet we are deeply affected. We say we don't believe we want to treat anybody differently, whatever the colour of their skin or background. But there's something very deep in us. In *Long Walk to Freedom* Nelson Mandela says that after he was freed, and was travelling the world to tell what was happening, he actually went on a plane in Kenya, saw the pilot was black and immediately felt unsafe. And he said: 'You see, even in me, with the colour of the skin the same, I still had endemic within me the feeling that the black man is inferior to the white.' It goes very deep in all of us. Desmond Tutu said of apartheid that it's not just evil, it's blasphemy; because if you believe every other human being is made in the image of God, then to treat them differently because of the colour of their skin is blasphemy. That is a very challenging statement. I'm afraid that favouritism is something very deep within many of us. At the time of the general election there was a piece in the *Evening Standard* showing nine faces of Tony Blair, wearing a range of clothes from the swish suit down to the cloth cap. It asked, 'Supposing one of these other faces had been projected, would he still have become prime minister?' The point was that we often judge by the appearance. We still do.

Behind all this lies Leviticus 19:15: 'Do not pervert justice; do not show partiality to the poor or favouritism to the great, but judge your neighbour fairly.' Bias to the poor is not a biblical injunction, except where there is a bias to the rich. And the reason why there is a bias to the poor in this passage, and needs to be in much of our world today, is that so often the bias is to the rich and powerful. But the Bible says we should not show any partiality to the poor or favouritism to the great; because before God they all stand the same. That's the idea here, that's what the ideal is. In the same chapter we have 'Love your neighbour as yourself' (Lev. 19:18), which James quotes (2:8), so he obviously has that passage in mind.

It's an important word, favouritism. It's doesn't actually occur in secular Greek at all, it only comes up in the New Testament. It's used in Romans 2:11 when Paul says that judgement is on Jew and Gentile alike 'for God does not show favouritism'. It's used in Ephesians 6, about masters and slaves: to the masters, it say, 'Do not threaten them, since you know that he who is both their Master and yours is in heaven, and there is no favouritism with him' (6:9). You'll stand the same, stripped of whatever you are; and you'll stand naked before God whether you are the highest or the lowest in the land, a king, a prospective king or an ordinary commoner: all that will go.

Peter is helpful here, though he uses a different word. In Acts 10 he had the vision of the unclean animals, on the roof in the middle of the day. The command came, 'Rise up and eat,' and he said, 'I won't eat any unclean thing.' God had to deal with him about that. Then Peter later said, 'I never realised till now how true it is.' And something begins to dawn on him that's been part of his makeup and upbringing, that he had not actually challenged. It's so easy for that to happen. I still hear my mother, I still react like her to some things. It's good, in some ways. But there are things deep within us that are part of our makeup, and it's important for us to challenge ourselves time and time again.

We needed to look both at the poor and the rich right across the spectrum in our diocese at Chester. We dealt with people, from those in sheer powerless poverty, to those who said, 'Don't you go to the races, Bishop? Everybody who matters goes to the races.' I can tell you we wept as much for some of the gentry as we did for some of the poor, who were floundering helpless without the knowledge of Jesus Christ, and dipping into all sorts of ridiculous other things. And so it's not easy, it's not easy at the door of the church if you have different sorts of people coming towards you. Can you actually look through the externals? Are we people who can look through the outside, through the wrinkles of the elderly if we are young, or through an exuberant person with a punk haircut—what does it matter?

A possible scenario (2:2-4)

James has finished the overture. Now he gets down to it. Suppose someone comes to your meeting. The word is 'synagogue' in the Greek here, but they used if for meetings for worship, as well as legal hearings, and obviously we would not apply it in that way. But verse 3 is about the fact that in the courts of those days judges could one make person stand and another sit. Now those of you in business know the game. You have the big chair behind the desk, and you sit the person lower in front of you so that you are in the power position—preferably with the window behind you, so they can't see your face. We still play that game, and they played it then. They could say where people sat and thereby could immediately create an advantage.

Clothes likewise. But by the second century AD the Jewish rabbis were ordering that both parties in legal hearings should wear the same sort of clothes, so one did not have the advantage of being in the fine suit and the other in poverty-stricken clothes; because people would favour the nicely dressed person. They were being fair. It was the second century, so they must have been listening to James a bit!

It especially applies to us in worship meetings. How much we can give attention to this person and not that one, or judge them because they are wearing this or not wearing that. Our son Andrew and his wife were at a church somewhere on holiday. They were wearing jeans. Behind them two ladies said, 'How absolutely disgraceful, coming to church in jeans!' He wanted to turn round and say, 'And I'm a bishop's son, too!'—But he didn't.

We notice the sort of welcomes that we receive. Sometimes at our church doors we are so frightening, so sophisticatedly posh, that we frighten many ordinary people off. This is why, when I was at All Souls Langham Place, one of the church wardens who was a consultant never wore a suit on Sundays, so that the students would feel more welcome. When we first went to All Souls, we thought, what on earth have we walked into? All these very poshly dressed people! Then a lad came in an Afghan ragged coat and long hair and we thought, 'Hallelujah, at least we've got some!'

Of course they were wonderful people underneath. We shouldn't have judged the others by the outside. My friends, look at the people around you. Seek to welcome and look out for the person who's there. The lonely person, the person in need. If you go as a visitor to a strange church, don't you often find it difficult afterwards to break into the little groups of Christians talking with each other? Remember how it feels the other way round.

The gold rings of verse 2 were worn by the Roman senate. They were the people who had power, so you put them in the best position in the hope you might get favours out of them. How easy it is to do that! There's a distinction about acknowledging that we have differing members, and regarding them differently. And we need to act on that, or (verse 4) we become 'judges with evil thoughts'. This is wrong. Douglas Webster says the church must be a competition-free zone, where instead of courting one another's favour, we rejoice together in God's favour. How true and important that is! Do we therefore still give respect to a

queen or a mayor, or for that matter a bishop? Well, respecting the office is a different thing to respecting the person; people wear a hat and the right clothes at a Palace
garden party, and that's appropriate. There is 'fearing the
Lord and the king' (cf Prov. 24:21), and 'showing proper
respect to everyone' (cf 1 Pet. 2:17). So we mustn't simply
go too far the other way.

But we need to be careful, and those of us who have
authority need to reach out. It's said that the Queen
Mother at a formal banquet noticed that the man next to
her was drinking from his finger-bowl. So he would not be
embarrassed, the Queen Mother did the same.

Bias to the poor (2:5-6)

We've already observed the need to balance bias to the rich
and powerful and to the poor. God sees the poor as often
'rich in faith' (verse 5). In the words of the song, 'Let the
weak say "I am strong", Let the poor say "I am rich", because of what the Lord has done for me.' Yes, it's Old Testament, but it goes on into the New Testament as well. He
looks through the outside, and how wonderful that is.

Not that anyone is outside God's mercy. I have to keep
reminding myself time and time again, as I work with
them and meet with them, that the rich, bless them, are
very nice people. But they are often in great need of the
Lord Jesus, and they can come to the Lord Jesus. It's a
ministry to extend to such people as well as to the poor.
There is a great need to reach to all sorts and conditions of
people.

In the Roman courts they favoured the rich, who could
afford to take legal action. The wealthy were allowed to
take legal action against 'inferior' people, but the lower
classes weren't allowed to take legal action against the rich.
We say, 'This was 2,000 years ago.' But what about today?
The Lord Chancellor recently suggested that the size of
legal fees can stop many people going to law. Of course it
does. Would you dare to go to law today unless you had a
lot of money behind you, or you could get proper legal aid?

There are many injustices throughout our own country. If you have the money you can go to law, or if you've got a big company or a big newspaper behind you; but if you are an individual you often can't.

So we are still in this power-injustice game, even though it's different to James's day. It isn't a level playing field in our own country. We need to see this, because often—even in New Testament times—it is the aristocracy who stir things up. In the city of Antioch, 'the Jews incited the God-fearing women of high standing and the leading men of the city. They stirred up persecution against Paul and Barnabas' (Acts 13:50). They didn't do it directly, they got at the top people and made them do it, because they had the power to do it. Lord, help us in this situation, it's not easy.

But James wants us to see as Jesus sees. He sees the weak and poor as rich in faith—He sees that they 'inherit the kingdom he promised those who love him' (verse 5) There is the ethos of the Sermon on the Mount: Blessed are the poor in spirit, for theirs is the kingdom of God. There's the message of Nazareth, and the reading in the synagogue: 'The Spirit of the Lord is upon me because he has anointed me to preach good news to the poor' (Luke 4:18). This is part of our commission, and part of our responsibility as people. And wherever we are we need to face it, and particularly in the societies around us. If you live in a very nice comfortable area, then you and your church should be very closely involved with a needy community nearby.

Once, faced with appalling need in part of my diocese, I was told by a man who was in a position of leadership high up in our country, 'The church should pull out of this area.' And I said, 'Look, I'm an Anglican bishop. Wherever you live in this country you are in a parish. We don't pull out, we pull in.' We raised a million pounds to rebuild the church right there for Jesus in that place. Because we have a responsibility.

In some of our parishes they said things like, 'You don't

want to give anything to people in Birkenhead. My husband used to be there and they were all layabouts there. You'll never get anything from this country parish.' In other parishes they said, 'Come on, let's go and see.' And they went, and some of their cars were vandalised during the visit, but they met love, they were overwhelmed by love; and they gave and they gave, because they suddenly saw that this was their responsibility, bless them.

So in practical terms it means mission, not just to the educated but to the non-book culture. Very often we need to consider changing church programmes. It means affirming the richness of faith in ordinary people. Think of the great testimonies of people who have never had education, who just love the Lord Jesus! They've got more to teach us than many others. It means social care and action. Some evangelical parishes have started credit unions, giving practical help about finance. Some parishes have furniture and clothing stores for Jesus, to help those in the poverty area. They are in action for Jesus, they want to reach out and preach the gospel and act for the Lord Jesus.

Involvement is needed in so many different ways. In political causes, for example, in which many of us, in the House of Lords and elsewhere, have an opportunity to speak and to act in all sorts of different ways; to encourage the rich and affluent to see what really matters. This is all part of working for the Lord Jesus Christ. And how important it is in the world in which we live.

I went once to Chequers with other bishops to meet Margaret Thatcher. I said to her, 'Prime Minister, if you came to some of the parishes in my diocese you would find that the only professionals (and I use that term in the technical sense) there after five o'clock on a weekday and throughout the weekends are the clergyman and his wife who live there for Christ's sake. You listen to them, and then you'll really know what it's like in these areas. These men and their wives and families are gold dust for Jesus. And so are the people who stick there with them for the Lord Jesus, to spread the gospel.' She said, 'Give me their names. I want to write to them.'

The noble name (2:7)

The commentary in verses 5-6 is sharp; it gets sharper. They say those who say that they are Christian believers and use power and position to squash and manipulate and exploit are not acting as believers in the glorious Lord Jesus Christ. Rather they are 'slandering the noble name of him to whom [they] belong'. Wow! That's pretty sharp.

Of course the Jews didn't like to use the holy name, as John 1:12 makes clear by specifying: 'Those who believed in his name.' The apostles rejoiced because they'd been counted worthy to suffer disgrace for His name from those who slandered His name.

Verse 6 says, they 'insulted the poor'. Does this hurt? I hope it does. It hurts me. The Scripture is sharp in James. But so often we glide along without seeing it. Of course many of you are involved in obeying these injunctions and you fulfil them wonderfully—perhaps all of you.

Love is the key (2:8-11)

Favouritism is deeply challenged by the basic principle of the second great commandment. The two commandments, of course, are reflected in this whole chapter.

When we mentioned earlier Leviticus 19:18 about justice and impartiality, only three verses later we found 'love your neighbour as yourself.' Our Lord of course quoted that; James calls it the royal law. Have you ever thought why? Let me suggest the reason. Those who had authority had power. They set up the rules, they wrote the rule-book in their own favour. So they had it all wrapped up; if you were poor and powerless, you felt you couldn't do anything about it.

'But,' says James says, 'there's one thing that rides above you all. It is an imperial edict, the edict of the King of Kings. And it rides over the lot of you, because the Lord Jesus Christ has echoed these as the greatest commandments. It is therefore the royal law of the King of kings, which over-rides everything else.' And, he says, this commandment is to love other people as yourself. How important that is—that we should love ourselves, but also reach into another person's situation.

Many moons ago we were at a house party and I became sick. The whole world was spinning and I was sick and couldn't stand up. I rolled about the whole time; people treated me as if I was mentally deficient. A year later we went back to the same place when I was recovered. And I heard someone say, 'Well he's quite intelligent after all.'

I'm thankful for that experience. My dear friends who are here, who are perhaps mentally ill, God forgive us if we ever treat you as of less value than anybody else. God forgive us if you've got MS or you are an epileptic, or you are blind or deaf, and we treat you as of less value. Sometimes when men are dreadful towards women, I wish I could make them change sex for a year and deal with the consequences. I must reach out to see what it would be like if I were there and not here, because love cannot be selective. Favouritism is not in the will of God.

Judgement and mercy (2:12-13)

In verse 11 we see that we can be very selective. The Zealots were people who would have got very angry about adultery—but they didn't hesitate to murder. And (this is important) you and I can get very upset about murder and adultery, but not so upset about bearing false witness or coveting what our neighbour has. And what this passage says is this: if you are going to be severe about one part of the law, remember we are answerable to the whole of the law. You've only got to disobey one point of the law to disobey the law. It is a reminder of how easy it is to be persuaded. How can you go to Mass on Sunday and kill as an IRA terrorist on Monday?

With judgement and mercy, therefore, the passage comes to at the end. There's got to be judgement and there will be judgement, but mercy is, in the end, greater. The great thing is that judgement will be 'by the law that gives freedom' (verse 12), because the parameters of God's law give us freedom to operate as human beings. But judgement without mercy is a terrible thing. When I was caught scrumping apples, I am thankful that a man took our names—and then tore up the paper and threw it away. It taught me a lesson, in my boyhood, of judgement and mercy. It's not easy ever, as headmaster, bishop, or anybody who has to exercise discipline, to do that; to hold, in all sorts of walks of life, the principle and the compassion.

And yet our Lord said, 'Blessed are the merciful, for they shall obtain mercy.' He gave us the parable of the unmerciful servant. 'Mercy triumphs over judgement!' In the end, yes, there must be judgement; but mercy is the greater, because of the mercy supremely from the Lord Jesus, that you and I have received.

Praise His blessed name!

3 : 'Have Integrity in Faith, Action and Word'
James 2:14-3:12

It was quite a ride yesterday, wasn't it! And today it's going to be more of the same—just like the weather. I can tell you that tomorrow, we start out with sunshine, though it will cloud over shortly afterwards; but in this morning's study it's more of the same as we had yesterday. Rather like the preacher who went to a new church and there preached the same sermon, week in, week out, until eventually they complained. He responded, 'When you start acting on it, I'll preach another one!'

Here the preacher is repeating the same theme, but coming at it from a different angle. He's making us face up to the responsibility of action in the midst of the world in which we live. You know the old Chinese proverb? That there are thirty-six options facing you in any circumstance, and the best is running away? You and I as Christians cannot run away—that's for when we go home to heaven. But for now, wherever we are living, serving and working, that is the arena where at the moment God has called us to be His witnesses and those who act in His name. So this is a very important passage, which I hope will encourage many of you but also will challenge us.

Faith without works is dead (2:14-26)

Faith vs works? (verse 14)

First we come to the question: is it a question of faith versus works? Here is James standing alongside his brother, speaking as his brother. What did our Lord say? 'Every tree that does not produce good fruit will be cut down and thrown into the fire' (Matt. 3:10). What did our Lord say? 'Not everyone who says to me, "Lord, Lord," will enter the kingdom of heaven, but only he who does the will of my

Father who is in heaven' (Matt. 7:21). What did our Lord say? 'Build on the rock and not upon the sand' (cf Matt. 7:24-27), because building on the rock is building by hearing and doing, not just hearing.

So when James begins to talk about faith and works, he is echoing entirely the force of the Sermon on the Mount. We are hearing our Lord, in a sense. But Paul did the same thing. The second part of Ephesians is the outworking of faith in words and actions. 'For we are God's workmanship, created in Christ Jesus to do good works' (Eph. 2:10). And in Romans 1:5, we are told to 'call people from among all the Gentiles to the obedience that comes from faith'.

Now very often, people say that James is against Paul; that Paul says, 'It's by faith you will be saved,' and that James is saying something different. In fact they spend ages discussing it in theological books. But there isn't any real problem there. It's partly the question of use of words. Even in this country, the use of words differs. When we first moved to Manchester, someone came to the door and said, 'Can we borrow your trolley?' Myrtle trundled out the tea trolley, wondering how the lady was going to get it round the streets of Manchester. The woman looked stunned. What she had meant is what we called a pushchair, or what the Americans call a stroller! You say the word, you hear something different. It's the same word. We were over in America and we said to our hosts after a meal, 'Can we wash up?' They showed us to the bathroom ...

So when Paul uses 'works' and James uses 'works', they are using the word that is translated the same, but they are using it in a completely different way. That is what removes any real conflict. I'm sure you are aware of that, but we need just to spell it out. Paul is against those who rely on the works of the law as the way to be right with God. Now that is English religion; I was brought up on the whole idea that if you were English, particularly if you lived in the South, and you went to church occasionally, that you were a Christian. So many people in this country believe that's so. A preacher once said, 'Stand up everybody in the church who knows they are saved.' Afterwards there was a great furore: 'All those people claiming to be "saved"!' Until someone pointed out that it was those who were sitting down who were the presumptious people, for they were saying 'We are good enough for God in any case. We don't need to be forgiven and saved.'

Paul was tackling the Jewish idea that this would be sufficient. He had learned that it wasn't. He'd had to learn what it meant to come to a crucified Saviour: 'I am crucified with Christ: nevertheless I live' (Gal. 2:20). And thus he is very concerned to point out that you are saved by faith in the Lord Jesus Christ, the one who gave His life on the cross as the sacrifice for the sins of the world, once and for all; those great words. Now James has no problem with that; indeed he has already spoken to us about being born again, about salvation and so on. For him, deeds are the outcome; he's talking about the holiness of life, the other side of the issue of faith, and how to relate to other people and work in the world. For Paul, being justified by faith was a judicial term; you are accounted righteous before God. For James, it is this moral outworking from that justification in which holiness is found.

James's first shock question

Now immediately James has a shock question. He asks, what use is a claim to faith that is not evidenced in deeds? He's tackling the empty profession of the lips. Does this ring bells anywhere?

There's the profession of the lips: sentimental, sincere, always at the fellowship, always there in the church services—give well, affirm to other people, have confidence in the gospel, have strong church involvement—but never, never, never care for anybody. Not for your neighbour, not in your office, not in your place of work, not even with your family.

This is what the world calls hypocrisy, and we don't like it. People say 'I'm not coming to church, it's full of hypocrites,' and we always say, 'Well, come and join us; there's room for one more!' But none the less, we know underneath that hypocrisy disgraces the Lord Jesus Christ, and often turns people off Him for ever. As a man said to me in one street, 'All the people who slink down the street with their big Bibles, but are never there when we need help!' Yet in contrast there are the Christians, like, I guess, so many people here, who have given their lives across the years. You are the ones to whom people turn in your street or in your area.

I think of when I had my first education in the north of England about the ministry and its tremendous demands. For me, it was a great shock coming from the South; seeing children without shoes in 1956, because all the money went on the drink on Friday night. There was sheer, utter poverty in those back-to-back houses in streets with extraordinary names like Paradise Row and Pleasant Row. I had to learn the hard way.

A local doctor and his wife threw open their house to the young people. They took them in and they put up with all sorts of conditions—for Christ. Those young men began to move forward. The doctor bought a climbing centre up in the hills above Eskdale, and took them there to challenge them—rock-climbing and mountain-climbing. It was terrific work. Today some of those young men, taken right out of the gutter and out of the dirt, are great men for the Lord—still tough, but they are tough Christians, wonderful to meet. But thank God, the man in the midst of it all had his house open, at great cost in many ways. And time and again, this is the sort of person that we meet. So I hope you are that sort of person. I'm sure you are.

John the Baptiser was announcing salvation. The crowd asked, 'What shall we do?' He said, 'If you've got two tunics then give one away. If you have food, share it. Tax collectors, look at the job you are in; collect only what is just. Soldiers, don't extort money or accuse people falsely' (cf Luke 3). He was saying, 'Look at where you are, in your job, in the place where you live, in the situation where you are. Is there integrity about your Christian life? The way in which this is worked out—look at it there first.' It makes such a difference, doesn't it? If you are in hospital and someone treats you as 'the ulcer in bed 5', you don't feel awfully warm about it. But if someone treats you as Mary or John or Bill, as a human being, it makes a huge difference. Often it's not just Christians who do that. But a Christian ought to always have that touch which is the caring touch.

Now, look more closely at this. We see that what is in question in verse 14 is not the person who has faith, but the person who 'claims to have faith'. In fact James is shedding doubt on the reality of the faith. If you look more closely still, you will find that the Greek form being used suggests constant repetition. It's what we call the present subjunctive. The people he has in mind are telling people how good they are *ad nauseam*, and how great believers they are, month after month and year after year. But you don't see any change in their lives. There is no fruit of good works.

James's second shock question

Now, just as we thought the argument was over, James starts again on a different tack. 'Can such faith save him?'

The listener might react by condemning James as downplaying true faith. 'By faith we are saved', but James is dubious and doubtful. But we know, as I was saying, that James's view of salvation is sound. In 1:17-18, 21 he speaks of the work of grace and rebirth and the gospel that saves. So what James is saying is that faith without works is insufficient for salvation; because it can't, it *can't*, it CAN'T be genuine. Come back to the Sermon on the Mount. 'By their fruits you shall know them' (cf Matt. 7:16). Not if they say just 'Lord, Lord'—by their *fruits* you shall know them. Do I have to say it again? It rams it home, doesn't it! And James does, in the same way.

So this is something which reaches to us very deeply. It's an enormous thing, as Paul says: 'If the love of God has got you, you realise Jesus died for you, you have no choice, you are constrained, you are compelled not to live for yourself but to live for others' (cf 2 Cor. 5:14). In other words, it must happen. And if it doesn't, how dwells the love of God in you? I don't believe it does.

And so we are involved in this. It is like being rescued from a sinking ship. After you've been rescued, you look at the ship sinking and you say, 'I have been saved.' You look at the lifeboat, and you say, 'I am being saved.' And you look at the shore and say, 'I will be saved.' All of that is there in Scripture. We are saved by the wonderful grace of the Lord Jesus, and His death once and for all; and when this process of the saved people, and the need to be people who shine for Him goes forward, then—as the Puritan John Owen says—'Faith alone saves, but saving faith is never alone. It completes itself in deeds.'

A possible scenario (2:15-17)

Now we come to a possible scenario. It's important to bring things out in stark reality. I remember the story of an American church, where the preacher was getting really excited. He said, 'If you've got two homes, give one away.'

A woman in the front cried, 'Hallelujah! Amen, Pastor.'

He said, 'If you've got two yachts, give one away.'

'Amen, Pastor!'

'If you've got two cars, give one away.'

'Amen, Pastor!'

'If you've got two televisions—'

'That's not fair! I've *got* two televisions …'

Well, James brings it into that stark reality. 'Suppose a brother or sister is without clothes and daily food.' If you've never been to Jerusalem, or have only been there in the warm months, go there in winter. It's a freezing cold place then. And here were people in the poverty of these cold winters, hungry and with inadequate clothing. And up comes some blessed soul who needs a kick in both shins and says, 'I wish you well. Keep warm and well fed. Good-bye.' Wow! Or better, How? *How* am I going to be warm and well fed?

When you look at the underlying form of the words

quoted in verse 16, you find that it is in fact a passive form
that is like a prayer. 'May you be warm, my brother. God
bless you, may you be warm, I'll be praying for you.' James
is saying, 'How on earth can you meet a physical need with
just a good wish or even a prayer?' Prayer is very important. But when Mary Endersbee wrote a book about Christian relief work called *They Can't Eat Prayer*, people didn't
like the title. It was too searching. And so many of us have
had to learn this truth. It is this that always disturbs us.

We've been looking at Malachi.[1] At the beginning of
Malachi, we were challenged to look at such questions as
'When did we love You? When didn't we love You? And
when did we despise Your name? How have we defiled
You?' In other words, excuses. It's the same as Matthew 25,
and the Great Assize: 'When did we see You hungry and
feed You? When did we see You thirsty and give You
drink? When did we see You a stranger and invite You in?
When did we see You needing clothes and clothe You?' (cf
Matt. 25:31-46) That's the people who did it. And the people who *didn't* do it were asking, 'Where on earth did this
happen? We didn't notice it.' Because the people who are
really living for the Lord Jesus with that caring love do it as
part and parcel of their life, without thinking. They don't
have to say, 'Tomorrow I'm going to go and visit the sick;
that'll be my job for this month.'

Those who never think in these terms, who are so bless-
edly caught up with singing 'Hallelujah' and standing on
their heads, having blessed fellowship and just wanting
comfort, don't even see it. The Great Assize—can you ever
read it without being concerned? I can't. God save me.
'Come, you who are blessed by my Father', who are like
this in your life. If you are like that, bless you, the Lord
blesses you, this is the sort of Christian He wants you to be.
The *agapé* of self-giving that has been poured out for us on
the cross is that which is to be poured out by us. Paul says,
'If I give all I possess to the poor ... and have not love, I

---

1. Three talks from this Convention series are included in the
present volume: see p.191, p.202 and p.218.

gain nothing' (1 Cor. 13:3). So it is the attitude, not just the giving. It's not just, 'I've done this,' it is the attitude underneath. And that's what makes it something that happens naturally.

In the same way John, 'If anyone has material possessions and sees his brother in need but has no pity on him, how can the love of God be in him?' (1 John 3:17). It's the underlying attitude, of love in action. It's very important to understand this, because it is possible for some Christians to close in on themselves and think, 'Well, I don't do this and I don't do that; and I'm perfectly OK.'

When I was first ordained we had funerals every week; in most cases you went to the home to travel to the church with the funeral cortège. Almost every time, they said, 'He (or she) never did any harm to anyone.' To which I wanted to say, 'Did he (or she) ever do any good?' It's not enough for us to say, 'I don't do this, I don't do that, I wouldn't do that, I wouldn't do this.' God says, 'What *do* you do that is positive, and real, reaching out and touching, caring and loving as I would?'

In verse 17, faith is now not just something claimed. It's not even something that doesn't save. It is dead, dead, dead. It's a graphic word here: 'useless, non-existent, invalid'. All this, of course, takes us back to chapter 1 and its aim of maturity, with a faith tested, of persevering and growing.

So pause to consider some of the implications of this in the passage. I'm speaking with great care here, because it's a sensitive issue. I was brought to Christ in a lovely church, with very good people and a good pastor, in the days of evangelicals in this country in the late 1930s and early 1940s. Looking back it was a lovely place, very encouraging, good in its witness, but—as far as I am aware—in the evangelical church of the day, there was almost no concept of social action or responsibility. That has now changed in most churches, although not in all. We've moved with things like Tear Fund and so on; we're aware of the great needs of the world. We've seen the material needs, as well as the spiritual needs, within our own areas. I'm thrilled to see the way in which things have happened in so many places, where people have said, 'What, in this area, should we be doing in the caring love of the Lord Jesus?'

At All Souls we did all sorts of things in caring for loneliness and so on; we gave up our Christmas Days and had meals with people there, and invited them to Christmas lunch with our families, and that was lovely. Or there was the All Souls tea run—they called it ASLAN (All Souls Local Action Network)—on Friday evenings to make sandwiches and go out before dawn, at the time when hypothermia was most prevalent. Other churches have done the same in areas where people are out on the streets. In 1992 at All Souls they went on to decide that it wasn't enough just to go out with sandwiches; these people were desperately lonely. So they started to organise events where people were invited off the streets to go to things together on a Saturday night. It was real practical action, and some 200 people were involved.

We have to ask ourselves, what is the situation we face? In a couple of months' time our son Andrew starts at St James Clerkenwell, and because he's only three years in the ministry I'm going to go as priest in charge. We'll be a father and son team for a year at least. He's absolutely bursting with good ideas; I don't know where he gets them but he's wonderful. It's very exciting. Just a congregation of thirty or forty, and 700 seats in the church, right by Farringdon Station. Quite a challenge; but there is such opportunity for the Lord Jesus there that he feels in his burning heart. But one of the things we've got to say is, 'What is the situation in this parish?' (Being an Anglican, one is used to working in one's parish boundary.) What are the social needs, what are the spiritual needs, what are the ways in which we reach people for Christ?

Luther said, in his *Preface to Romans*: 'It is a living, busy active thing, this faith. It is impossible for it not to be doing good things incessantly'—there's the Matthew 25 teaching we mentioned earlier. 'Whoever does not do such works, however, is an unbeliever. He gropes and looks around for faith and good works but knows neither what faith is nor what good works are, yet he talks and talks with many words about faith and good works.'

There's something deeper here. I go again on very sensitive ground. Since that terrible time in Rwanda where Christians killed Christians, many of us have had to ask what went wrong. I sat with an aged archdeacon back in our diocese who had managed to be brought out. He went off one morning to feed his cow. When he came back to the edge of the tree clearing in which he lived, his wife, his brother and all the members of his family were being killed with machetes in front of him, by Christians. Then they came for him. They stopped short of doing the same thing to him with the machetes, because one of the young people who were doing it had been baptised by him, and couldn't bring himself do it.

Now he lives, as many people in Rwanda live, with that nightmare. In 1995 the Evangelical Fellowship of the Anglican Communion published these words from Christians living and serving in Rwanda: 'The blood of tribalism went deeper than the waters of baptism.' That is a very big issue. We can say it in Northern Ireland, we can say it in our own selves. Exiled Tutsis of over thirty years were never allowed back into Rwanda. All the Anglican bishops were Hutus. And they said, 'One of the problems is that we have left a legacy of no social engagement.' Missionaries have tried to be apolitical, bless them; wonderful people, but retreating into pietism rather than teaching how to be engaged in public life. There was no concern for human rights, it was never on the church's agenda. And the Scriptures were never applied to social and practical questions.

There was also a failure to give systematic instruction. Because of the revival that happened wonderfully in Rwanda in the 1930s, people were keener to testify than to study Scripture. There was a limited doctrine of sin: sin was, 'Do not lie, smoke, or commit adultery.' It didn't go further to talk about structural evil. And somehow there was a naive obedience to the idea that if the State told you to do something (an interpretation of Romans that was pushed too far), you did it. When they were told to kill the others, they did it. And yet the conflict was not seen.

I only repeat what others have written, people who understand better than I do. Forgive me if that was too painful. But none the less, it is something that we as Christians find very difficult to explain. Very often tribalism still goes deep in our own hearts and lives, and we have to ask ourselves: How much needs to be changed in us? How much needs to be moved in us, from some of the positions we might be in? It's very, very easy, as I say, to be involved in Christian things, and not to wash feet or care for one's neighbour.

But then you go over the history of the years, and you realise the incredible sacrifice of men and women who have gone out into impossible lands for the Lord Jesus. And you ask, have we lost some of that courage? In many quarters, no. But when I first went to Chester I had one very difficult place to fill. It was a parish where I needed to put in a vicar; where, once the previous vicar had gone, the vicarage was vandalised from top to bottom overnight. They ripped everything out; all the wiring, the bathroom— it was a smashed-up building. And there in Merseyside I took thirteen different people to see it, all of whom said no. In the mercy of God, the fourteenth went and turned it upside down—Paul Kirby, at Bidston, for Christ. And God blessed him and honoured him.

At the same time I was asked to go and preach at the two-hundredth anniversary of the birth of Reginald Heber, who wrote 'Holy, holy, holy', and 'From Greenland's icy mountains'. At the age of thirty-three he was asked by the Archbishop of Canterbury to go with his wife and small daughter to be the bishop of the whole of India and Ceylon. It took him some months before he said yes, then he went out on that dangerous voyage. In his speech to his clergy on arrival he said, 'Anybody coming to this part of the world knows full well that ere long they will need to leave to the care of Him who cares for the ravens, those whom he loves most.' His first journey took a year and a quarter by ship going in all round India. He died in three years, his successor in six months.

You think of the Congo, you think of all the different parts of the world where people knew their life would be shortened to do this. And sometimes I think we are pretty soft in comparison.

You come back to our own country. I think of groups like the Church Pastoral Aid Society, who in 1836 saw the desperate needs of industrial cities, and said, 'We must do something; put people in, build churches.' And this has been true of so many organisations who have seen the need.

Are there two sorts of Christians? (2:18-20)

Now James introduces another scenario: someone stands up in the synagogue and makes an assertion. 'You have faith, I have deeds.' So the question is raised: Are there two sorts of people—one chooses faith, another chooses action? Well, there is a gift of faith mentioned both in 1 Corinthians and Romans, but really James is postulating a false question so he can knock it down, for it is for him a diversionary tactic that misses the main point of the argument.

So he turns it around. He speaks to the 'I have faith' section—without deeds, doctrinally sound, orthodox, respectably religious, and all the rest of it—and says (verse 19), 'You believe that there is one God.' Absolutely, that was the basic daily confession of the Jewish faith. 'Hear, O Israel, the Lord our God, the Lord is One.'

'Of course,' says James, 'I agree. Good! Good!' It's the same as 2:8; they are doing well, they are doing right as regards the royal law. He says it here, 'Excellent, well done, you believe; you've passed your theological exam perhaps, you can say the Creed and mean it. Good. Have a warm glow, have the strings playing behind you and go out with the credits running up the screen.' This is a nice scrubbed Christian who believes in God.

Then comes the sting (because this man's a preacher).
'Even the demons believe that—and shudder.' Ooff! It's a
nine-pin bowling smasher, a sword to the heart, a blast of
cold air in the warm glow; a preacher's soundbite that you
don't forget in a hurry.

In Mark 1 the evil spirit cried out, 'What do want with
us, Jesus of Nazareth? Have you come to destroy us? I
know who you are—the Holy One of God' (Mark 1:24).
My friend, whether you have a blessing from Timbuctoo or
wherever it happens to be, if your life isn't demonstrating
Christ then we don't believe you. And here in James is the
application of faith pressed home: total Christianity, those
who do, and change, and believe, and act. Praise God for
every one of you lovely people like that here. Bless you!
Praise the Lord for you!

But there is a further twist of the knife. 'You foolish
man,' he says in verse 20, with a preacher's directness.
'Faith without deeds is useless.' The word is *arge*; it means
'inactive, ineffective, worthless, sluggish'. The only other
time it's used in Scripture is in Matthew 20 in the parable
of the workers in the vineyard when men stand in the market place doing nothing. That's the same word. Your faith
is something that does nothing. And he attacks this with all
his force.

The Abraham evidence (2:21-24)

The Abrahamic evidence that follows is important if we're
to understand what's going on here. We know, when we
understand Paul, that faith is that which is accounted
righteous before God. We know that that is what comes in
Genesis 15, a supreme moment which is very meaningful
to all of us; the covenant relationship between Abraham
and God. But James moves us on also to Genesis 22, where
Abraham is challenged to offer Isaac upon the altar. In
verse 12 God says, 'Now I know that you fear, God because
you have not withheld from me your son, your only son.'
And how important it is to understand, therefore, says
James, that you don't just stick with Genesis 15 but that

you also see it worked out in Genesis 22. 'Of course you are accounted righteous,' says James. 'But also it's proven in the way in which you are prepared to lay your life on the altar.'

Many people would be challenged about that; your life for the Lord Jesus. God may sometimes lead you down one way for a time, but He wants you to be prepared to go down another way for Him. My wife Myrtle was prepared for, and felt the call of God to, missionary service. She laid her life open to Him, and then suddenly He closed the door. And she's ended up as the most marvellous partner of an Anglican minister for forty-one years. Wonderful!

But you often have to be prepared to go down a road that may not be the apparently right one.

The Rahab evidence (2:25)

Now come, James, you constantly shock us! Rahab 'gave lodging to the spies'. Why bring in Rahab? Because of her hospitality, or something else? What was it?

Rahab fascinated the Jews, probably because she was a pagan convert and came in with a rather fresh style. How many of you remember in the 1950s the shock of seeing at the Harringay Crusade the wife of the American evangelist wearing makeup? That was a shock in this country! (It's brightened up a few faces since then, I must say …) Rahab was regarded as one of the four beauties: there were Sarah, Abigail, Esther, and Rahab. They extolled her obedience. She gets a mention in Hebrews 11. But do you know where else she's mentioned? She appears in Matthew 1:5, in our Lord's genealogy—most people say that this is the same Rahab, the mother of Boaz. If that's so, James is bringing the family in. And what better example of someone who loved the Lord, and worked for Him in a glorious way?

The summary (2:26)

The summary is a pretty powerful one. It's a straight repeat, and one that we need to take hold of because it is an important issue.

Some people remember the Lausanne Covenant of 1974. Many of us were at Lausanne, it was a very moving time. Under item 5, on Christian social responsibility, the Covenant said:

> We affirm that God is both the Creator and the Judge of all men. We therefore should share his concern for justice and reconciliation throughout human society and for the liberation of men from every kind of oppression. Because mankind is made in the image of God, every person, regardless of race, religion, colour, culture, class, sex, or age, has an intrinsic dignity because of which he should be respected and served, not exploited. Here too we express penitence both for our neglect and for having sometimes regarded evangelism and social concern as mutually exclusive ... We affirm that evangelism and socio-political involvement are both part of our Christian duty. For both are necessary expressions of our doctrines of God and man, our love for our neighbour and our obedience to Jesus Christ. The message of salvation implies also a message of judgement upon every form of alienation, oppression and discrimination, and we should not be afraid to denounce evil and injustice wherever they exist .... The salvation we claim should be transforming us in the totality of our personal and social responsibilities. Faith without works is dead.[1]

James would have approved.

---

1. Quoted here from John Stott, *Explaining the Lausanne Covenant* (Scripture Union, 1975), p.15 [Ed.]

The tongue (3:1-12)

Its responsibility (3:1-2)

Firstly, the tongue's responsibility. We all have a tongue. How important it is in tongue and pen to use our words rightly! It's so easy for us to use words wrongly.

We start with the responsibility of the tongue in teaching, because obviously God calls apostles, prophets, teachers, evangelists etc. And there is a huge responsibility upon everyone who teaches. Those who teach must be judged more strictly. I am constantly reminded by Paul that 'in Christ we speak before God with sincerity, like men sent from God' (2 Cor. 2:17). Ouch! It's an awesome responsibility. It took me a few years to cease to be afraid of numbers and large congregations, but I always tremble deeply, as I did this morning coming here; because I have the awesome responsibility of opening the word of God. God forgive me if I've done it badly, or if in any way I mislead.

So James says, 'Not many of you should presume to be teachers.' Presuming was of course what was happening to some extent in the early church. There were itinerant preachers who went round with almost no teaching, spreading things that were detracting from the faith (and also obtaining free hospitality!) And today there are many who are deliberately misleading us. I tremble for such people and what will happen when they come before God. But we have to call ourselves not to be so. We have to be people who are very concerned about the use of our tongue in teaching. I look back and I tremble and cry to God for the many, many, many occasions when I wish I could have said something differently. Sometimes the words that you happen to say are with you for ever; people never forget that phrase, that statement; they never let you off the hook.

Now, God is wonderfully merciful. But it is awfully important that we should together pray for one another, particularly for those who have the responsibility of teaching. I know that so many of you are praying for those who are speaking. You pray for your pastors every week as they pre-

pare to preach. When you pray, it makes a huge difference
to preparation and presentation. And this huge responsibility is one we have to face and hand on to other people.
How important it is, the whole process of teaching!

I like the American idea of the all-age Sunday School.
It's rare in this country. All different ages gather to worship
together, and that's tremendous. I very much hope it will
happen here, as we experiment with more churches. Some
churches do it, with all the training and so on that is
needed. This is responsibility! And James says, 'We who
teach will be judged more strictly.' Indeed, our Lord said,
'If anyone causes one of these little ones who believe in me
to sin, it would be better for him to have a large millstone
hung around his neck and to be drowned in the depths of
the sea' (Matt. 18:6).

J. B. Phillips wrote *Ring of Truth*—an incredibly good
book that I still use—because an elderly clergyman, hearing one of those rogue bishops talking about not believing
in the resurrection, had committed suicide. Phillips was
rightly so angry that he wrote his very powerful book. We
have such responsibility, all who teach, and we will appear
before the Lord. The Zealots were of course teaching up-
rising, killing, revolt. They were the people he had in
mind. But we are very conscious of those who demean the
incarnation, or the atonement, or the resurrection of our
Lord Jesus Christ. I weep my heart out, as you do.

And so teachers have this responsibility with the tongue.
As Proverbs says, 'The tongue has the power of life and
death, and those who love it will eat its fruit' (Prov. 18:21.)

There's much said about this in the Scripture. For example, 'From everyone who has been given much, much
will be demanded; and from the one who has been en-
trusted with much, much more will be asked' (Luke 12:48).
Or again, from our Lord's lips, 'Anyone who breaks one of
the least of these commandments and teaches others to do
the same will be called least in the kingdom of heaven'
(Matt. 5:19).

But there's also understanding of frailty. We all stumble

in many ways. 'If anyone is never at fault in what he says, he is a perfect man' (verse 3). And this is the wonderful grace of God, that though the perfection standard is the one we all need to aim at, we stumble, you stumble—stand up, anybody who doesn't stumble!

We have to be people who are concerned for the very best for God. And I am thankful that He understands and forgives, even though it goes on burning in my own heart when I've failed Him or let Him down in some way. 'But I tell you that men will have to give account on the day of judgment for every careless word they have spoken. For by your words you will be acquitted, and by your words you will be condemned' (Matt. 12:36-37). Wow!

Its power (3:3-5)

It was a common illustration, that of bits in horses' mouths and of ships' rudders. It was like saying you can lead a horse to water but .... It was a well-known phrase, which James picks up and uses. The tongue 'makes great boasts'. My friends, the tongue can be for good or evil, you can encourage or discourage, you can criticise or you can help. You can be bitter or you can be kind. You and I, every one of us in this tent is like that. Our words can actually build people up or knock them down.

Words can move mountains positively, and they can split nation aparts (cf eg 1 Kings 12:11). One spark, says verse 5, can bring wholesale destruction. One spark, one word.

John Humphrys, presenter on BBC Radio 4's *Today* programme, has said that the whole success of the programme depends on whether you can put words into someone else's mouth and get them to repeat them back to you. Then it's on the headlines by six o'clock. Only the clever people resist using the words being put into their mouth. It's reported that 'The minister said,' but it was actually the interviewer who put them into his or her mouth. It's all in order to get a spark, to obtain publicity. So we see that in so many different ways, one word, one false untrue word, can be something terrible.

The Zealots set people on fire with their tongues. They
whipped them up in bigotry and hate. What does James
say? That this is merely bad? No, in verse 6 he says it
comes from hell. That the word 'hell' in our English
translations comes both from Gehenna, the smouldering
rubbish tip outside Jerusalem where the flames didn't
cease; and also from the place of departed spirits, Hades. In
the Creed it's Hades (Matt. 16:18); here it's *gehenna*, the
word the Lord used when He said, 'It is better for you to
enter the kingdom of God with one eye than to have two
eyes and be thrown into hell' (Mark 9:47). So James is using a very severe word. He is saying that when you allow
these things to happen, it is actually hellish.

We live in an unrighteous world, with so much evil and
wrong around us. We can be polluted by it (verse 6); we
need to keep ourselves free from that. Otherwise 'it cor-
rupts the whole person'. And we are all walking, all the
time, with this danger.

Our use of words, our discerning, our rejection of the
rotten things around us, the extent to which we seek to use
our tongues to help others; to speak, to witness, to build
people up—my friends, these things are of the heart. Jesus
said, 'The things that come out of the mouth come from
the heart, and these make a man "unclean". For out of the
heart come evil thoughts, murder, adultery, sexual immorality, theft, false testimony, slander. These are what make a
man "unclean"; but eating with unwashed hands does not
make him "unclean"' (Matt. 15:18-20). For many of us for
whom this is a constant problem, here is James. We have
heart trouble, and we need constantly to come back and cry
to our Lord to cleanse us, to change us and renew us with
the integrity that there should be in a Christian life.

The searching comment: 'This should not be' (3:9-12)

'My [friends], this should not be. Can fresh water and salt
water flow from the same spring?'

Now, I know we are not perfect and won't be until

heaven. We are wrestling with the stuff that is within us. When we moved to our second curacy we found a plant in the garden called ground elder. Somebody said to us, 'I've just heard on the radio what to do if you have that.'

'What?' I asked.

'Move,' she said ....

But you and I have the ground elder of sin within us. We're only going to be free of it when we move to heaven. So we have to cut it back and back, or the world will say, 'This should not be! How can you say you are a Christian when you are so bad tempered, when you let rip like that, when you don't actually find out what's going on and you speak with a mouth that brings people down? How can you have this bitterness and this constant criticism?'

You see (verse 12) the fig tree doesn't bear olives, the grapevine doesn't bear figs, the salt spring cannot produce fresh water. Time and time again we have to ask ourselves, are we like John Bunyan's character Talkative—a saint abroad and a devil at home? God forgive me and cleanse my mouth and your mouth. And I believe many of us may have to come back, and not just today but time and time again, as Isaiah did in the temple, saying, 'Woe to me! .... For I am a man of unclean lips' (Isa. 6:5). And the angel takes the coal from the altar, and touches our lips.

We have to come back and back and back to the altar of God's gracious forgiveness, to His mercy and to the cross of the Lord Jesus Christ, and receive forgiveness. We have to pray again for the Spirit to go on cleansing us and cleansing us, touching us and renewing us—that our tongues might bless the Lord, rather than curse people. God help us with that tongue, and with our lives; to have the integrity of the Lord Jesus, so that in everything we may say, 'May the words of my mouth, and the meditation of my heart, and the action of my life, be pleasing in Your sight, O Lord my rock and my redeemer.'

4 : 'Seek True Wisdom, Submit to God: Think Christianly' (James 3:13-4:17)

To some extent James has been so far rather like a Lakeland train journey—every now and again great views, but then pressing on again. Well, my friends, we are almost at the top of Shap Fell! We are going to enjoy some beautiful scenery—but not for long.

Seeking true wisdom (3:13-18)

We have here a beautiful picture of the search for true wisdom. 'Who is wise and understanding among you?' He's going to attack pretty strongly in chapter 4: the Zealots were the people who didn't show wisdom, and needed great repentance. But we start in a fairly gentle way.

The proper test (3:13)

'Let him show it by his good life, by deeds done in the humility that comes from wisdom.' May I ask you directly: do you live a good life? I don't mean in the TV sense of living comfortably, but of living with the wisdom of God in humility and grace. In 1 Timothy, Paul says, 'I also want women to dress … with good deeds, appropriate for women who profess to worship God' (1 Tim. 2:9). Do you—men too—dress in good deeds?

The good life is of course that which James had heard his brother speak of time and time again. The Sermon on the Mount was not something delivered like machine-gun fire. Sitting on that hillside above Capernaum, hearing the supreme teacher of all time, the Lord, the Son of God, must have been an incredible experience. Day in and day out people heard Him. He would have retold the same stories, and in different ways; hence you hear them often from the different evangelists. But what permeated them was the great theme on which He must have spoken so many times: 'Blessed are those who are poor in spirit'—this is the good life—'those who mourn, the meek, the humble, those who hunger and thirst for righteousness.' Hear James. He's been on about that all this week! The merciful? In James mercy triumphs over judgement. The pure in heart? Here this morning, purity is the theme. The peacemakers? All the time, James is pleading for peacemakers; and 'blessed are those who are persecuted for righteousness' sake'. We are standing with James alongside our Saviour. Here in his epistle we see it put into action in the turmoil of Jerusalem, and the turmoil of the very different world in which you and I live today. This is the good life.

What did our Lord say? 'Take my yoke upon you and learn from me, for I am gentle and humble in heart, and you will find rest for your souls' (Matt. 11:29). This is the Lord you and I follow. Our life is to be the good life that portrays Him. The staggering humility of the Lord Himself in Philippians 2 leaves us gasping: that He laid aside His glory and came into this earth and took the form of a child, a human being, a servant, and then died upon the cross for you and for me. When Paul writes of that (cf Phil. 2:6-11) it is supremely to teach the church to be humble.

If you look at that supreme example of humility, how can you ever think in other directions? God has honoured people of great humility, people like Billy Graham. Why has God so honoured him? Because of his sheer, utter clarity of Christian living and humility. He and Ruth were here for the centenary Keswick. Richard Bewes and I were taking the youth meetings. Ruth was taking notes at every meeting. You'd have thought, 'An evangelist's wife?' Not at all, she was there, thanking God, drinking it in, and still, when you meet her and Billy, still so open.

When Billy first came to this country, there was a great deal of razzamatazz. Reporters crowded round him from the moment he arrived. The one thing all the national newspapers could not get over was his integrity. They couldn't break it. And they realised that this was a humble man, not one for razzamatazz.

That is wonderfully true of so many people, for example my dear friend John Stott with his tremendous humility and all his gifts. You ask him what his greatest ambition is; he will tell you. 'My greatest ambition is to be more like Jesus.' This is why God can use people like that.

False wisdom (3:14-16)

By contrast, there is false wisdom. The Greek word is *zelon*, which translates into 'Zealots'. He is turning the Zealots' word for themselves against them, arguing that Zealots are often people driven by sheer envy. It's not just a matter of righteousness. They envy this aristocracy, and want to see them out of the way.

There's a difference between saying, 'We want right between the poor and the rich,' and being driven by envy and spite. That's the wrong spirit, as far as the word of God is concerned. So James points back at them their bitterness, harshness and selfish ambition. 'But we are not Zealots!', you say—no, but it is very easy to have selfish ambition and bitterness towards people with whom we disagree, even within the Christian church, and that should not be.

'Such "wisdom" does not come down from heaven but is earthly,' he says (verse 15). It has no eternal significance, it is unspiritual and it is 'of the devil'. That's why our Lord could turn on Peter, after his amazing confession at Caesarea Philippi—'You are the Christ, the Son of the living God' (Matt. 16:16)—and, when he tried to stop Him going towards the cross say to him, 'Get behind me, Satan! You are a stumbling-block to me; you do not have in mind the things of God, but the things of men' (Matt. 16:23). Peter's reaction, which was a natural one in many ways, was certainly not in the wisdom of God. And so he is told off for it, quite rightly; it is exposed to him.

So we need to see this negative again for just a moment, before we get to the top of Shap Fell and ease back a bit. 'The results prove the point,' says James in verse 16. It causes 'disorder and every evil practice'. You can see it from one end of the world to the other: envy, hatred and bitterness have driven country against country, people against people, brother against brother, family against family, time and time and time and time again—it goes on and on and on and on. All over the world it's still true: there's bitterness and envy, fighting and power.

True wisdom (3:17-18)

But what about true wisdom? Ah, the sun's coming out! Now here's something beautiful for God. This is the heavenly wisdom, the wisdom that comes from above. It's very similar to the whole idea of the fruit of the Spirit: love, joy, peace, longsuffering, gentleness, goodness and kindness— have you ever considered taking one of those each week and going through each of them asking yourself, 'How much am I like this? How much do I need to be made more like this?'

This wisdom is pure, says James. It rings absolutely true, there's no hypocrisy in it. There is about this person an integrity, and a transparent reality. There's no hidden agenda, nothing hidden underneath. So often there is a hidden agenda behind people's reactions. You have to dig and dig and dig and say, 'What is it that's *really* getting at you? You're saying this to me—but underneath, there's something else.' But the pure wisdom is that which doesn't have that hidden agenda. It is very open before God, and this is an important thing for us as fellow Christians.

I remember, in the earlier years of my ministry, talking with a number of visitors to All Souls. 'In the church where I am,' I was told, 'you can never ever confess that you are depressed, or have any doubt or difficulty. We're all supposed to be hyped up and on top every week. And I long to be able to just share my problems with somebody.' If we are going to be pure, we need to be open, and not people who make a pretence. Some people say, 'I have the peace of God.' But you know jolly well they haven't, because they are pushy, difficult and intense. They don't relax.

So there is a great genuineness here in the purity of God, as a person wrestles with the word of God and is changed by the word of God.

Now come seven quite difficult things that I want to help you to grasp. The passage that follows is extremely harmonious. It's rather like music. As you may know, I've been involved a lot in music, and have written tunes and hymns including 'Lord, for the years' and 'Name of all majesty' which some of you know and sing. In those early years of hymn writing, it was very much a partnership with Timothy Dudley-Smith, who as many of you know is a great hymn writer. When he sent me the words of a new hymn and I read them for the first time, they were literally music to my ears. And in the same way, as we read these words of James, the reading of the seven words should indicate a great harmony, with the very words themselves speaking together. I can't communicate it to you in music, but the sense is that the word is actually speaking what the content is: true wisdom. James achieves this by using four Greek words that all begin with the same letter: *eirenike*, *epieikes*, *eupeithes*, *eleous*. The he adds three more that start with 'a': *agathon*, *adiakritos*, *anupokritos*. He is using alliteration, as preachers do.

Let's look at James's list of the qualities of true wisdom.

It is *peace-loving*. The only other place this word is used in the New Testament is in the Epistle to the Hebrews, in the context of discipline. 'No discipline seems pleasant at the time, but painful. Later on, however, it produces a harvest of righteousness and peace for those who have been trained by it' (Heb. 12:11). This is the important issue. As we allow the word of God to take hold of us, and as God touches us and often corrects us—we don't like that, but He's loving us—the more we are prepared to submit, we will find, James goes on to say, that this is actually the good life. The more we submit to His moulding hand as the Master Potter, this is the good life. And if we want to stand on our particular ambition, we will find it is the other way round. Take the upper room, and Jesus's washing of the disciples' feet in John 13. See the contrast. What were the disciples doing? Standing on their dignity. 'You are not going to wash my feet.' What does our Lord do? He takes the towel and washes their feet. Why? Because the apostles still hadn't worked out their position, they were still insecure perhaps and had the wrong ideas of ambition; these, after all, were the guys who said, 'We want the best seats in heaven.' But our Lord knows who He is, our Lord is secure in His Father's will, our Lord is secure as the person that God has made Him. So He can get up and wrap Himself with the towel and wash people's feet, because He doesn't need to make a point other than the humility point.

Do you see what I mean? When you are insecure, you tend to be more full of yourself and push yourself and exploit opportunities to do so. But when you have a peace within with your Lord, when you are assured of your value as a child of God, someone who's valued by Him, loved by Him and within His will—then you can take the towel. You can step back because you don't need the limelight.

Someone said to me once when I was at All Souls, 'I want something to do in this church.'

I said, 'Right, come and help us with the refreshments.'

'Oh no,' she said, 'I don't mean that.' She wanted something important.

Then, are we *considerate*? This is the next word, which simply means fair, moderate and gentle. Titus 3:2 says we are 'to be peaceful and considerate, and to show true humility towards all men.' That is the Christian life—a quality required in overseers and leaders in 1 Timothy 3. It isn't easy to be fair and considerate. In the General Synod, I often get emotionally worked up, as a Christian and as a bishop, with some of the issues I've had to face. But when you do that, you often lose the point, unless you have consideration and fairness with which to make your point. That's something that I've had to work on with God, and seek from Him; the ability not to be too provoked, but to be able to reach out towards other people, to reach towards them with a gentleness and fairness that honours the Lord.

Then, are we *submissive*? Are we compliant and ready to obey? To submit not just to a leader, but to *the* Leader and

His word? For many of us that's part and parcel of the way we've been brought up, or the way in which our Christian life has developed. But I went as a bishop to a certain theological institution and attended a lecture which was an introduction to the New Testament. The person began by saying, 'There are only a few stepping-stones in the New Testament on which you can actually rely.' Well, I didn't keep my calm, I can tell you! And this of course is the supreme difference: not submission to the word of God as something relevant to us today, but treating it as something from which you stand back from, and dissect, saying 'It's only a first-century document.'

If we mean business about submitting to the word, it means living under it and having a desire to grow under it. A common criticism of evangelicals is: 'The evangelical church is growing because people simply want certainties, and you can't have certainties in this world.' What a load of tripe! The New Testament *leads* you to certainties. 'No condemnation now I dread' ... 'I am justified by faith' ... 'I have peace with God'. But if you are a totally liberal thinker and dispense with the word of God as having any real authority (I'm talking of extreme liberals, for there are some very good people in the liberal position who do take the Bible seriously)—if you go out there, then you are going to get into that position. There's never going to be certainty. There can't be, when you are trying to walk in a marsh.

But the more you submit to the word of God, the more you find it to be true. The more you find it to be something trustworthy, the more you go on in your Christian life. I'm only sixty-seven, but the great thing about growing older is that the older I grow the more I'm convinced that this is the only word that can bring the answer to humankind. And I'm prepared to defend it and stand up for it, because I know that this is the way in which we can see the way through, and nothing else actually can answer the world's need.

We know that, the more we go on. That is why I believe

in the certainties of the Scriptures, because God confirms them in His action. Therefore we need to be people who submit to it rather than to stand above it—that's the different position. It's like the Indian who wanted to be ordained. His bishop was a very liberal bishop, who said, 'This isn't true in the Bible ... That isn't true in the Bible ...' and wouldn't ordain him, because he believed the whole Bible. So he gave the bishop a pair of scissors and the Bible, and said, 'Would you mind cutting out the bits you don't believe? Then I'll know what I'm supposed to believe.' So he ordained him.

Are we going to submit to the word? Not of course without intelligence, but as people who wrestle with it, dig under it, and believe that this is the word of God.

Then, *full of mercy*. This is a wonderful picture. Mercy triumphs over judgement, and how true that is of our Lord Himself. With the tax collectors and sinners, He is criticised as He sits with them. The Pharisees attack Him, and He answers them, 'It is not the healthy who need a doctor, but the sick. But go and learn what this means: "I desire mercy, not sacrifice." For I have not come to call the righteous, but sinners' (Matt. 9:12-13). How important it is that this mercy reach out, that movement should be made to reach the person outside the kingdom, rather than just spend all the time within having a blessed happy time of fellowship. It is that movement that wants to reach out with the mercy of God towards those outside Him. And this mercy often softens our hardness of principles. We have to balance mercy and judgement.

Do you remember how our Lord, when the disciples were hungry on the Sabbath, picked grain while going through a field. 'Oh! You can't do that,' they said. 'What is the greater thing?' our Lord replied. 'Settling the hunger, or keeping the Sabbath rule?' So mercy comes into the judgement situation. Again, he condemned the Pharisees, reminding them of how David and his companions were hungry and ate the consecrated bread. He said to them, 'If you had known what these words mean, "I desire mercy, not sacrifice", you would not have condemned the innocent' (Matt. 12:7).

Is mercy something which is in you? Time and time again the matter arises. The Pharisees again, in Matthew 23; Jesus says to them, 'You give a tenth of your spices … but you have neglected the more important matters of the law—justice, mercy and faithfulness …. You strain at a gnat and swallow a camel' (Matt. 23:23-24). Mercy, mercy, mercy.

The Good Samaritan—who was the neighbour, to the man who fell into the hands of the robbers? 'The expert in the law replied, "The one who had mercy on him." Jesus told him, "Go and do likewise."' (Luke 10:37). Mercy, mercy, mercy. It's part of the wisdom of God. How merciful are we?

People sometimes tell me that they expect the church to say 'No' when you approach it. I believe we need to have that quality of mercy that has a 'yes' face. Do you have a 'yes' face? Do people expected you to say automatically judgemental things—or merciful ones?

And *good fruit*. There are echoes of Matthew here: 'Every good tree bears good fruit', but 'by their fruit you will recognise them' (Matt. 7:17, 20). Well, good itself is good in itself; a good act is good regardless of its results, but is also good in its results. God saw that His creation was good, and He wants His people to have that goodness. One of the great descriptions of one of my favourite characters in the New Testament, Barnabas, is that he 'was a good man' (Acts 11:24). Because of his goodness, people were encouraged and attracted by him. He went into a hornets' nest of a situation, but his goodness, his 'yes' face, were such that the church grew and responded. Oh for more Barnabases in the church! Men and women of the Barnabas quality, of the goodness, the attractiveness, the loveliness of Jesus.

And then are we *impartial*? That means no fudging, no mixing up; this is someone who is actually able to think very carefully before they come to a decision, but is then quite firm and clear in that decision.

When I was Rector at All Souls in 1978-79 John Stott was Rector Emeritus. I asked John him to preach a series on major issues. He welcomed the idea, and it grew into his book, *Issues Facing Christians Today*[1]. The way he tackled it was to gather people from each subject area, including non-Christians, so that he could hear the world's attitude as well as that of the church. He produced a magnificent series of sermons that resulted in the book. He was able to judge, having looked at things objectively and not started with some bigoted, preconceived ideas.

Then, *sincere*. No pretence, no play-acting, no hypocrisy. Love must be sincere. So often there is insincerity in the world. Time and time again people can lie directly to your face, because it's the only way of getting you off their back. When people do that you distrust them. But the Christian's word must be clear. You need to be someone who is known for telling the truth with utter sincerity. It's not good enough just to be sincere; sincerity has to be clear, and part of your desire to follow the Lord.

I hope you've got the feeling of harmony in this pasage, underlying the beauty of the good life. Are you like these lovely people? Are you good people, my friends? Are we, am I, peace-loving, considerate, submissive to the word, full of mercy, good fruit, impartial and sincere? Wow! Are you that sort of person? I do hope you are.

Submit to God (4:1-10)

The person who divided the Bible into chapters did so while riding on a horse. Sometimes I think he was jogged by the horse! But he was perfectly right to put a break at the beginning of chapter 4.

We've been enjoying the sunshine and, I hope, the beauty of 3:13-18. But this is the Lake District! The sun has gone, the cloud and rain have come, it's grown dark, the music has stopped and we are back into the real world.

---

1. John Stott, *Issues Facing Christians Today* (Marshalls, 1984).

Bang!

The wrong spirit (4:1-3)

'What causes fights and quarrels among you?' Here we
have the wrong spirit, the spirit that causes so many problems, quarrels and battles. 'You want something but don't
get it. You kill and covet, but you cannot have what you
want. You quarrel and fight.'

It is the spirit that was released by the Zealots, but it's
one that is still around. It's an awful spirit, not least
amongst Christians' it's a disgrace when we allow it to ex-
ist. We know it happens, and we know it's wrong. It all
comes from the world in which we are, a world that suffers
from coveting, from advertising glitz. Even if you are very
poor you probably have a TV set, so it is constantly thrown
at you what the good life is supposed to be. You're told you
should have this, and this, and this. An incredible amount
of money is put into the Lottery every week by people who
have the sheer hope that they will win the jackpot. I don't
know how anyone can believe it's likely to happen to them.
I like the story of the man who suddenly said to his wife,
'Oh, I've forgotten to buy my lottery ticket.' She stopped
the car by a drain and said, 'There we are, this will save
time. Throw the money down there.' This coveting world!
We know it's true; but we are caught up in it even so, and
if we are not careful we are affected and moulded by it.

Now this is something, of course, that causes quarrels
and fights. When you think about it, 'I want that country'
has caused wars—Hitler's greed, and all the rest of it. Today it's much the same. There's so much that causes pain,
difficulty, murder and suffering in the world. It's the world,
not part of the Christian life (or it ought not to be), but we
have to face up to this wrong spirit that creeps in.

James indicates (verse 3) that sometimes we come to and
ask things of God and we 'do not receive, because [we] ask
with wrong motives, that you may spend what you get on
your pleasures'. For many, many people that is what prayer
is. A recent poll found that about 75% of people in this

country claim to pray. But what do they pray? Well, what did you learn to pray? Very often it's 'God bless Mummy and God bless Daddy, and please give us sunshine on our sports day, and during the Keswick Convention', and so on—we ask God to deliver what we want. But when we do that we are actually rubbing the Aladdin's lamp which we call prayer, and we expect the Lord appear saying, 'Yes master, what do you want me to do?' So you ask: 'I want a Cadillac for Christmas, I want to be free of cancer, I want to live a good life until I'm ninety.' Isn't that what most people do with prayer? Until you wake up and as a Christian you see it the other way round. And you kneel before the Lord and say, 'Master, what do You want?', and you put your life at His feet and offered to His will.

In James 4:3 they ask for their own pleasures, and so they don't receive. People sometimes take Scripture right out of context. 'Ask and it will be given you,' they say. 'Look, this is what the Bible says.' But where does that come from? It comes in Luke 11, the Lord's Prayer. What is the context? 'Our Father which art in heaven—may I have what I want?' No! It says '*Your* kingdom come .... *Your* will be done .... *Your* glory' (cf Luke 11:2-4). My spiritual life—'Lead us not into temptation'—and only then my physical needs; those are the parameters in which you ask, and it's an important arena to understand. So James is describing a whole arena of wrong treatment of our God, that should not be true in the Christian church but still enters it through prayers of that sort. And the more we come to know the Lord, the more we are attuned to His will and how to pray.

Friend or Foe? (4:4-6)

You must decide whose side are you on. God's? Not if you act only by human standards. Verse 4 uses the term 'adulterous'. If you know your Old Testament, you know the book of Hosea, where Israel is called an adulteress because she's been unfaithful and broken her relationship with

God. The same thing happens in Isaiah. And so it is here. The situation is that you have been put into a relationship with God, established for us in Christ, and now you act as though you're not in that relationship. You act as if your first love is to other people, or to the world, or to things. Are you an adulterer, my friend, in New Testament terms? Someone who's unfaithful to God, whose friendship with the world is more important than friendship with God?

James is the preacher. He's a stinger. He doesn't just say that's wrong. He says that you actually hate God (verse 4). Again, you are an enemy of God if you are someone whose main friendship is with the world, its standards, ambitions and thinking, rather than with a deep desire to be a person immersed in the word of God. 'You are my friend,' said our Lord, 'if you do what I command.' You want to be a friend of the Lord? That's how you do it. And how important it is to do so, and how often we have to stop and see that we have drifted, and need to come back across the line to God in repentance.

A strange phrase now follows. 'Or do you think Scripture says without reason that the spirit he caused to live in us envies intensely? But he gives us more grace.' (verses 5-6). What does that mean?

The NIV has a marginal note here that suggests, *'that God jealously longs for the spirit that he made to live in us*; or, *that the spirit he caused to live in us longs jealously.'* They are alternative translations; we're not quite sure. But the RSV says, 'that He yearns jealously over the spirit he has made to dwell in us'—God loves us, and He's jealous for us with the true jealousy of God, that we might be faithful to Him, and love Him, and yearn for Him. He wants to give us grace. It may mean that. Or it may mean that all of our problems tend to spring from a jealousy in our own hearts. One way or the other, God still wants us to take this issue seriously.

Taking God seriously (4:7-10)

Verses 7-10 continue down that line. 'God opposes the

proud but gives grace to the humble', who really want to
walk with Him. There may be some who are here this
morning in rebellion against God. You know full well that
friendship with the world is more important to you than
friendship with God. Why you are here I don't know—or
do I? Perhaps you, particularly, have got to hear what
comes next, because here James is talking to the Zealots,
who have gone overboard against God. And he is still saying to them, 'There is still time to repent.' In fact, it'll be
the final word tomorrow morning.

There is still time to turn, however far you've gone.

> There's a way back to God
> From the dark paths of sin;
> There's a door that is open
> That you may go in.

We used to sing that, and it is a great truth; there *is* a way
back to God. It's true for all of us if we are going to take
God seriously; it demands a readiness to think through
with God what is important.

Submit yourselves, then, to God. Let us review ourselves
for a moment, and check that we really do submit to God.
One of Lord Nelson's conquered foes, knowing his reputation for graciousness and kindness in victory, offered
Nelson his hand. Nelson refused. 'Your sword first, sir, and
then your hand.' Thus our Lord says: 'Your sword first—
Submit. And now your hand, in friendship.' First we must
submit to Him as God.

That was the issue for me when I was twenty. Is He
God—or not? If He is, then I submit my whole life to
Him. If He isn't, then I give it all up. And if we submit, the
one thing we want to say is, 'Your will be done—what is
Your will?' Some people wish they had been called to Africa, but they need to be right where they are, in their
house, caring for someone in their street for the rest of their
life. We may not like that in the same way. It may not have
the same glamour. For others it does mean uprooting and
going out in a different direction of service. But we submit

day, after day, after day. We should pray, 'Your will be
done. This day, help me to do Your will. And in contacts
with people where I am, in my office, in my place of work,
in my sports club, wherever it is, help me to do Your will.'
Submit to God. You are His servant, this is His day. You
are the person who may be able, in some particular way, to
fulfil His will today.

Resist the devil. The devil is subtle, someone who twists
and turns. We are told in Ephesians 6:12 to 'put on the full
armour of God', so that we can stand our ground. We need
to resist, and it will mean a fight. This is especially so for
young people. You who are students are under enormous,
enormous pressure from the devil's agents around you to
submit to the standards of the world. If you leave home and
go to any institution you'll be under enormous pressure
there too. The world wants to press you, it is restless until
it's got you into the same way as they are.

The Christian who is to stand against that needs to be
able to resist the devil, as Joseph did; to run away when
temptation is put in one's way. How important it is that we
resist! Instead of falling to Satan, we go closer to God. We
need to weep with God, to spend time with Him, to draw
near to Him day after day in all that we are.

Sometimes it's only as we see God that we really see sin
properly. Isn't that true for all of us? It's true of Isaiah in
the temple, when he sees the vision of God: 'I am ruined!
For I am a man of unclean lips' (Isa. 6:5). It is only as we
see more of God that we see ourselves as we really are.
When C. S. Lewis came to faith, he said, 'I then saw what I
really was, a zoo of lust, of bedlam, of ambitions.' You see
yourself. It's very difficult to do that before. Most people
come to faith by looking at the Lord and coming to Him
first, and then following it with repentance and holding to
the cross, because you only begin to see your need of salvation when you've actually come to Him and seen yourself
in His light. So constantly we need to come near to Him.

That demands time. It means helping people to grasp
the majesty, reality and holiness of God. That isn't always

achieved by a happy-clappy rave-up; much as I like happy-clappy rave-ups, they are not enough in themselves. There needs to be quietness and a waiting upon God as well, and often we've lost that in a sense of irreverence. We don't even start church services formally now, we all have to be friendly, and that's great in one way. But there's a sense in which you need to come in reverence to worship God. We've lost a lot of that, and we need to bring it back now— the sense of the reverence of God. The other day I was confirming a law student, and I asked him, as I ask all people being confirmed, 'What was it that brought you to God?' He said, 'I was in the cathedral, and the incense was going up against the stained-glass window, and I realised that God was for real.' Here he was with the Lord Jesus as his Saviour, and he was really raring to go.

God had to touch him with the majesty. Don't always wear ragged jeans at the front of your chancel. There is the majesty of God.

Wash your hands, you sinners. This is a very strong word. James is talking about hardened sinners, but they can still wash their hands and come back to God.

Purify your hearts, you double-minded. This is a word to those who fool around with God. They want Him and yet they don't want Him. They want Him on Sunday, but not on Monday; in the church, but not in the home. And this double standard, that so often disgraces God in the world, is something to which we are tempted all the time. I am, you are, we are.

Grieve, mourn and wail. And so we grieve with deep regret, real repentance, absolute misery because we've let God down. How often you and I have felt that! 'Lord, O Lord, if only I could re-write what happened yesterday, or last week, or even years ago!' And we mourn with deep sadness that we've hurt God, we've failed God, we've run away from Him and let Him down. And there's wailing and bitter weeping.

When we did BBC World Service Broadcasts from All Souls, I received a letter from an American girl in the Peace

Corps in Liberia. 'I don't know why I'm writing to you.'
She poured out her heart; why she'd given up Christianity,
it was to her like marriage, suffocating, and so on. It was a
long, long letter. I wrote back enclosing a copy of a book I
used to send to a lot of people: *A Severe Mercy* by Sheldon
Vanauken[1], and one or two other books as well. I had no
immediate reply. A long time afterwards she came back to
Christ, and then she wrote to me. But one thing she could
not get over. In letter after letter, she wailed: 'How I must
have grieved my Lord.' She's now serving Christ in the
back streets of Washington DC, with a great love for the
Lord Jesus.

Change your laughter to mourning and your joy to gloom.
We are not to all go round with miserable faces; but the
wrong sort of laughter is cheap laughter. All this seems very
strong, but James is talking about taking God seriously.
This is the person who really does want to be humble under God.

Humble yourselves before the Lord, and he will lift you up.
And that too is a tremendously important passage, which
time prevents us exploring.

Think Christianly (4:11-17)

Attitude to others (4:11-12)

'Brothers,' he begins the final section (I'm sorry he's always
on about brothers, but there we are, brothers and sisters.)
'Do not slander one another.'

This is Christian to Christian. Let it be written right
across the media and across church after church; 'Do not
slander one another'. How often do you or I weep when we
see quoted in the national press one Christian slandering
another? How can that possibly further the kingdom of
God? The world wants to hear it, to be able to say, 'That's
what they're all like.' So we give opportunity to the devil.

---

1. Sheldon Vanauken, *A Severe Mercy* (1977). A moving love
story in which C. S. Lewis appears as spiritual guide.

James is so emphatic about it because we expect the world to slander us. We were warned about it in 1 Peter 2:12, 'Live such good lives among the pagans that, though they accuse you of doing wrong, they may see your good deeds.' The accusation is of slander. In 1 Peter 3:16, the same thing. You need to have such a clear conscience that even though they are slandering you, your life will still stand up to examination. Who would ever want to be Archbishop of Canterbury? This beloved man of God George Carey and his lovely wife Eileen who love the Lord Jesus with all their heart, have had to stand up to so much. I long that we in the church might learn to have the love that expects the best, not the worst; that doesn't run to judge' that doesn't say, 'There must be more to it than that!' Because this is a man of God. The press cannot break George Carey, because he's a man of God with integrity. They can't rake muck on him, because in God's mercy he walks humbly with his God.

My friends, this is an important issue. It's the royal law, that you should love your neighbour as yourself. You need to love your brother and sister as yourself, in the Lord Jesus. And if we do have something we need to say about someone, say it to them personally, not in public.

Attitude to life (4:13-17)

In these lovely and perhaps more familiar verses we come to the business of trading.

One of the things we learned in Chester was to do with the gentry. There were all sorts of conditions of people there, some of them very aristocratic and very nice—solid silver cruets, that sort of thing. Yet I was interested when somebody in the gentry said, 'Most of these people aren't proper gentry.' Apparently 'the gentry' are only those who actually own land. The others are just middle-class people who've made money.

In trading (verse 13)

But in this little section we are dealing with middle-class

people who've made money. Tomorrow we begin with a
nice torrent of rain on the other lot, before we get into a
nice passage about healing.

So here are the traders who lived to trade to make
money. There's nothing wrong in trading, but if you only
live for that, it consumes you, says James. Well, we know
that's true; we know, and James would have known, the
parable of the rich fool—who said with satisfaction 'My
barns are full,' and to whom God said, 'You fool, this night
your soul will be required of you' (Luke 12:16-20). James is
echoing his brother all the time. This is a man who's putting the Lord's words into action. Here he is picking up the
presumption of the trader, that he is master of his life and
destiny. But remember when the bubble burst in the Stock
Exchange? Or the collapse of Barings Bank? Am I master
of my destiny?

Some people, even some Christians, read the *Financial
Times* at breakfast, lunch, tea, and dinner. They sleep with
it under their pillow and wrap their fish and chips up in it
the next day. But there are more important things in life.
It's very important if you are in the business world—but do
you live for it? No. The important thing is that the person
in the midst of that environment is able to see that the values of the Lord Jesus are bigger than that. Even though he
needs to be a good employee or employer and good at the
business world, it must not consume him. How many people in exactly that position have said, 'There must be more
in the world than this'! As a Christian, I cannot devote my
whole life simply to making money and not have time to
serve God in other ways.

Well, these are big issues. So often in churches we've not
addressed the issue of work properly. We need to preach it,
teach it, study it, organise groups to discuss it. It's terribly
important, because this is how the world thinks.

Do you know the story of the man who was enjoying the
sunshine alongside his little fishing boat, moored at the
quay? A passer-by said, 'What are you doing lying in the
sunshine? You could be getting more fish and making

more money.'

He replied, 'Why?'

The man answered, 'So that you can increase your income, get a second boat and get more fish.'

'Why should I do that?'

'So that you can expand your business and go on making more money till eventually you can retire and be able to sit in the sunshine.'

And the fisherman said: 'What do you think I'm doing now?'

In much the same way, we as Christians somehow have to see what really matters in the end. God has to touch our hearts. What of those outside the church; can we challenge the non-Christian on this? Yes, we can. I believe in values. To ask somebody, 'What do you really value, what is important to you?' is these days a powerful evangelistic method, and is a way in for Christ that I've found extremely valuable.

In uncertainty (verse 14-15)

Now James comes to the whole uncertainty and fragility of life, which you and I know about. So we don't say, 'I'm going to do this tomorrow, or the next day.' We do in practice, and to some extent—but who knows, who knows? Who knows whether I shall be here even tomorrow morning? None of us knows. We live always at the present moment. So we should say, 'If it is the Lord's will, we will live and do this or that.' It was a well-known phrase in Christian circles, and James includes it here.

At the time I began researching this section, we went to Bosnia, during the conflict, for Operation Christmas Child. We'd been warned to take Mars Bars, sleeping-bags, and as much water as we could for our needs, and a tin hat. We needed all that. It was all very uncertain. One of my friends said, 'If you don't come back we'll give you a lovely send-off in the Cathedral'—very encouraging!

But it was a reminder of the fragility of life. What is our life? It's important that we measure it out. In the old days one used to say 'DV' endlessly: 'I'll come, DV.' It stood for *Deo Volente*, which is Latin for 'God willing'. In the end people became modernised, left the Latin behind, and began to say 'God willing' in English. They abbreviated that, too. There's a story of a person from London who was invited to speak in Chester. He sent a telegram: 'I shall come, GW.' They wired back. 'No, come LMS, it's quicker.' You have to be a certain age to understand that joke (it's about railways).

Unfortunately we reacted against over-use of the phrase and we don't use it any more. But we should still see the idea as part of our thinking, and occasionally remind ourselves, as Paul did: 'I will come to you very soon, if the Lord is willing' (1 Cor. 4:19), and so on. It's important. We live under the will of God, and we need to say it from all of our hearts together.

In the face of all this, and in spite of submitting to the will of God, we have in verse 16 the traders boasting about how much money they're making and rubbing their hands. We have the arrogance of these people, often against the humility of people being trampled underfoot in Jerusalem; the failure of them to think of the oppressed; their one desire to make money. Well, my friends, you and I may not be in that league. But we are people who need to live under the gracious will of God. He's given us one life to live. None of us knows for how long. My father died at a much younger age than I am now, my wife's father earlier still. We don't know.

But if we want to live for the Lord Jesus, may we this day resolve afresh to ask Him to help us to live the good life—the good life on His terms; to humble ourselves unto the mighty hand of God, to seek His will and to know what it is to be cleansed and renewed, and to say, however much of our life is still there for us on this earth, 'If it's Your will, if it's Your will—and above all else, may I do Your will and glorify You, my blessed Saviour. Amen.'

5: 'Always Keep an Eternal Perspective'
James 5:1-20

The end is in sight! And that's exactly what this chapter's all about—keeping an eternal perspective.

When I was fourteen I was evacuated to Syston in Leicestershire. During the summer holidays we youngsters filled in our time trying to think of things to do. Several of us set off to ask the local farmer if there was a job. 'Oh yes,' he said. So we turned up next morning, and he said, 'You go down to the field at the end of the lane and you start weeding.' It was an enormous field. It seemed to have hundreds of furrows and thousands of weeds. He said, 'I'll be down later on to see how you're getting on.' We worked like Trojans and exhausted ourselves. He didn't come. The next morning he said, 'Back to the same field, I'll be down later to see how you're getting on.' We didn't get quite so far the next day. And so it went on. And on the day we were lying in the sun, he came.

My dear friends, we need to have the eternal perspective before us. The Lord is at the door, always, at any moment, for any of us; at any moment we may meet Him. We are always within an eternal perspective, and James has it.

Maybe we'd like it to be like modern aeroplanes. Where flight details and time of landing are displayed in front of you. If life were like that, we'd certainly not trust in the same way. But as it is, we don't know when the landing will come. This thought runs underneath the whole of James's letter. The more you read this letter the more it impresses you; just like in the teachings of his brother, the Lord (for example the parable of the foolish virgins, or of the stewards, or of the returning master, or of the talents). Indeed that very description that we looked at earlier in the epistle, of the Lord of glory, is, we saw, very much a reference to the judgement and to the coming of our Lord.

So underneath all this, there's a great sense of the ulti-

mate. The rich man will fade away (1:10). 'Blessed is the
person who perseveres under trial because the crown of life
is ahead' (cf 1:12). Or 2:12—'Speak and act as those who
are going to be judged by the law that gives freedom'; remember, you're going to be judged. Or 4:12, which we
rapidly skimmed yesterday—'There is only one Lawgiver
and Judge', so don't judge one another. Our Lord said,
'Judge not that you be not judged' (Matt. 7:1). And he said,
'For in the same way as you judge others, you will be
judged, and with the measure you use, it will be measured
to you' (7:2). Wow! When you are quick to judge people,
remember the same judgement comes back to you.

So we have this encouragement in chapter 5 to move
forward with the purpose of God all the way, because we
are going to meet Him. Verse 4, the Lord knows what's
going on. Verses 7 and 9, don't take judgement into your
own hands, because 'The Judge is standing at the door!'
The Judge knows the absolute truth, and no-one else does.
Not even our closest friends know the truth about us. The
Lord, the Judge, is standing at the door.

The theme of the ultimate meeting with the Lord, then,
underlies the whole chapter. Although it's pretty obvious
here at the beginning, keep it in mind when we get on to
the business of healing, and you will begin to see how some
false interpretations have led us up the garden path.

Those who make others suffer (5:1-6)

So let's now come to the first passage, these first six verses.
We may wonder what they have got to do with us. Then
we hear of such things as Cambodia and the killing fields
and how almost the whole Christian church there was
murdered. Not one of us here would have survived. And it
wasn't just killing, it was butchering and torture and terrible, terrible, terrible things. How our brethren must have
cried out to God in the midst of that oppression! So let's
feel it, my friends; this is not just the time of James, it is
also for many people the time of this generation, where

man is still abominable to man. Such is the sin that comes, even sometimes as we have already thought about Rwanda, from people who name the name of Jesus. And that makes it all the worse.

James says, 'Now listen, you rich people.' You remember, it's not just a matter of riches, but of people who have power. James does not approve of the methods of the Zealots. He said that the way to fight this wrong is not to take up arms and go round murdering people. Would, under God, that should be said in Northern Ireland. Would, under God, that should be said in every part of the world. You don't solve problems by the gun, necessarily. Some would cite World War II, but I think that's a separate issue. Here we are talking about oppression, and James reacts against that; rightly or wrongly, that's how he feels and we are dealing with his epistle.

But that doesn't mean he sits down like a wimp. Here's a man who has a righteous cause in his heart that has fired him through this epistle. So it's been very uncomfortable to read, and has reminded us of the huge responsibility we should have for righteousness, justice, fairness and peace in the world. Far from sitting down, he's been right out there in the forefront to bring every pressure he could bear. And people like Baroness Cox, who's with us today[1], and others like her from the House of Lords, have a lot of influence they have brought to bear in the name of Christ, to try to reach into these situations. And it is right to do so.

James was called 'James the Just'. That was how he was known on the streets of Jerusalem, such was his reputation for standing in the name of Jesus for justice. And here was the injustice of the day. About 90% of the land was held by these rich aristocrats. If you held the land, you held the power. Of course you can see the same in medieval England with its feudalism, serfs and slaves and all the rest of it. The aristocrats wielded the power. Hence James says. 'What on earth are you giving them special places in the

1. Baroness Caroline Cox gave an afternoon talk at the Convention, on 'The Persecuted Church'.

synagogue or the meeting for? These are the people who
are exploiting you and dragging you into the courts' (cf
2:6). Money brought power, and it was used to oppress. We
need to imagine ourselves in that situation: trampled down
in some of the filthy back streets of Jerusalem, downwind
from the sewers, with inadequate clothing to get through
the winter. They were cold and hungry. And some of these
rich people simply said, as we have already seen, 'Well, the
Lord bless you. Go and get warm' (cf 2:16). We need to sit
there with them in imagination. We have to know what it
is to be in the fields, to not know whether we are going to
get our wages at the end of the day, and to know that if we
don't, we and our families will starve. This situation was
condemned in the Old Testament; but, it seems, it was
happening here.

The need to weep and wail (5:1)

So James says, 'You need to weep and wail, you people
who are doing this, you need to have this terrible misery'
(cf 5:1). We would want them to feel the terrible misery of
what they're doing, though so often the arrogance and
power they possess means they don't worry. But when we
identify with those suffering, *we* weep and wail.

A little while ago we were out in Thailand. We visited
the River Kwai, and saw one of the huts where captured
Allied soldiers were held prisoners. It was filled with
memorabilia, and it was all awful. But what finished me
was a photograph of an English soldier, totally naked,
bound to a post with barbed wire. I cried my eyes out, I just
couldn't take any more. What man does to man! And no
wonder James says to these people who are doing it, 'You
need to weep and wail for what you've done.' Propheti-
cally, of course it came true. Within a few years, because of
the Zealots, Jerusalem was destroyed and almost every rich
aristocrat in Jerusalem lost everything.

Now, how do we learn from it?

The need to see the uselessness of hoarding wealth (5:2-3)

In the next two verses James tells us that possessions in themselves are not of great value. Our Lord Himself spoke about them in the Sermon on the Mount, which James constantly echoes: 'Do not store up for yourselves treasures on earth, where moth and rust destroy, and where thieves break in and steal. But store up for yourselves treasures in heaven, where moth and rust do not destroy, and where thieves do not break in and steal' (Matt. 6:19).

James adopts the same approach. Gold and silver, which are valued precisely because they don't corrode—even these will be destroyed. They hoarded wealth (verse 3), hence the loss of it will be extremely bitter; whereas we should hoard the wealth of what is really valuable to us in life. 'Think on these things,' says Paul, 'whatsoever is true, noble, just, pure, lovely, admirable, excellent, praiseworthy' (cf Philippians 4:8)—these are the lovely things of the world. And we play around with the sordid so often, even as Christians.

So we need to come back with James to weep and see the significance of this. Some of us are blessed with possessions. Sometimes I think that in retirement we find ourselves better off, some of us, than we've been all our lives. And sometimes, for those of you who've been on the minimum in earlier years, it takes some adjusting to. But our Lord also told us to enjoy and also to be responsible. And so together we often have to work these things out.

The need to see the eternal significance of injustice (5:4-6)

We need to realise what it was like for the person who had worked all day in the heat, and then has to go home and tell his family, 'We can't eat tonight because I depend on each day's pay to buy enough food to keep you alive'—while his employer was saying, 'I'm going to use this day's profits to build a monument to myself.'

In verse 4, James says, 'The cries of the harvesters have reached the ears of the Lord Almighty.' Wham! The Lord is the Judge. You can't do this thing and the Lord not know about it. You may call yourselves religious people (and they did), and yet you are exposed before God. You cannot do this, He is the perfect Judge, the righteous Judge.

So this passage is a very strong warning against the injustices of the world. And to many people going through deep oppression there must be some sense that the word of God in the Old and the New Testaments' understands what we are going through.

'You have lived on earth in luxury and self-indulgence' (verse 5). Remember how Amos describes the rich: they lay on beds of ivory, drank bowls of wine and had the best meat, and they thrust aside all thought of the evil day (cf Amos 6). Even Amos saw it. James echoes him in attacking the softness of luxury. The point is not just that luxury is wrong, it's a luxury that ignores the cries of the needy. My friends, this is an uncomfortable epistle. We have to ask ourselves, what is the balance between what we spend on ourselves and what we spend on others? I find that worrying, and so it should be; it should disturb us constantly if we follow the word of God.

In the New Testament again, Paul says, 'Command those who are rich in this present world not to be arrogant nor to put their hope in wealth, which is so uncertain, but to put their hope in God, who richly provides us with everything for our enjoyment' (1 Tim. 6:17). Hallelujah! That's true. Sometimes we are embarrassed by the way He gives us so much to enjoy! 'Command them [the rich] to do good, to be rich in good deeds, and to be generous and willing to share. In this way they will lay up treasure for themselves as a firm foundation for the coming age, so that they may take hold of the life that is truly life' (6:18-19).

Indeed that's true. Paul, James, our Lord, Amos—time and time again, the message comes across to us. And though we may not stand in the same situation as existed in Jerusalem, and we don't, most of us; yet the issues arising from it challenge us in the affluence most of us have in this country, compared with the desperate situation of many in the world, and not least many of our brothers and sisters in Christ.

In verse 6, there is the trampling of innocent people, 'You have condemned and murdered innocent men, who were not opposing you.' That was almost James's epitaph for himself: in AD 61, the aristocratic power-bodies determined to get rid of James, and together with the High Priest they had him stoned to death. There are a great many such mafia-style groups in today's world. I often encounter what is almost a secret society when I deal with some councillors and others in various places. It exists sinisterly as an undercurrent and it demands first loyalty before justice and fairness. That's in our own society.

Such a society ganged up to get rid of James. The ordinary people in Jerusalem thought James was a hero; they demanded that the person who authorised his death should be removed from office. They achieved it, because of the strength of feeling arising from James's popularity. He had stood for the poor in the midst of the oppression.

But is there something else in that phrase: 'You have ... murdered innocent men, who were not opposing you'? Of whom else is that true, but his brother and our Lord? There is a sense in which the Lord Jesus Christ is being referred to. He too died as a martyr, as an innocent person at the hands of those who wanted to get rid of Him because He was in their way. And so the Bible speaks of the innocent one, our Lord Jesus Christ, the Lamb without blemish, who knew no sin and became sin for us; they killed the Prince of Life. In all the murders of Cambodia, in all the terrible events of the killing fields, in all the martyrdoms of our brothers and sisters across the world even in this very day, they align with the Lord who died that way first, for you and for me.

Those who suffer (5:7-12)

So James now comes to those who suffer. And he says that this needs patience.

The need for patience (5:7-12)

The troubles will end. It may be that it will only be when the Lord comes back. But look forward with this. Have this assurance; one way or the other this will come to an end. You may be tempted to join the Zealots and embark on murderous escapades, but remember, be patient, don't join the violent lot. The Lord's coming (it is almost a technical term here) approaches and He will gather His own unto Himself. There's something about the sort of pregnant atmosphere here, the excitement—the sense that it's going to happen. 'I know you can't actually see it this moment, but be patient; until the Lord's coming, until He meets with us.'

He uses the example of the farmer. I loved meeting the farmers in my diocese. On the whole they are pretty patient people. They have to be; it's no good running round in frantic circles just because it isn't raining. It will come tomorrow, or the next day. It doesn't turn a drama into a crisis. So wait, see the farmer. They were all people who worked in the fields, so they understood the example.

In verse 9 he speaks of grumbling. You see, pressure produces unrest, and then we have a nasty habit of blaming each other. People who once were in fellowship begin to fall out because they are under pressure. Rather than attacking the wrong, we start to get angry and vexatious with each other. James says, 'Watch it. It's no good, you've got to be patient and avoid this business of grumbling and judging each other, because (verse 9), 'The Judge is standing at the door!' Here it is again. The judgement seat of Christ.

Then in verses 10-11, he gives further encouragement from the prophets when he uses Job as an example. And how much there is in Jeremiah, who will be the subject of next week's Bible Readings.[1] In particular, he speaks of Job's perseverance (verse 11), the quality of having your feet on the rock and standing there, whatever's hitting you,

---

1. These Bible readings are included in the present volume: see pp. 112-190.

rocking you or moving at you.

Job was not, in one sense, a persecuted prophet. Perhaps that helps many of us to identify with him more, to identify with the blizzard of troubles that he experienced in his life. I realise ours is not the same catalogue of troubles, but often we have illness, and problems, and ups and downs of life; and we can therefore perhaps identify with him. So thank you Lord, and thank you James, for giving me Job in this passage; because it pulls us in as well, as people who often go through difficult times.

Job had to learn the difficult lesson that you have to trust in God always; that 'Though he slay me, yet will I hope in him' (Job 13:15); that 'I know that my Redeemer lives' (Job 19:25). But at the end of it all he had to say, when he really woke up to it, 'My ears had heard of you but now my eyes have seen you. Therefore I despise myself and repent in dust and ashes' (Job 42:5-6). And out of this terrible experience came a vision of God as never before. As the Bible says, the Lord blessed the end of Job's life more than at the beginning. So Job is also a real encouragement. And James gives us this wonderful phrase, one of the great key phrases of the New Testament and the Old Testament: 'The Lord is full of compassion and mercy' (verse 11). Is that true or is it not?

An elderly lady in our church in Manchester, a sweet soul whom we absolutely loved, was hospitalised very suddenly and became very severely ill. Her faith went through the window, bless her, during her illness. It happens very often; we can't think properly, we need other people alongside us. Our lady worker sat with her for the whole of one afternoon and said to her, 'Until I hear you say, "God is love", I'm not going to move out of this hospital.' And our friend came to that point where she could say it. When she was recovered she stood in church and said to our worker, 'Thank you Mary. You held my hand. And when I got back to that truth, then the sun came out and here I am.' God is love. He is full of compassion and mercy. And we hold on to it in spite of all the problems around us. This is our God.

How wonderful!

Then in verse 12 there is warning about oaths. James is not talking about law court procedures. He is talking about the pressures of persecution again, and how not only can you react against each other or cease to be patient, but you can also start using language that you shouldn't be using. He says, 'Above all'; it's obviously following on from what's gone before. And how often under stress people use language that the world uses. James is concerned that we ourselves should not adopt language that drags God into our oaths and into our expressions and into our frustrations. He is not talking about legal oath-taking; I believe that the man I knew who refused to take his ordination oath because of this text was wrongly interpreting it. It's about something much deeper.

It's so common today. If the name of Allah is used as a swear word—obviously very offensive for Moslems—there's an outcry. But you can hear the name 'Christ' used a thousand times an evening on TV, and our Lord is blasphemed day after day, in office after office, in home after home. And it's very easy for us just to pick it up. So, under the frustration, beware. Keep your eyes upon the Lord, know you are answerable to Him, keep the patience you need to have. Don't react like the Israelites did, who started moaning, 'What on earth have you brought us into the wilderness for, with this wretched manna we have to have every day?' and forgetting they'd been liberated from oppression. How easily we moan! We must hold back from that, we must hold on to God, look to Him, and know that we are running a race set before Him and that we shall meet Him; and that the landing may come at any moment.

The need for prayer (5:13-16)

We come now to the passage for which most people know James, about suffering and healing in this context. It's so often pulled in different directions, and cases are built upon it. But I'm going to try to take it as carefully as I can.

There are seven references to prayer in this passage, so we know what it's all about: prayer. But remember what the context is: the Lord's second coming and the ultimate end of life and of meeting with Him. That underlies everything. And if you keep that in mind, as I've said earlier, it does help us to keep the context.

First of all, *'Is any one of you in trouble?'* You need to know that two Greek words are combined here; one means 'evil', the other 'suffering'. What we for some reason translate 'trouble' is, in the Greek, 'trouble which means suffering evil'. Back in 5:10, the prophets' 'patience in the face of suffering', the same word is used: suffering evil and persecution. It's the same in 2 Timothy 2:9, when it speaks about suffering for the gospel even to the point of being chained like a criminal: the same word. Does that help us to understand it? It's obviously what we should be thinking about in the persecuted church session: enduring hardship.

That's the context. However we may wish to interpret more widely, that is what James is actually talking about. And there's a sense in which he is telling us that in the midst of this suffering of evil we do not just sit there, and we don't—in James's book—engage in violent resistance or guerrilla warfare: but we pray. We pray for our enemies, we pray for our persecutors, we pray for the situation which is around us, we pray for God's hand in this situation. Suffering evil is not just standing there saying, 'Isn't this awful?' It's getting on our knees and saying, 'God ...' It's that sort of suffering of evil, of persecution, of hardness and bitterness, which brings it to God.

And how important that is for us all, particularly when perhaps there's bitter opposition to your work for God, in your missionary society, or your church, or in your fellowship; and you come and you start to pray for the opposition, and for those standing against you. This is what James urges you to do.

Secondly, *'Is anyone happy?'* says the NIV, rather pathetically. 'Let him sing songs of praise.' It's a bit more than that. James is a serious man. The actual phrase is 'in good heart'. That's much better than 'happy'. For instance, when Paul is in the middle of the shipwreck, in the middle of the raging storm at sea, this is the word he uses. He doesn't come up on the deck and say, 'I am H.A.P.P.Y. ....'. What he says is this word James uses here: 'be of good cheer' (Acts 27:22,25). Be of good heart; though the storm rages round you, God is going to do something amazing.

This is the way in which this word is used, and that is why he uses it here. So if you are of good heart in the midst of this situation, if you're looking to God, sing praises. Actually, 'sing psalms' is what the word means. It means that we rejoice in God in all circumstances. I mentioned earlier that our favourite family wedding and marriage text is 'Rejoice in the Lord always; and again I say, rejoice.'

And for what do you give praise? The circumstances? 'Oh thank you Lord, we're all being persecuted'? Not so many years ago, you may remember, there was an appalling movement that told us to praise God for everything. If you didn't praise God for your cancer, you wouldn't be healed. It was an abominable misuse of Scripture. How can you praise God for evil? You can't. But you praise God that in the worst evil, He is still with you. That is what we give praise for. A man rang me up while that teaching was current. 'You're the rector of All Souls, I must talk to you. My son used to be a fine Christian and a member of the church, then he got married and now his marriage has broken up and he's been divorced. He's an alcoholic, he's on drugs and he's lost his job.' I listened sympathetically. And then he said, 'Of course we're praising God that his marriage broke up and he's on drugs and ...' Lord, have mercy. My heart went cold, my back shivered.

No, we don't praise for the circumstances, we praise that God is with us in any circumstances. Be joyful always, pray constantly, give thanks in all circumstances, for this is God's will for you in Christ Jesus. And this is a fundamental thing. For James's readers, the psalms were what you used for praise. Today we have many hymns. Find out which are useful to you, to sing and make music in your heart to the Lord, and for giving thanks to Him.

'*Is any one of you sick*?' comes next. The word is *astheneia*, the word that Paul uses in 2 Corinthians 12, where he prays for this *astheneia*, this 'thorn in the flesh', to be removed. And God says, 'This isn't going to be the way.' So Paul says, 'Therefore I will glory in my *astheneia*.' So Paul teaches us that this is not always removed.

Now, if you look too loosely at this text you can take it in a way that can mislead people very much. I remember a group of medical students in one of the London hospitals during the years we were serving in London, who got carried away with the idea that all you had to do was lay hands on people, anoint them, and they would be healed. They became absolutely hyped up with it. They said, 'We are going to clear out the wards of St Thomas's Hospital by going down there with this text in our hands.'

That leads people into all sorts of extraordinary positions. If you demand that God must heal because the Bible says so, you are going to be in real difficulty, even though God gloriously heals. But the passage here is about very serious illness. The normal Christian life in the church is that when we are sick and ill, we pray for each other. If you are in a fellowship group, that's where we carry each other. We pray for each other, and that's right. And in churches, there are often special times when we have healing prayer. At All Souls, every three months we had a special evening, but there were always times to pray for people individually in the corporate prayer gathering, as well as in the fellowship group. Thus there is this important element for praying for one another, and how wonderfully God meets with us! There are times when we are overwhelmed by the way in which He heals and touches beyond our expectation. But very often, that isn't the way; and we have to stand together with our Lord, looking to Him and trusting Him.

But here in particular it says that '*he should call the elders of the church*'. That's the clue, isn't it? It doesn't mean 'I've got a sore throat, I'll nip into bed and ring the pastor up and he can come round.' The reason they have to come to his or her bedside is because the patient is too ill to go to the church. There's no other reason; we are talking about someone seriously ill. And that is the context. The Lord is standing at the door. That is what is underlying the chapter and helps us to ease back to understand what this is all about. The particular case here must be people near that point in their lives when they are 'at death's door'—it's a special moment.

In the synagogues in the Jewish tradition the elders came together at such a time to a household. So James was just Christianising the Jewish tradition. He transfers it from the synagogue to the *ekklesia*, the church, and he sees this as the task of the elders of the church. Now the elders come in caring love, to pray over the person. It is a responsibility, in particular, of leadership. In Chester the son of our archdeacon was caught in a terrible accident and was lying in a coma at death's door. And there came the moment when I went to the hospital, with the knowledge of the whole diocese. We asked everybody in every church in the diocese who would do so, to stop at five o'clock on that Sunday and pray with me, and that I would pray over him and anoint him at 5 p.m. We did it together as a church. We couldn't take the church to the bedside, but the church came to the bedside with me. And how often that's important, in this serious arena!

Now the elders have come to the bedside. Imagine you are the one in bed. You're possibly weeks or days or hours from death's door. What do you want? Somebody to stand over you and say, 'Unless you have enough faith you'll die'? Or do you want someone to say, 'We're going now to pray that you'll be delivered and healed'?

Now, the task of the elders is to sense the situation. And when we look at the passage here we find out one or two important things. First, they should pray—yes, but also anoint him with oil. That's a lovely, strengthening thing to do for any person. Oil is that which is used for healing: the Good Samaritan bandaged up the traveller using oil. Oil is even to be put on your head when you're fasting, so that people don't know you are fasting, you look normal. When the disciples were sent out they were anointed with oil. But in no sense does anointing with oil act as a magical healing potion.

When I've been praying publicly for somebody who's seriously ill, people have sometimes said to my face at the church door, 'Unless you anoint them with oil they will not be healed.' Or they say, 'Unless you lay hands on them they will not be healed.' In each case I said, 'You believe in magic. I believe in a God who heals, and answers prayer.' The oil is important, it is a comfort, it is a strength, it is a sign between us and God, yes; and the laying on of hands is that which identifies. These are important elements. But to say, 'Unless you do that...', is to turn it into some sort of magical trick. Of course these things are helpful; but don't make them the things that heal, because in James we find that it is the prayer of faith that saves the sick. So we have to be careful, though these things are important and helpful, and it is all 'in the name of the Lord' (verse 14).

Then we come to verse 15, and the prayer of faith. Now James is always the surpriser, and we need to follow him quite carefully. He decides not to use the word for 'prayer' even though the translators do. The word he uses is only used elsewhere for a vow. Listen. In Acts 18 Paul had his hair cut off at Cenchrea because of a vow he had taken. Acts 21:23 mentions four men who made a vow. That is the word that James uses here. It is the vow of faith. So why translate it 'prayer', which can be very misleading?

It is, I think, helped by our understanding of Matthew 18:19. 'If two of you on earth agree about anything you ask for, it will be done for you.' And the following verse: 'Where two or three come together in my name, there I am with them.' The task of the elders is to be people who are mature in the discernment of the grace and will of God. As they come to this bedside, prepared in heart, cleansed and ready to meet with God and to wait upon Him, they— men, women or whoever they are—have to say to God, 'Is this going to be a moment when You want to move in a dramatic way; or is this the moment when we come with great comfort and stand with our brother or sister as they come towards the glorious radiancy of Your glory, as we read Scripture and pray with them, and see the wholeness of their soul restored in readiness to meet their Lord? Which is it, Lord?'

It is this vow of faith that has to discern it. There are times when we know that God is in this—there have been many times when I've known that with my staff, and we sense from the word 'go' that God was in the situation. So we prayed with a faith that was supremely confident because God had, in a sense, told our hearts. And although we know we could be wrong, in all cases where it's happened that I've experienced it's been right, and there's been a remarkable recovery even from the jaws of death. Other times, I don't get that peace as I stand with someone at their bedside. And often I'm more blessed than I can possibly say, as I read passages like 2 Corinthians 4 that speak of the glory, and going to be at home with the Lord. The room seems to fill with light, and I leave feeling I've just been on holy ground, as my brother or sister has walked into the presence of the Lord.

So when you come to the bedside, you have to sense with God what He is saying. That is what the word means, I suggest. And when you are on target with God, something happens. What is it?

Well, according to the NIV, James says, *'And the prayer offered in faith will make the sick person well.'* Now with due respect to the NIV translators, that is not what James says. If you've got an older version, you will see that it says, 'will save the sick'. What does the Greek say? 'Save'—*sozo*. It doesn't say, 'will make him well'.

Some people say, 'But I'm already saved.' Just a minute—we are talking about something deeper. Salvation is also connected with healing, and I can understand how the translators may move into that sense. But we want God's best for this person. And it is right and proper to say, 'If this is the way in which God wants to bring this person back to physical life again, and to fullness of life, hallelujah! This will be the work of the Lord Jesus; in His grace and by His Spirit that will save him from the jaws of death.' But it's also right to say that if God gives us the conviction that He's actually calling His child home, then we are also part and parcel of helping them, in their spirit, to hear the word which they cannot read because they are so ill; to pray for them because they cannot pray at that point; and, in the glorious fullness of the Lord Jesus, to give them the great bathing of Jesus in their hearts, that they may be healed and saved within, in readiness to meet Him.

You can take it both ways—whichever way it happens at that moment, God leads you so to pray.

So this is much more than saying, 'You pray, they will be well. This is what the Bible says.' And I'm sorry the translators, for some reason, have not kept to that word 'save'.

Then it says, *the Lord will raise him up*. He will raise him up if there is to be physical healing; but will also raise him up in the glorious resurrection, if this is the going home and you are preparing the heart to meet Him. Some of us have had the privilege of hearing others say, 'The music, the music, the music!' as they've gone across to meet Him. And you think what it's going to be like, when you come towards Him and the glorious wonder of His grace and love, as He comes to meet you. And we are there with them to help them at that moment, to bring a wholeness.

That's why the business of confession comes next. It's very important. And it is often important for a person, at the moment of passing into the presence of the Lord, to be able to hear one say, 'In the name of the Lord Jesus, my dear friend, you've shared that. The Lord knows. He's forgiven and cleansed you.' And to be able to bring them the peace of His assurance of forgiveness which they couldn't find themselves, in the illness that was consuming them.

So confession to one another can be a great blessing. The amazing thing is that this is where James uses the word 'healing'. Such is James the preacher; he uses 'saving' over the sickness and 'healing' over the confession, because the full healing of God is of your whole being. As an old phrase says: the loss of gold is much, the loss of health is more, but the loss of Jesus Christ is such that no man can restore. And those are the priorities all the way down the line. Healing is never to stand in the way of the full saving grace of the Lord, because this body is going to be thrown away. The real person is eternal with his Lord and her Lord.

So there's great sensitivity here in this beautiful passage of Scripture. 'The prayer of a righteous man,' it says, 'is powerful and effective.' Again, this is a beseeching prayer. Verse 16 is reminds us that elders should be righteous people, people who are walking close to God before they enter that sick room. They shouldn't just dash in, fitting it in between this and that, and say, 'Right, I'm going to lay hands on you, anoint you with oil and have a prayer; then off I go, because I've got to go and meet my child from school.' These are people who come ready in the Lord's name to wait upon Him in the sick chamber. The righteous person is the person right with God and prepared for this time of healing, or of restoration, or preparing their brother or sister to meet with the glorious Lord for ever.

The powerful and effective example of Elijah comes next. He is cited as an encouragement, and that's good, because Elijah had a lot of doubts and faltering alongside everything else. It helps us to know that he wasn't an armour-plated Christian. He wept his heart out and suffered spiritual depression. He was a person like us; and thank you, Lord, for that.

'He prayed earnestly,' it says. By the way, that does not mean 'in a trembling voice'. Some people interpret it like that: 'Unless you pray e-e-e-e-e-earnestly, with a quavery voice…' It just means 'fervently'. And 'fervently' means 'God help us.' But why did he pray it for three years? Because God had brought to him the conviction that this was what God's will was, and that's why he prayed in that particular way.

So finally we come to these last two verses. James is looking to the end, and still in the last two verses of this letter is longing that the Zealots and those who've run away from God should still come back to Him: there still is a way back to God. So he doesn't end with trumpets, he ends with evangelism. He ends with a desire for his brother who has wandered from the truth, that someone, someone, should bring him back. 'Whoever turns a sinner away from his error will save him from death and cover over a multitude of sins' (cf 5:20).

Yes, in spite of all that he thinks is wrong about the Zealots he still longs for them to be saved. And so we do with rebellious young people from our families, and rebellious people of our acquaintance who have run away from God, and trampled on Him, and thrown things at Him and said things about Him: 'O God, may someone, someone, someone, bring this sinner back.' Our hearts bleed with the desire that they may be saved in the fullness of salvation, back to the Lord Jesus and His saving grace.

So there's no greeting, there's no farewell. This is a staccato style of letter. It has been described as the 'ouch!' book. Would you agree with that, at the end of five mornings on this letter? Ouch! This is a moving, challenging and sometimes very disturbing epistle.

One modern development in the Church of England's liturgy is that these days we do not end with the blessing and our heads buried in our hands in the pew. It's followed by a challenge: 'Go in peace to love and serve the Lord. Now go out and serve.' James started his epistle by calling himself a servant of God and of Jesus Christ. If we are prepared to go out and fulfil that title, then James's epistle will have found its mark, and we will go out afresh to be the servant of God and the Lord Jesus Christ.

And so let me say: 'Go in peace to love and serve the Lord.'

'Studies in Jeremiah'
by Mr Charles Price

1 : 'Jeremiah and the State of his Nation'
Jeremiah 7-9

A lady was given a Bible commentary for Christmas. She found it very dull and hard going, as commentaries are if you just read them on their own. But when she next met the person who had given it to her, she said, 'I've been reading my Bible. It throws an awful lot of light on the commentary you gave me!'

Sometimes we do things that way round. But what we have to say in these Bible Readings has its origins in the Bible, and specifically in Jeremiah.

I don't know how excited you felt when you discovered we are going to look into the book of Jeremiah in these studies. Some of you may not know where it is in the Bible. But if you know anything about Jeremiah at all, you probably thought, 'How miserable!' Jeremiah is known as the 'weeping prophet'; you probably thought to yourself. 'We're in for a mournful time.' The *Oxford English Dictionary* defines 'Jeremiad' as, 'A writing or speech in a strain of grief or distress: a doleful complaint: a complaining tirade: a lamentation.' It adds that it comes from an allusion to Jeremiah in the Old Testament. Then it cites a sentence in which the word is used: 'I could sit down and mourn and utter doleful Jeremiads without end.'

So this is really cheerful stuff, isn't it? Yet despite its melancholy, it is one of the longest books in the Bible—fifty-two chapters. It's not the easiest book to read. If you read right through the Bible, you probably speed-read when you come to books like Jeremiah. Nor is it an easy book to understand. It's no obvious chronological or topical structure to the book. Almost every commentary gives you a different outline and a different structural analysis. It's a mixture of poetry and prose, and you interpret those, of course, in different ways. The text itself doesn't always explain its context. Sometimes you haven't a clue what's going on behind the scenes when Jeremiah says certain things, and without an appreciation of its circumstances, much of its message is lost and the main thrust of it is difficult to get hold of.

The Background

It's not an easy book. But the man and his message are inseparably bound together, probably more so than with any other prophet except Hosea. To understand the message we need to know something of the man, and to understand the man we need to know something of his message. Jeremiah lived in a specific time and he had a specific message that he addressed to specific people in specific circumstances. I want to explore some of that this morning, looking first at 1:1-3 and then concentrating in our main study on chapters 7, 8 and 9.

Firstly, then, 1:1-3. Jeremiah sets his story in a forty-year period of the history of Judah. 'In the thirteenth year of the reign of Josiah'—that is very significant, because something very important was taking place around that time. In 2 Chronicles we're told, 'Josiah was eight years old when he became king, and he reigned in Jerusalem for thirty-one years' (2 Chron. 34:1). He was the son of Amon, who was a bad king, like his father Manasseh, Josiah's grandfather, who was one of the most evil kings to ever reign in Judah. Manasseh reigned for fifty-five years and undid all the good that his father King Hezekiah had done before him. He installed pagan gods in the temple in Jerusalem, he sacrificed his own sons in pagan ceremonies, he was heavily into the occult, he practised witchcraft, sorcery and divination, he consulted mediums and spiritists, and he left an appalling legacy of vice, corruption and idolatry.

Manasseh was dramatically converted in the last days of his life, but too late to influence the nation for his son Amon who succeeded him and was equally evil. Two years into his reign Amon was assassinated and his eight-year-old son Josiah came to the throne.

But 'In the eighth year of his reign, while he was still young, he [Josiah] began to seek the God of his father David' (34:3). At the age of sixteen he was converted, we would say in New Testament terms: he began to seek after God for himself. And he began to purge the nation. 'In his twelfth year he began to purge Judah and Jerusalem of high places, Asherah poles, carved idols and cast images. Under his direction the altars of the Baals were torn down; he cut to pieces the incense altars that were above them, and smashed the Asherah poles, the idols and the images.' You can read some of the detail later on.

It was a year later, in the thirteenth year of his reign, that Jeremiah, he tells us, was called to his ministry.

In 2 Chronicles 34:8 we read, 'In the eighteenth year of Josiah's reign, to purify the land and the temple, he sent Shaphan son of Azaliah and Maaseiah the ruler of the city, with Joah son of Joahaz, the recorder, to repair the temple of the Lord his God.' At the age of twenty-six, he began to clear out the temple which had been neglected for several generations. He paid money to the priests who employed people to do the job. In the process (verse 14), 'While they were bringing out the money that had been taken into the temple of the Lord, Hilkiah the priest found the Book of the Law of the Lord that had been given through Moses.' In cleaning out the temple Hilkiah found this book tucked away somewhere in a back room, blew off the dust, took it to the king, read it to him, and the king tore his robes and said, 'God has given us instructions and we have not known what they were' (cf verses 14-21). It's very likely that the book they found was all or part of the book of Deuteronomy.

And so (verses 29-34), calling the nation together with

its elders, Josiah read parts of this book to them and then commanded them to renew the covenant that they had neglected. The people were all assembled together. And (35:1), 'Josiah celebrated the Passover to the Lord in Jerusalem, and the Passover lamb was slaughtered on the fourteenth day of the first month.'

Verse 7: to the ordinary people, Josiah gave 30,000 sheep and 3,000 cattle to participate in this great celebration of the Passover. Verse 8: to the officials, he gave 2,600 offerings and 300 cattle. Verse 9: to the Levites he gave 5,000 offerings and 500 hundred cattle. According to my arithmetic, there were 41,400 animals sacrificed over the sevenday period of the Passover. Verses 18-19: 'The Passover had not been observed like this in Israel since the days of the prophet Samuel; and none of the kings of Israel had ever celebrated such a Passover as did Josiah, with the priests, the Levites and all Judah and Israel who were there with the people of Jerusalem. This Passover was celebrated in the eighteenth year of Josiah's reign.'

Jeremiah's Temple Sermon (7-9)

Why am I taking the time to tell you all this? Because the discovery of the lost book of the Law precipitated in the eighteenth year of Josiah's reign this great celebration, such as they had never had for centuries—since the days of Samuel, it says. It was a wonderful time, the whole nation turned out, there was a carnival atmosphere, there was great joy in Jerusalem, everyone was excited, everyone was enthusiastic, revival was in the air. 'We're getting back on track with God,' they were saying. And the nation threw in its lot all together.

All except one man. One man stood on the periphery of all of this and smelt a rat. His name was Jeremiah. Although Josiah was genuine in his reforms (cf 2 Kings 23:25—there was no king like Josiah who genuinely turned to God in this way), for the people the reforms were superficial. They were following the lead of a popular king, they did all the right things, they enjoyed the celebration, they joined in the fun. But something was wrong.

Jeremiah 7-9 is his famous temple sermon. He doesn't put a date to it, so people have all kinds of opinions about when it was preached. There is a very similar message in chapter 26 that is dated as being in the reign of Jehoiakim, one of the later kings; so some people say that chapter 7 is the same message. I don't think it is. It is slightly different, and in any case, if it is the same message—why put it in twice? I believe, and it would take too long to give you all the reasons, that in chapter 7 Jeremiah is speaking at this time of spiritual renewal we have been reading about— where there was revival in the air. Everybody was excited once again about the worship of God, so it seemed.

In verses 7:1-11 the main thrust of Jeremiah's message is simple and direct. He says, 'You people who come into this place…' The place, of course, is what God describes as 'the house that bears my Name'. God can be met in the temple. He didn't then live as He does now in human beings—we, now, are the temple of the Holy Spirit. If you wanted to meet with God then you had to meet Him in the temple, in particular through the priesthood, in the Holy of Holies. It was called the Holy of Holies for one reason. God was there, symbolically made present by the Ark of the Covenant which represented His presence. Of course it was only symbolic, as Solomon said at the dedication of the temple: 'But will God really dwell on earth? The heavens, even the highest heaven, cannot contain you. How much less this temple I have built!' (1 Kings 8:27). But the temple at Jerusalem, which followed on from the tabernacle that God gave Moses to build in the wilderness, was the place where people came to meet with God.

The People's Worship (7:1-3)

He says to them, 'Hear the word of the Lord, all you people of Judah who come through these gates to worship the Lord.' You come into this place, he says, to worship God. Now—why? Why do we worship God? Have you ever asked that question? Why does God demand our worship? Is it because He has a big ego and we need to stroke it? To tell God how great He is? Many of us would be tempted to be godly if that was what being godly was—having your ego stroked. Are the demands of God like those nauseating demands of a tinpot dictator like Saddam Hussein, who insists that cars stop when he drives down the road? Is God's ego at stake? Of course not. The suggestion that God needs us to boost his ego is blasphemous. So why do we worship?

There are two reasons, both relevant to this message of Jeremiah. The most obvious one is: so that we might be aware of God in His power and His strength, and might find our security in that. Later, in 7:23, He says, 'Obey me, and I will be your God and you will be my people. Walk in all the ways I command you, that it may go well with you.' That is: if you know Me and you trust Me and you obey Me, then you'll be secure and things will go well with you.

The second reason is the more important one in this passage and probably, from our point of view, the most important one anyway. When God created human beings He created us to be in His image. People debate the nature of that image, but whatever else is involved, the image in which God created man is essentially His moral image. In other words, He created human beings to act and behave in such a way that our actions and behaviour give evidence of what God is like. Whatever else it means, it means, 'Look at the image, and it reminds you of the real thing: God.'

If we are created to be in God's image, we can never discover the true nature and function of human beings without knowing God. Hence to know what human beings are designed to be like, we need to know what God is like. And it is in worship, in acknowledgement of who God is, in all His moral attributes, His kindness, His love, His mercy, His goodness, His faithfulness—it is in recognising and acknowledging that, that we discover what we are supposed to be like, having been designed to be in His image. Which is why in Scripture, and here in Jeremiah's message in particular, the effects of true worship are always moral. The result of worshipping God is that the character of God is being seen in the way we live, behave, act and react.

That's why Jeremiah says in the middle of verse 3, 'Reform your ways and your actions, and I will let you live in this place.' The whole point of you meeting here to worship, he says, is that there should be a moral transformation in your life and behaviour.

I suppose true worship always expresses itself in moral character. In 2 Corinthians 3:18 Paul says, 'And we, who with unveiled faces all reflect the Lord's glory, are being transformed into his likeness with ever-increasing glory, which comes from the Lord, who is the Spirit' (2 Cor. 3:18). We reflect, that is, as we expose ourselves to the Lord Jesus Christ—like, the Amplified Version suggests, a mirror. A mirror only throws back what you put in front of it. And as we expose ourselves to God, the consequence of genuine worship is not that we have had a good time, but that when I go back home the way I treat my wife begins to show what God is like.

The principle also holds true for idol worship (2:5). 'This is what the Lord says: "What fault did your fathers find in me, that they strayed so far from me? They followed worthless idols and became worthless themselves."' Their idols were worthless: and they became worthless. There is no dichotomy between genuine worship and behaviour. If you genuinely worship a worthless idol, you become like your idol—worthless. If you genuinely worship the living God, you become like God in your moral character.

Thus John says, 'If anyone says, "I love God," yet hates his brother, he is …'—what? 'A liar,' says John. 'For anyone who does not love his brother, whom he has seen, cannot love God whom he has not seen' (1 John 4:20). That's pretty emphatic. To love God is to love His character; to love His character, to be conformed to His character.

And back in this apparent revival and renewal in Jerusalem, Jeremiah speaks the Lord's word to the people: 'Therefore, what I did to Shiloh I will now do to the house that bears my Name, the temple you trust in.'

You see, the temple was never designed to be an object of trust. It was designed to be the means by which they might know God. All the rituals that God gives are designed to portray a reality. All the activity in which they were to engage in the temple was designed not as an end in itself, but to reveal to them things of God's character and His purpose, His willingness to commune with them. When you detach the ritual from the reality to which it points, you may still engage in the ritual, as these people did. But what happens then is that instead of the ritual pointing to the reality, ritual replaces the reality. It is the temple of the Lord that you trust in—not God Himself.

It is so easy for it to happen today. The Old Testament covenant was full of rituals and regulations they had to observe, based on the temple and the priesthood, which we don't have. But God has given us symbols: we participate in the Lord's Supper, we take the bread and we break and we eat it, we take the wine and we drink it, because Jesus said, 'Do this in remembrance of me.' The ritual is the eating of the bread; the symbol is the bread. The symbol is the wine; the ritual is the drinking of it. But the reality to which it points is Christ.

The danger is this. You can participate in the ritual, but if the whole point of the exercise is not that we remember Him and think of Him, you can still participate—but instead of the ritual pointing to the reality, the ritual will replace the reality. The all-important thing will not become Christ, but 'Have I had the bread and the wine?' We'll become superstitious about it.

Another example is baptism and the new covenant; a beautiful picture. There are different views on this. Some see it as being like a wedding ring, a demonstration that by the act of baptism a person has been united with Christ and His death, His burial and His resurrection to walk in newness of life. Others see it as being like an engagement ring, that says, 'Our trust and prayer is that this person will one day for themselves marry the Lord Jesus, and make

Him their own.' But in either case baptism is a symbol designed to point to something of substance. It's a ritual designed to point to a reality, our union with Christ; we identify with Him in His death, burial and resurrection to walk in newness of life. But supposing you don't know Christ. Can you still be baptised? Of course; but the difference is, instead of the ritual pointing to the reality, the ritual will replace the reality and the all-important thing will become not my union with Christ but 'Have I been done?'

Jeremiah stands on the sideline of the crowd of people congregating into the temple. He says, 'You are engaging in all the right outward forms of worship, but you've detached the rituals from the realities. And it's dead.' He brings them God's own words in 7:21-23, where God says, 'Go ahead and engage in all your burnt offerings. Do it any way you want, I couldn't care less. Eat the meat of the burnt offerings, if you want.' (They were never meant to eat the meat of the burnt offerings, it was supposed to be entirely burnt.) 'Eat it if you want. Because all the outward form has been detached from the reality it's designed to portray.'

There's nothing more boring than a Christianity that's become detached from Christ. Yet so many engage in such a Christianity, where Christ is the patron, the One in whose name we seek to do it—but He's not the substance.

The People's Words (7:4-8)

It's always easier to learn a language than it is to discover life. These people learnt all the right words. Jeremiah says: 'You are trusting in the fact that you've learned the temple vocabulary.' We talk a lot about professions of faith; that's fine, but God is more interested in living by faith.

We can learn to say all the right things. The New Testament says so several times in John's first epistle: 'If we claim to have fellowship with him yet walk in the darkness, we lie …. If we claim to be without sin, we deceive ourselves …. If we claim we have not sinned, we make him out to be a liar …. The man who says "I know him," but does not do what he commands is a liar …. If anyone says, "I love God," but hates his brother he is a liar' (1 John 1:6, 8, 10; 2:4; 4:20). John says, you can learn the language, you can say all the right things.

Just because we have grasped that something is true doesn't mean that we have grasped the truth. The Bible is true—but it isn't the truth. Jesus said, 'I am the truth.' What is the difference? Consider a rail timetable. It may tell me that a train leaves Penrith at 15:14 this afternoon and gets to London at 20:05 this evening. Suppose that to be true. It might even be inerrant. But the timetable won't get me anywhere. The truth to which the timetable bears witness is the train. It's that which will get me to London.

You can study, know and memorise the Bible and yet separate it from Christ Himself. That's why Jesus criticises the Jews for studying the Bible—have you ever noticed that, in John 5:39? He told them: 'You study the Scriptures in order to know the Scriptures, you study what is true, but you don't understand that it's designed to point you to the truth, and that I am the truth. And so what does it do? It makes you Pharisees. It gives you a weapon with which you can hit people over the head. It doesn't bring you life.'

This book detached from Christ becomes a dead book, even though it's the inspired word of God. I sat on a plane recently for about twelve hours. A fellow in his mid twenties and his fiancée (as I later discovered) were sitting next to me. After a while I got my Bible out to prepare something I was having to speak on when I arrived at the other end. When I began to read, he said to me, 'It's nice to see somebody reading their Bible.'

'It's nice to meet someone who thinks it's nice to see somebody reading their Bible,' I replied. 'Are you a Christian?'

'Well, I would say so, but you probably wouldn't.'

'Why ever not?' I replied.

'I'm a Christadelphian,' he explained.

'Then you're right,' I responded. 'I'd probably conclude you're not.' Christadelphians deny the deity of Christ and all kinds of similar fundamental issues.

He got out his Bible, a well-worn Authorised Version, well marked. For several hours, sitting on that plane next to each other, he ran round his Bible in a way that left me exhausted. He found all kinds of rabbit-holes in different verses and disappeared down them, reappearing in Leviticus and all kinds of places. But it was a book detached from Christ, and though it was the inspired word of God it was a dead book in his hands.

Jeremiah says to these people, 'You are deceived. You have learnt the language, but you have never discovered the life that that language is designed to represent.' Jesus gives us that most solemn warning in Matthew 7:21-23, where He warns that many will come to Him 'on that day'; they've learned the language, they say, 'Lord. Lord …'. Not only that, they've learned to jump through all kinds of evangelical hoops, to prophesy, even to perform miracles. But the response of Jesus is, 'I never knew you; because although you have the language, you never knew life.'

Jeremiah says to these people, 'Your language means nothing because it's never been translated into life.'

The People's Works (7:9)

It is possible to learn all the right religious activities to please those around us in the temple, or in our church, but for it to be little more than a sort of Christian house-training exercise.

My wife and I have two cats at home. When they came to live with us we had to house-train them. They didn't know how to conform to our culture. We don't do things on the floor; so when they did, we put their noses in it and put them out of the door. They learned it's not acceptable. We taught our cats that they don't eat in the house. We got them because our house is in the middle of a field and the field-mice like to visit our house. I estimate that our two cats between them catch around 400 mice each year. We feed the cats outside the back door, not too much—enough to keep them alive but to leave them slightly hungry so they'll go off to catch mice. They know there's no food for them in the house. The dining table and kitchen bench are out of bounds. If you observed our cats you'd be suitably impressed, because we've trained them to behave perfectly.

As long, that is, as we are there. But if we are not? They couldn't care less. If we leave in a hurry in the morning and the food isn't put away, there'll be footprints and tongue prints in the butter when we get back. They don't have any moral conscience. They have simply been house-trained; they've learned to conform to the culture we've imposed on them on the basis of reward and punishment—mainly punishment.

I meet Christians who have been evangelically house-trained. They can jump through all the hoops that their local church puts up for them, they can do all the tricks. But behind closed doors it's a different story. When they leave home and maybe go away on business and no-one knows them, it's a different story. When they go away to university, give them three months—it's a different story.

Jeremiah stands outside the temple in this time of apparent spiritual renewal and revival, and he says, 'You're kidding yourselves. You've substituted ritual for realities, language for life, internal reality with external behaviour, and true spirituality with superstition.' And he says, 'Go now to the place in Shiloh where made a dwelling for my Name, and see what I did to it because of the wickedness of my people Israel' (7:12).

You have to go to 1 Samuel 4 to read about that. Psalm 78:60 summarises it: 'He abandoned the tabernacle of Shiloh, the tent he had set up among men.' God abandoned that which he had ordained, because God is never committed to His people, He is committed to His own programme, and it's His people who have to be committed to Him. Because, as it says in 2 Chronicles 15:2, 'The Lord is with you when you are with him.' It's a good verse. So what's our business? To say, 'Lord, please be with me'? No. Our business is to make sure we are with Him, in touch with Him.

We don't have time now to look closely at chapters 8 and 9. But in chapter 9 Jeremiah presents the antidote to this superficiality that he's diagnosed.

> Let not the wise man boast of his wisdom or the strong man boast of his strength or the rich man boast of his riches, but let him who boasts boast about this: that he understands and knows me, that I am the Lord, who exercises kindness, justice and righteousness on earth, for in these I delight. (9:23-24)

Don't boast of your wisdom, says Jeremiah. Don't boast of your strength or your riches; and I'll tell you why. You can never be too simple for God, but you can be too smart for Him; you can boast of your wisdom. You can never be too weak for God but you can be too strong for Him; you can boast of your strength. You can never be too poor for God, but you can be too rich; you can boast of your riches. That's why God has a vested interest in stripping us of our own sense of wisdom and strength and riches. With empty hands we must make our boasts. 'Let him who boasts boast about this: that he understands and knows me.' To boast about Him means this; that He is the Lord, who exercises kindness, justice and righteousness, and that the moral character of God is being reproduced in your life.

The real test of your spiritual life is not what you do on a Sunday morning or the enthusiasm with which you may throw yourself into acts of worship. The real test is the way you treat your wife behind closed doors, the way you talk to your kids, the way we talk to our neighbours—or, probably more telling, the way we talk about them when they're not listening. The moral character of God, being restored in us, so that once again people looking at you and me see something of what God is like.

I think we can say this: that God has no agenda for His people other than the reproducing of His own character in them. The goal of the gospel is Christ-likeness. When every Christian stands before the judgement seat of Christ, it's not going to be a theological examination. God's not going to ask you what your view of baptism was. That won't get you any points. 'What was your understanding of the Second Coming? Did that catch you by surprise, or did you get the month right? The Holy Spirit was a bit controversial in your time, did you manage to sort that one out?' He won't ask you those questions, though they are important questions. He will say, 'I was hungry—did you feed Me? I was thirsty—did you give Me a drink? I was in prison—did you visit Me? I was naked—did you clothe Me?' The answer may come back, 'But I didn't know it was You!'

Of course, had you known it was Him you would have played the game and performed. But it's when you don't know it's Him that the reality of the spiritual life is demonstrated.

This message of Jeremiah is about rediscovering reality. In a day of superficial renewal, when it became trendy to be in the temple and trendy to worship God, it took the prophet to stand on the sideline with a long face and say, 'God isn't pleased.'

What is the substance of your spiritual life? Is it coming to meetings, your annual visit to Keswick, being in church? Or is it waking up to every new day and saying, 'Lord Jesus Christ, whatever is my agenda today, may your agenda reign, so that in me today, the character of God is evident'?

Because 'It is in this,' says God, 'I delight.'

2 : 'Jeremiah and his own Life and Ministry' Jeremiah 12:1-17

Yesterday we looked at the state of the nation when Jeremiah came to his ministry. There was a renewal taking place—a superficial one so far as the people were concerned, though genuine so far as King Josiah was concerned. We looked at Jeremiah's message to that situation. But today I want to look at some of Jeremiah's own personal circumstances, and I would like you to have before you the first five verses of chapter 12 where he addresses himself to God.

Jeremiah's situation

Jeremiah had a very tough task. He preached for the last forty years of Judah's history, until the Babylonian army moved in and destroyed the nation and took the people into exile. During those forty years there was no response to Jeremiah's preaching. God had told him in advance there wouldn't be. Three times, in chapters 7, 11, and 14, He had said, 'Don't pray for the people that you're going to preach to.' Then in 15:1 He said, 'Even if Moses and Samuel were to stand before me, my heart would not go out to this people. Send them away from my presence! Let them go!'

If God had told me before I came here, 'Don't pray for these folks at Keswick. They are going to be so hard, so set in their ways, nothing's going to happen. They're not going to respond. But preach anyway!' I'd find it very difficult to get up enthusiasm to preach for five mornings. Yet for forty years Jeremiah preached to a brick wall.

Moreover, he was a very lonely man. He wasn't a loner, quite the reverse. He was the kind of man who craved friendship and companionship. Yet in chapter 16 God imposed three prohibitions on him.

1. *'Don't marry and have children, because if you do you will give the impression there's a future for this land.'* This despite the fact that we can deduce from much of what Jeremiah says that Jeremiah was a romantic.

2. *'Don't go to funerals and show sympathy. I have withdrawn my blessing from the people. Though you weep over their agony, I am going to let them go to the natural destruction to which they are heading.'* We'll talk about this tomorrow.

3. *'Don't accept any invitation to a party. Don't enter a house where there is feasting and sit down to eat and drink. Just sit on the sidelines, Jeremiah, and be miserable. Don't participate in expressions of joy and feasting and marriage.'*

Not only that: throughout those forty years he experienced persecution. When He called Jeremiah, God made him a promise. 'They will fight against you. They will not overcome you, for I am with you and will rescue you,' declares the Lord. 'But they will fight against you, they are not going to be indifferent to your message' (cf 1:19). Let me give you one or two of the references that run right through the book. In chapter 11 it says that the young men of Jeremiah's home town of Anathoth, his own contemporaries, plotted to take his life. In chapter 15 he describes himself as a man with whom the whole land strives and contends: 'Everyone curses me.' In chapter 18, 'They attacked him with their tongues, they slandered him, they plotted to kill him.' In chapter 20, the priest Pashhur heard Jeremiah prophesying; he had him beaten and put in the stocks at the upper gates of the Lord's temple. In chapter 26, as soon as he had finished prophesying on one occasion the priests, prophets and people seized him and said, 'You must die.' In chapter 32 he was thrown into prison, in chapter 37 he was beaten and put into a vaulted cell where he remained a long time, in chapter 38 he was thrown into a waterless cistern where he sank down into the mud. In Lamentations 3 (which is a postscript to the book of Jeremiah), he says, 'They hunted me like a bird, they threw me into a pit and I almost drowned, the waters came over

my head' (cf 3:52-54). 'They mock me in their songs'—
they used to tell Jeremiah-jokes; and Jeremiah says, 'I
laughed until I realised they were about me.'

Jeremiah's temperament

These are some of the external struggles and difficulties
that Jeremiah faced. They would have been bad enough,
but he was racked by internal struggles as well. Jeremiah
was depressive by nature. He had what we would call today
a melancholic temperament.

We call him the weeping prophet. 'Oh, that my head
were a spring of water and my eyes a fountain of tears! I
would weep day and night for the slain of my people' (9:1).
When you go somewhere to preach these days there's usually a glass of water provided in case you dry up. When
Jeremiah arrived to preach, they probably put a sponge in
the pulpit to clean up afterwards. He wept because of the
inner anguish that he experienced.

He had moods that swung like a pendulum. Sometimes
he was high and then a few moments later he would be
low. It's particularly well illustrated in chapter 20. He has
taken a clay pot and smashed it on the ground, and said,
'This is what God says: I'm going to do the same to your
people.' The people responded by being angry, and that
was when they beat him and put him in the stocks. And
Jeremiah said, 'O Lord, you deceived me, and I was deceived; you overpowered me and prevailed. I am ridiculed
all day long; everyone mocks me' (20:7). He is really dis-
couraged.

But he goes on, 'But if I say, "I will not mention him or
speak any more in his name,"'—I say I'll quit, I'm throw-
ing in the towel—'his word is in my heart like a fire, a fire
shut up in my bones. I am weary of holding it in; indeed I
cannot' (20:9). If I say I'm going to give up, he says, there's
this fire in my bones that begins to flame.

Verse 11, he's getting high again: 'But the Lord is with
me like a mighty warrior.' And in verse 13 he hits a real

high spot: 'Sing to the Lord! Give praise to the Lord! He rescues the life of the needy from the hands of the wicked.' But look at verse 14, the very next verse; he's swung right down to the bottom again. 'Cursed be the day I was born!'

There's a line in a John Denver song: 'Sometimes I fly like an eagle/Sometimes I'm deep in despair.' That was Jeremiah. You never knew what kind of mood he was going to be in, because within his own heart and life there was turmoil. We know more about the personal life and problems, the struggles, fears and disappointments of Jeremiah than about those of any other Old Testament character. And there is something interesting to be found in Jeremiah's book; all his fears, complaints and questions are expressed alone before God, in secret. When he's out amongst the people he is fearless and uncompromising: he says, 'Thus says the Lord.' He delivers his message with boldness. Then he goes home, closes the door, sits down and weeps. 'God, why did you tell me to say that? Are you playing games with me?'

Jeremiah's problem

That is the background against which we must understand chapter 12. The people in Jeremiah's home town of Anathoth at the end of chapter 11 are plotting against his life, they want to kill him. I love Jeremiah's honesty: 'You are always righteous, O Lord, when I bring a case before you. Yet I would speak with you about your justice' (12:1). 'I have to be very honest with you God—I have a problem with your justice.'

There's his problem. 'Why does the way of the wicked prosper? Why do the godless live at ease?' Jeremiah wasn't the first to raise the question, and he won't be the last. Why is it that someone can turn his back on God, and life seems to flow smoothly for him? 'Yet,' says Jeremiah in contrast, 'here I am; I seek to please you and honour you, and I'm in trouble all the time. My life is threatened, I'm going through emotional torture.'

Asaph (who used to play the percussion in the temple in Jerusalem in Solomon's day) wrote in Psalm 73, 'As for me my feet had almost slipped; I had nearly lost my foothold. For I envied the arrogant when I saw the prosperity of the wicked' (Ps. 73:2). He goes on, and it's very much a generalisation, 'They have no struggles; their bodies are healthy and strong. They are free from the burdens common to man; they are not plagued by human ills ...' (73:4-6). And yet, 'They scoff, they speak with malice' (73:8); 'Surely in vain have I kept my heart pure; in vain have I washed my hands in innocence. All day long I have been plagued; I have been punished every morning' (73:13-14). Asaph says, 'You know, I almost backslid over this very question, because as I seek to serve and please and honour God, God doesn't seem to respond to me. Life is difficult. Yet outside of Christ, outside of God, people are living in total lack of interest in His purposes, and yet they seem to be having such a good time.' David raised the same issues in Psalm 37. Job asked the same questions. His friends of course didn't help, because they said, 'If you do trust God, life will go well for you,' which God said, at the end of the book, was nonsense.

Well, we sympathise with Jeremiah, I'm sure. There are probably some folks here this morning in whose lives things have gone wrong again and again. Yet folks who don't seek to trust and love God seem to be having such an easier time. Why should the godly suffer? Why shouldn't God intervene and make life easy, and demonstrate His blessing on us by lifting us out of these trials and troubles?

Jeremiah's solution—and God's answer

There are two possible solutions to the dilemma in chapter 12. The first is Jeremiah's solution (verse 3), and then God's solution (verse 5).

In verse 3 Jeremiah suggests that God should butcher the ungodly. A slip of the tongue? Jeremiah having a bad day? Look at 17:18, where he asks that his persecutors be

destroyed with 'double destruction'. Be very careful,
Jeremiah; there's a little self-righteousness sneaking in
here. In the next chapter he says, 'God, don't forgive them,
don't cleanse them, don't offer them any hope and don't
just deal with them when You are in a good mood, God,
deal with them when You are angry' (cf 18:23). In Lamentations, which is a postscript of lament written after the
destruction of Jerusalem, Jeremiah says, 'O Lord ... Look
at them! Sitting or standing, they mock me in their songs.
Pay them back what they deserve, O Lord, for what their
hands have done. Put a veil over their hearts, and may your
curse be on them! Pursue them in anger and destroy them
from under the heavens of the Lord' (Lam. 3:61-66).

Well—it's a very simple solution, Jeremiah! We've all
shared his sentiments, haven't we? Sometimes we see pa-
raded on our TV screens those who've been made heroes.
We know that they are godless and their example is godless. We say, 'God, why don't You do something, why don't
You strike them?' That was Jeremiah's solution.

In 12:5 God speaks. As the NIV heading puts it, it is
'God's answer'. He says to Jeremiah, 'If you are complaining now, running with men, what are you going to do
when I run you with horses? If you are complaining now
you have fallen down in safe country, how will you manage
in the thickets by the Jordan?' (cf 49:19). 'In other words,
Jeremiah,' says God, 'toughen up.' He doesn't mean overcoming weakness, for it's in weakness that we discover
God's strengths. He means overcoming that self-pity that
feels entitled to an easy time from God. 'If it's hard now,
it's going to get worse. Running with horses is going to exhaust you.'

As servants of God we have no grounds for expecting to
be freed from difficulties. God's promise is not that He
changes our environment, but that He changes us. He
doesn't take us out of the difficulties, He equips us to go
into them, and often the intensity of the battle is not a sign
that things are going wrong but evidence that things are
going right. What did Paul write to Timothy? 'You want to

live a godly life? Not only are you going to experience persecution, but those who persecute you will get worse' (cf 2
Tim. 3:12). That's a promise that I've never seen on a cal-
endar, because we are very selective about the promises that
we want to read every day. I don't know anybody who
claims or memorises this one. But it's part of our Bible.

In Matthew 10 Jesus sent out the disciples for the first
time. Up till now they'd been with Him. He had done all
the preaching and performed the miracles and they had
simply picked up all the pieces left after the feeding of the
5,000 and—though Jesus didn't ask them to—kept the kids
away when they tried to overcrowd Him. Now Jesus said,
'I'm sending you out; you are going to preach the gospel,
the kingdom of heaven; and you are going to raise the
dead, you're going to heal the sick. Freely receive, freely
give' (cf. 10:5-8). They probably got very excited. 'At last, at
last,' Peter probably thought, 'I can do something.'

Then He added, 'I am sending you out like sheep
among wolves' (10:16). What happens when sheep and
wolves meet? The sheep get into trouble. 'Now,' says Jesus,
'you're the vulnerable sheep.' Sometimes we boast, 'We are
going to conquer.' Yes, that is true and we need to believe
it. But I tell you this; in the process, many of us are going
to be beaten and hurt. You see, being on top won't always
be our prerogative. We may get tired, we may get scarred,
we may get hurt, we may get lonely, we may be misunderstood. But don't opt out when that is so.

That's why I believe it's a very important principle to see
the guidance of God as positive. He leads us to things,
rather than from things. I am for ever meeting people who
want to go away from things because they are difficult. But
normally God's guidance is not given negatively. If you
want to leave something, hang on in there till God calls
you to something else. Probably some of you are unhappy
in your church and longing to leave. Hang in there! God
leads positively, He calls you to things.

But where is God in all this? How do you survive? Of
course God is not indifferent. He is never indifferent.

Psalm 56:8 says, 'List my tears on your scroll.' I like the AV rendering: 'Put my tears in your bottle.' Why does God keep our tears in His bottle? Out of some morbid interest? No. It is because He knows that our tears are almost always an investment. You learn far more from your tears than you ever learn from your laughter.

Despite the tears that Jeremiah shed (the title of his second book, Lamentations, means 'crying'), he needs to know something that you and I also need to know: that God is doing something, even when we cannot see it. Jeremiah never knew what God was doing through his life. What he did know was that God had called him, because it's recorded—and I'm so glad it is!—in Jeremiah 1. God called Jeremiah as a young man and said, 'Before you were ever born I set you apart as a prophet.' And when Jeremiah said, 'I'm only a child, I'm young,' He said, 'You must go to everyone I send you to and say what I command you. I am putting you into this prophetic role, this ministry, and I will give you what to say.'

Yet after forty years of preaching there was nothing to show for it. No-one listened. When King Jehoiakim was on the throne (chapter 36) Jeremiah dictated his prophecies to Baruch his scribe and directed him to read them at the temple. A report reached Jehoiakim that somebody was reading prophecies threatening the future national security. The king ordered the prophecies to be brought to the palace. He had the prophecies read to him, as he sat in front of the fire, and as these prophecies were read it says that King Jehoiakim cut them from the scroll and threw them on to the flames. By the end the whole scroll had been burned and Jehoiakim and his attendants were totally unmoved. Baruch and Jeremiah and his friends had to go into hiding. Jeremiah was so angry that he sat down and rewrote his prophecies: and this time he added 'many similar words' (36:32). He wrote them in anger, and in his book the anger as well as the compassion of God comes through.

At the end of those forty years Judah was overrun, and after an eighteen-month siege the city of Jerusalem was

captured, devastated and virtually razed to the ground by
the Babylonian armies. Most of the people were taken off
into exile. As Jeremiah, chained with others, waited to be
marched off to Babylon, Nebuchadnezzar king of Babylon
sent word to the commander of the invading army. 'There's
a man in Judah called Jeremiah. He's been preaching for
forty years about the doom of the nation. He's undermined
their morale—if you find him, treat him well.'

The commander found Jeremiah amongst the exiles as
they were going back (chapter 40). A few of the poor people
had been left in Judah to till the ground and keep it tidy
under their Babylonian overseers. The commander said,
'Jeremiah, if you want to go to Babylon with your people,
you can; if you want to stay and go back to Judah, you can.
You can live wherever you please and do what you like.'

Jeremiah didn't like the implication; he'd been serving
God's interests, and no else's. But he decided to go back to
Judah, where the Babylonians had appointed a governor,
Gedeliah, whose story is told in the latter chapters of the
book. He set up his headquarters in Mizpah, a town about
ten miles north of uninhabitable Jerusalem. There the
Babylonian government of Judah was established.

After seven months some of the Jewish remnant in
Judah planned a coup under Ishmael who was of royal
stock. They went to Mizpah and asked for an interview
with Gedeliah and with his soldiers, during which they
drew their weapons and assassinated them all. Ishmael
filled a cistern with the bodies. Then they went to
Jeremiah. 'Jeremiah, you are a man who listens to God—
what shall we do now?' Jeremiah asked God; ten days later
God answered him (42:7). But during those ten days the
assassins began to panic. 'Now word has gone back to
Babylon that we have assassinated the governor and tried
to retake the province. They are going to come and utterly
destroy us; they'll wipe us out and show us no mercy.'
They decided to go to Egypt.

After ten days Jeremiah told them, 'This is what God
says, "Stay here in the land, don't go to Egypt. Whatever

you do, don't run away.'" But they said, 'Jeremiah, you've taken too long to get your message. We've made our plans already, we're going to Egypt.' They kidnapped him and marched him off to Egypt, where he probably died. We have no record of Jeremiah after he had walked through the city of Jerusalem, written his laments and was then taken off to Egypt. If you or I had met him in Egypt and said: 'Jeremiah, God called you more than forty years ago. What have you accomplished?', he would probably have burst into tears and said, 'Nothing.'

There had been just a few sympathisers. Baruch was his secretary, who had to write out chapter 45: 'Should you then seek great things for yourself, Baruch? Seek them not' (45:5). There was Ebed Melech, an Egyptian who once saved Jeremiah from a pit; later God said to him, 'You trust in Me.' So Ebed Melech was, if not a convert, a sympathiser—but in any case he wasn't a Jew but an Egyptian. There was Ahikam, who supported Jeremiah when people wanted to kill him (chapter 26). 'A few sympathisers?' Jeremiah might retort. 'Forty years of tears, hardship, persecution, loneliness, isolation—and even the fear that God had been playing games with me and deceived me.'

Others saw fruit during that time. Daniel did. He was a few years younger than Jeremiah, who had already been preaching forty years at the time of the exile; Daniel was one the aristocratic young men of Judah taken off to Babylon. But he saw fruit. He even, remarkably, saw King Nebuchadnezzar himself converted. Daniel 4 is the king's official testimony, published as a tract to tell the whole Babylonian world of his conversion. Yes, Daniel saw fruit. But Jeremiah never did. When he died in Egypt, he left behind in his tent nothing more than a rolled-up scroll of prophecies to which no-one had ever listened.

But he didn't know that in that rolled-up scroll was one of the longest books of the Bible. He had no idea that 500 years later, Jesus the Messiah, whom he anticipated, would sit one day with His disciples in Caesarea Philippi and say, 'Who do people say that I am? What are the rumours about Me?', and be told, 'Some say you are Jeremiah.' Jeremiah would say, 'Well how in the world would they know about me?' He had no idea that 2,500 years later we would sit in a tent in the north of England one hot Tuesday morning, hoping to benefit from this man.

God sometimes gives us the privilege of seeing lots of fruit. When He does, always say thank you to Him. But many of us never see it. When you see what God is doing in your life be grateful, but don't take it too seriously. Most of us reap what other people have sown anyway. We are all workers together in this. But the lesson from Jeremiah regarding fruitfulness is this: Never try to measure your value or effectiveness by the results of your life. Measure your value and effectiveness by the cause of what you do. If we go by the results of what we do, we'll probably be tempted to manipulate the results. But if we go by the origin and cause of what we do, God will direct us. Back in Jeremiah 1, God says: 'You must go to everyone I send you. Jeremiah, you are not just a loose cannon wandering around trying to do your own thing. I'm sending you. I'm putting you in the place where you are, and I will give you what to say. And you must say whatever I command you.'

When you know you are where you are because God put you there, and you are doing what you are doing because God called you to it, you don't have to see the fruit.

Sometimes we say glibly, 'God has a wonderful plan for your life,' and we are in danger of deceiving ourselves. God does have a wonderful plan—but it's a wonderful plan for God, not necessarily a wonderful plan for you or for me. A number of years ago Jim Elliot and four colleagues were martyred and their bodies left in a river in Ecuador. Jim was twenty-nine years of age. God had a wonderful plan for Jim Elliot. It wasn't very wonderful for Jim.

I read that 10,000 people have gone to the mission field because of Jim Elliot and his colleagues and the story that Elisabeth Elliot has written about them, and the story of Jim in particular. I quoted that statistic at a conference of missionaries in Ethiopia. Afterwards somebody came to me

and said, 'I'm here because of Jim Elliot.' I was at a conference of European missionaries on the Adriatic coast last
year and I mentioned it again. Two people afterwards told
me, 'I'm here because of the life of Jim Elliot.'

When Jim Elliot said, 'Lord, have your way in my life,'
God said, 'Thank you, thank you, Jim. At twenty-nine,
your body will lie in the river martyred. Your widow will
have a broken heart, your orphaned daughter will never
know her father, but—thank you, Jim. It's not very good
for you, but it's wonderful for Me.'

If the blessing of God is to be measured by the evidence
of goodness in your own experience, Jeremiah would have
to write his whole life off. But God has an agenda far bigger than what was evident in those forty years. My wife
Hilary pointed out to me John 13:7, where Jesus, washing
His disciples' feet, replies to Peter's objections: 'You do not
realise now what I am doing, but later you will understand.' Maybe some of you today have no idea of what God
is doing. You have prayed and pleaded with God to intervene in some way, and it seems as if heaven is locked. 'You
don't know what I am doing,' says Jesus. 'But one day
you'll understand.'

When I get to heaven I plan to sleep for the first million
years, then I'm going to knock on Jeremiah's door. Of
course I won't be the first to do so—but suppose I were. I'd
say, 'Jeremiah, I just want to thank you for your ministry.'

He'd probably look at me and say, 'That's very kind of
you; but I don't recognise you. Did you live in Jerusalem?'

'No, in fact we weren't contemporaries at all. I lived
2,500 years after you, but—'

'I thought you were thanking me for my ministry!'

'I was. I read your book.'

'My book?'

'Yes—you wrote a book, Jeremiah. It's part of the Bible,
inspired every word of it by the Spirit of God. Jeremiah,
you blessed me so much.' Of course it won't be news to
him, he'll know all about it already by then. But I'll say,
'Thank you for your faithfulness. Thank you, Jeremiah.

You didn't quit.'

I talked to a widow who'd been a missionary with her husband for something like thirty-five years in Tunisia. She said, 'In those years we were there we only ever saw one convert. My husband used to run boys' camps; we saw a number of boys make a profession but they never stuck. Only one did. We'd come home on furlough and we'd say "It's hard, it's tough." We'd try to think of things to put in our prayer letter for which people could praise God, and we couldn't think of anything. People back home were very suspicious. Were we really doing the job? Then one day,' she said, 'this boy said to us, "I'm going to leave Tunisia and go to Israel"—for he was a Jewish boy. That boy's name was Victor Smadja.'

Some of you who may be familiar with the scene in Israel will know him. He runs a printing press, amongst other things. He does a great work amongst the locals. I know him because I've spoken at conferences he organised. And that lady said to me, 'We had no idea, God sent us to Tunisia to evangelise Israel a generation later.' But she said to me as she told me that, 'But it was hard, very hard.'

Do you know what God's doing in your life? If you do, that's great. Remember Job said, 'If I go to the east, he is not there; if I go to the west, I do not find him. When he is at work in the north, I do not see him; when he turns to the south, I catch no glimpse of him' (Job 23:8). 'If you ask me where is God in all this,' says Job, 'I don't know.' Sometimes we've got to die to the right to an up-to-date testimony. Maybe we don't have one because we're out of touch with God. But maybe it's because God is doing something. We walk by faith, not by sight. Job says, 'I can't see where God is, I can't tell what God is doing in my life.' But then he said this: 'But he knows the way that I take' (23:10): 'I don't where God is, but God knows where I am, God is doing something.'

To six of His disciples whose calling is recorded, Jesus said the same two words: 'Follow me.' Isn't it interesting that nobody asked Jesus, 'Where are we going?' Why? Because where we are going is actually irrelevant. What matters is with whom we are going. Had they asked, of course, He might have said, 'James, I'm sorry to tell you this but you are going to have your head chopped off by Herod, in Acts 12, and that's not far off. And Peter, take that smirk off your face; you are going to be crucified upside down. Judas, you won't live to see the real purpose of this anyway—you will commit suicide. John, you are the only one who will die as an old man in your bed; and you will have such dreams as an old man on the Isle of Patmos that they'll probably drive you crazy—visions of all kinds of strange things you won't understand.' If God told you tonight where you'll be this time next year you might panic, so might I. It's not where we're going that's the measuring stick, it's who we're with.

Last night, Don Cormack spoke very movingly to us of Cambodia. He spoke of Major Taing Chhirc, who was martyred by the Khmer Rouge.[1] Didn't he say to us that the soldiers may have washed their feet in his blood? His last words were, 'The Lord is with us and we praise Him, because we are on the victory side.' This was a man about to die. I knew Taing Chhirc, we studied together in Glasgow. He was in a room two doors from me on the same floor. I remember when he went back to Cambodia and left his wife and daughter in Edinburgh, fearing for their safety. But he said, 'God wants me to go back.' He died. It wasn't a very good plan for Chhirc, it was a good plan for God. He was doing something.

'Blessed are those who mourn,' as Don reminded us. And yet the picture is not complete there. Those who mourn will be comforted. Comforted by whom? Well, it's obvious isn't it, the Comforter. And who is the Comforter? The *parakletos*, the Holy Spirit. It is as true for us as it was for Jeremiah; as it is for every one of us in this place. You've come in humility and said, 'Lord Jesus Christ, I do surren-

---

1. Don Cormack is the author of *Killing Fields, Living Fields: an Unfinished Portrait of the Cambodian Church—the Church that Would not Die* (Monarch, 1997).

der my life to You. Have Your way in my life.'

Then He will. You don't have to plead and beg for it; He will. He doesn't always tell us what He's doing. Sometimes He does, and when He does, be glad. He doesn't always—mostly, He doesn't. We usually only see the activity of God in hindsight, looking back and seeing that God has led us. But you can be absolutely sure of this; that if you are mourning, if like Jeremiah there's grief, disappointment and even anger at God, if there's confusion and turmoil within you—hang in there. You'll be comforted. Because, you'll see one day, He does all things well.

'Jeremiah—you're running with men, I know it's tiring. I know it's wearing. I know it's difficult. But you're going to run with horses. Toughen up, Jeremiah. Jeremiah, this is the real world. It's a battle, it's a conflict. But I'm doing something.'

3 : 'God's Discipline in People's Lives'
Jeremiah 13, 18, 19

This morning I want to talk about the theme of the discipline of God in the lives of the people of God, and look at four parables that were either enacted by, or watched by, Jeremiah. It's said that a picture is worth a thousand words, so we are saving 4,000 words this morning!

If ever you want biblical grounds for the effective use of drama, you need go no further than the prophets. Some of their most effective messages were dramatically conveyed. Poor old Ezekiel had on one occasion to lie on his side for 390 days (that's thirteen months), having drawn a picture of Jerusalem on a clay brick and then built a ramp up to it and set up a few toy camps around it and a few little battering rams. Then with an iron pan between him and his little model he had to lie on the ground for 390 days. And when he finally got up, no doubt to the great relief of everybody in Jerusalem, to their amazement he turned round and lay on his other side for forty more days. He was depicting the 390 years the northern kingdom of Israel would be in exile, and the forty years the southern kingdom would be. Once he had to shave off his beard and his hair and divide the cut hair into three equal parts on a scale. Then he had to burn one third, scatter another third to the wind, and then put some of the remaining third in his garment and then throw the rest away. Another time he had to eat a scroll in front of everybody and tell them how nicely it had tasted—'Like honey in my mouth,' he said, to show what the word of God should be.

Isaiah would probably have never been invited to come to speak at the Keswick Convention. For three years he had to walk around in bare feet and with bare buttocks, to show the humiliation of those who trusted in Egypt.

Hosea, you remember, had to marry a woman who was an adulteress. Then God gave them three children. These three children had names all of which described or explained the message that Hosea's life was, to the nation of Israel, the northern kingdom.

There were Elisha, Zacharia and many others. Jeremiah once had to put a wooden yoke round his neck and say, 'This is what's going to happen to the people of Judah.' A false prophet, Hananiah, seized Jeremiah, smashed the wooden yoke, and said, 'There lies Jeremiah.' Jeremiah said, 'That feels better! I'm glad it's smashed.' And God said, 'Make another one. But this time make it out of iron. Walk around with it around your neck' (cf chapter 28).

There's plenty of drama in the Old Testament prophets. And I want to look at these four examples with you and see them as a progressive message that God is giving to the nation about the nation.

Diagnosis: The Linen Belt (13:1-11)

The first begins very simply. 'This is what the LORD said to me; "Go and buy a linen belt and put it round your waist, but do not let it touch water." So I bought a belt as the LORD directed, and put it round my waist' (13:1).

That's very simple. The 'belt' was probably some kind of undergarment worn against the skin, because that is what the picture is going to refer to in due course. We don't know how long he wore it. But, 'The word of the Lord came to me a second time: "Take the belt you bought and are wearing round your waist, and go now to Perath and hide it there in a crevice in the rocks." So I went and hid it at Perath, as the Lord told me' (13:3-5). There's some debate as to where exactly Perath was. The Authorised Version says 'the Euphrates', which is certainly a strong possibility for its location. That would be a 700-mile return journey. 'Go 350 miles to Perath and there,' says God, 'hide it in a crevice in the rocks.' Jeremiah did so and returned home.

Many days later God spoke again to Jeremiah. 'Go now to Perath and get the belt I told you to hide there' (13:6).

He did as he was told and found the belt, unsurprisingly, 'ruined and completely useless'. He went back home again.

What was that all that about? Fortunately verse 8 explains. 'These people,' said God, 'have a purpose and a function: to be as close to Me as the belt was close to you round your waist.' The first reason God called Israel to Himself was not to give them a function but to enjoy fellowship with them. They did have a function, but it grew out of the relationship of fellowship that He was to enjoy with them. Fifty-two times in the prophecy of Jeremiah, God refers to Judah as 'My people'. It's a warm, intimate term. He speaks of Israel as being like a bride to Him.

Back in chapter 2 He says, 'I remember the devotion of your youth, how as a bride you loved me and followed me through a desert, through a land not sown .... Does a maiden forget her jewellery, a bride her wedding ornaments? Yet my people have forgotten me, days without number' (2:2, 32). God is saying. 'My covenant with Israel is not simply a legal document; it's a romance, a marriage, an intimate fellowship where I love you, and you love Me.' The first terms of the covenant were: 'Love the Lord your God, with all your heart and soul and strength.'

But, He says throughout this book, they have committed adultery. 'Worse,' He says in chapter 3. 'You lived like a prostitute with many lovers. In other words you have violated the terms and purpose of My relationship—not simply that you have in the world a special role as the people of God, but that you are on intimate terms with Me in a love relationship.' Over fifty times in Jeremiah His invitation is, 'Return, return. Come back to where you belong.'

Isn't this exactly the terms of the relationship of the church with the Lord Jesus Christ? He didn't come into the world simply to rescue us from hell, His mission complete as long as you get into heaven by the skin of your teeth. He came to find a bride—those with whom He enjoys that intimacy of fellowship and communion.

The Christian life is union with Christ. The first invitation of Jesus is 'Come to Me,' the second is, 'Abide in me.'

Those two invitations encompass the whole of the Christian life. But Judah has violated this purpose; 'and My people,' says God, 'will be like this belt'. Away from the intimacy of their relationship with God, they are still legally God's people, but they are ruined, they are useless for the purpose for which He called them.

This is a pretty negative message, isn't it? And it's a very true one. It's a very accurate diagnosis, not only of Judah, but—you recognise its accuracy—of the church of Jesus Christ, of our own hearts.

Chapters 14, 15, 16 and 17 go on to explain the implications of the first parable, preparing us for the second parable in chapter 18. A drought comes upon the nation and God doesn't respond to their cries for mercy. He tells Jeremiah, 'Don't even pray for these people. Even if Moses and Samuel were to come, I wouldn't see them.' There's a growing sense of alienation. God says He intends to send four kinds of destroyers: the sword to kill, the dogs to drag away, and the birds of the air and the beasts of the field to devour and destroy (15:3). He warns Jeremiah (chapter 16), 'Don't you give any hope, don't you marry.' We saw the reason yesterday: if you have children you are giving the idea there's a future; and don't mourn, because God has taken His sympathy away from these people.

It is all designed to explain the linen cloth perishing, useless, unfit for the purpose for which it was created. In chapter 17 Jeremiah speaks of the deceitfulness of the heart and the curse that comes from depending upon man. The climax of verse 12 prepares us for chapter 18: 'A glorious throne, exalted from the beginning, is the place of our sanctuary.' In spite of all He has spoken of in the preceding chapters (the destruction that is coming, the alienation of the people from God) He says, 'But there's a place of sanctuary, a place to which you can run, a glorious throne.'

Discipline: The Potter (18:1-12)

What does that mean? 'Go to the house of the potter,' God

tells Jeremiah, 'and you'll understand what that means.'
Jeremiah doesn't enact the second parable, he observes it.
Verse 1 describes how he watched the potter discard a
faulty pot and make it into another one, 'shaping it as
seemed best to him'. The key is in 18:5-6: 'Then the word
of the LORD came to me: "O house of Israel, can I not do
with you as this potter does?" declares the LORD, "Like
clay in the hand of the potter, so are you in my hand, O
house of Israel."'

He goes on to explain how He is going to mould the
people like clay. The clay Jeremiah saw in the hands of the
potter is the nation of Israel. It's marred, something's gone
wrong. The potter, says Jeremiah, is the sovereign God; the
one who occupied that glorious throne that is the place of
our sanctuary. And the shaping of the clay is the pressures
of life, which God in His kindness and sovereignty brings
into our circumstances.

The government of God in our lives is not expressed in
a willingness to manipulate circumstances to make life
easy. So many of our prayers are along the lines of: 'I've got
a problem; please, God, move it out of the way for me.'
That wouldn't demonstrate the sovereignty of God. The
sovereignty of God as depicted here is the potter bringing
pressure into our lives to mould us; and the wheel against
which his hand moulds represents the circumstances of
life. Paul says, 'We rejoice in our sufferings, because we
know that suffering produces perseverance; perseverance,
character; and character, hope' (Rom. 5:3).

In my Bible I've underlined those two words, 'suffering
produces'. It doesn't mean that we are impartial to our
suffering, nor that God is. We saw yesterday that He keeps
our tears in His bottle. But He does so because our tears
are an investment. Suffering produces. Hebrews 12:7 says,
'Endure hardship as discipline.' Why? Because God has
somehow neglected you? No, but because God in His sovereignty is bringing into your life situations you would
never have chosen—and is then moulding you.

Of course the discipline of God is not only corrective

and remedial. It's not only a discipline because things are
wrong. He's refining what is right. The Lord Jesus Christ
Himself was subject to the disciplining of His Father:
'Though he was a son, he learned obedience from what he
suffered' (Heb. 5:8). The Father brought into the life of
His own Son suffering, from which He learned.

Events in your life and mine may be satanic in origin.
But remember Job; it was Satan who attacked him, who
brought about the destruction of his livestock, workforce
family, and then inflicted sickness on his body—but it was
only with God's permission. As far as Job was concerned
there was no evidence of God: 'I look east, west, north,
south, I don't see God.' Yet at the end of the book, he says,
'My ears have heard of You, but now my eyes have seen
You. Something's happened. I've seen God' (cf Job 42:5).
Of course it was Satan who attacked him. But when your
life is in the hands of God even the devil will do you good.
Because the end result of Job's life was, 'I've seen God.'
Not because he had been to some great Convention or had
some great spiritual experience, but because he had been
under satanic attack and endured thirty-eight chapters of
suffering. He said, 'I've seen God,' because although the
devil was active, behind the scenes—giving him permission
and laying down the boundaries—was the sovereign God.

Our sanctuary, security and hiding place, says Jeremiah,
is not in the fact that God gives us everything we want—
He's not our Sugar Daddy—but in the discipline He
brings into our lives.

Not getting what you want is actually good for your
character. Last week I was at the sports day of the school
that two of my children attend. I was sitting between my
wife and another mother. As certain children ran and won
races, the other mother frequently said, 'That will be good
for their confidence, winning the race.' I was feeling a bit
frustrated by her continuous comments, but my wife who is
wiser and braver than I am leaned over and said, 'Winning
may be good for their confidence, but learning to lose will
be good for their character.'

God sometimes lets you lose, as far as the recognition of the world at large is concerned. He lets His people lose repeatedly, to all appearances, throughout the Scriptures. Do you remember when Paul complained about his thorn in the flesh? 'To keep me from becoming conceited because of these surpassingly great revelations, there was given me a thorn in my flesh, a messenger of Satan, to torment me' (2 Cor. 12:7). He is unambiguous about its origin: this is from Satan. He doesn't tell us what the thorn in the flesh is of course. But it sounds to me as though it's something physical. We know he had poor eyesight, because he mentions that. Others think it may be something else, perhaps the fact that he wasn't married. Some suggest that it was that he was married! But whatever it was, he called it 'a thorn in my flesh'. It was uncomfortable, and he recognised that it came from Satan. So he did the obvious thing that you and I would do. He pleaded with the Lord to take it away—in three periods of intercession. But God said, 'Paul, I've a vested interest in keeping you weak. It is your weakness that provides the opportunity for the demonstration of my strength.' So Paul concludes, 'I will boast all the more gladly about my weaknesses, so that Christ's power may rest on me. That is why, for Christ's sake, I delight in weaknesses, in insults, in hardships, in persecutions, in difficulties. 'For when I am weak, then I am strong' (12:10). The very thing he asked God to remove, because he saw it as his enemy, is what he now rejoices in.

Sometimes what we consider our biggest enemies are actually our biggest friends, because their role in our lives, like the hand of the potter in the clay, moulds us for that which is God's interest in us and is usually different to our own interests. Hebrews 12:10 says, 'Our fathers disciplined us for a little while as they thought best; but God disciplines us for our good, that we may share in his holiness.'

That's God's agenda. It is not our happiness but our holiness. Don't confuse the two! A holy man or woman is a happy man or woman. A holy home is a happy home.

Let me quote, from memory, the gist of something

Elisabeth Elliot once wrote. 'Parents used to want their children to be good. So they taught them to be good, and as a result most children, as they learnt to be good, were happy and secure. Now parents want their children to be happy. And usually, in the short term, being happy doesn't mean being good.' There's some very real wisdom there.

God's agenda is our holiness. 'O house of Israel, can I not do with you as this potter does?' (18:6). 'Like clay in the hand of the potter, so are you in my hand, O house of Israel'—and I am going to mould you, even hurt you, in order to bring in you the holy character of God.

In God's dealings with you and with me, that statement in verse 4 is very significant; that the pot that the potter was shaping from the clay was marred in his hands. He doesn't tell us about the marring, but from that earlier parable we can take it that things are wrong. 'So the potter formed it into another pot, shaping it as seemed best to him.' That's a very important statement; because the sovereignty of God is there in making it into another pot. Don't think of the sovereignty of God as some fixed, predetermined blueprint for everything that's going to happen, so that if you've blown it you've blown it. God's plan changes with the realities of the situation, and God remoulds the clay.

Remember in the Garden of Eden, when God said to Adam and Eve, 'Do anything you like except one thing. Don't eat of the tree of the knowledge of good and evil.' On the day they ate of that tree, they became embarrassed. They became aware of their nakedness. And God came walking in the garden. 'Where are you?' He knew where they were of course, but He wanted them to acknowledge where they were. When they said, 'We were embarrassed because we were naked,' He said, 'Who told you? Have you eaten from the tree that I commanded you not to eat?' Of course they had.

And then it says this. 'The Lord God made garments of skin for Adam and his wife and clothed them' (Gen. 3:21). God clothed them. Was that God's original purpose? No. But He remoulded the clay. He didn't say, 'You disobeyed what I commanded you, therefore—Pow!' He didn't zap them on the spot and start again. He remoulded the clay.

When the nation of Israel wanted a king, like every other nation around them had, God said to Samuel (who was the prophet and judge at that time), 'It's not you that they've rejected, Samuel, it's Me. This is a rejection of God. But I will remould the clay. I'll tell you what king to give them.' Saul. He was a disaster of course. And then, David. Do you know how Jesus is introduced in the New Testament? 'The genealogy of Jesus Christ,' it says, 'the Son of David' (Matt. 1:1). The throne of David should never have been in the ultimate purpose and sovereignty of God. That was not what His will was. But He remoulds the clay.

You see, this is the marvellous thing. Failure is never final. Never ever write anyone off. We can go wrong, they can go wrong. But a glorious throne, exalted from the beginning, is the place of our sanctuary. And on that throne is a potter, and He brings His hand against the clay and remoulds it. Into something different, yes, because there are some things you can never go back on; you can do things and can never undo them, you will live for ever with the consequences. But He'll remould the clay.

Isn't that wonderful! Is He remoulding you today?

Destruction: The Clay Jar (19:1-15)

The third parable is a very sobering and frightening one, but it follows on from the second.

God says, 'Jeremiah: go back to the potter's house, get a pot. In the potter's house you saw them soft, pliable and reworkable—but now the pottery is hardened. It can't be remoulded now. And I want you, Jeremiah, in front of the people, to smash the jar on the ground.'

In chapter 18 the focus is the potter at work, his interest, his purpose, his power, his actions, his moulding of the clay. But chapter 19 focuses on the clay jar. 'Then while the people are watching,' He says, 'smash it in such a way that it cannot be repaired.' There's a helplessness in this pic-

ture. The pot is unable to resist the action against it as it's
hurled to the ground and smashed—there's a finality about
this. The sovereignty of God is ultimately irresistible.

The end of the story; the pot lies in a thousand pieces on
the ground. What is the meaning of this for Judah? Well,
God says there's going to be a destruction of this nation.
Jerusalem and Judah are going to be invaded by the Babylonian army of that pagan king Nebuchadnezzar, though
God calls him, 'My servant Nebuchadnezzar.' This was
unbelievable news. Read on. When Jeremiah had smashed
the clay jar the priest Pashhur was so angry he had
Jeremiah put in the stocks and they beat him and flogged
him.

Jeremiah himself was confused by this. In chapter 20 he
says, 'O Lord, you deceived me, and I was deceived' (20:7).
'Surely, surely God, You won't smash the people to pieces.'
But He does. The judgement of God is a frightening and
very real thing. You don't hear much about it these days.
It's not what we're into. But of course there will come a
judgement day one day in the future. 2 Corinthians 5:10
says. 'We must all appear before the judgement seat of
Christ, that each one may receive what is due to him for
the things done while in the body, whether good or bad.'
There's going to come a judgement day from which none
of us will be exempt.

But at the same time Paul says to the Romans, 'The
wrath of God is being'—present tense—'revealed from
heaven against all the godlessness and wickedness of men'
(Rom. 1:18). What is the wrath, the judgement of God in
the present tense? How does God show His wrath? How
do we see His judgement? I don't think we see it through
train crashes, earthquakes, drought and sickness. We're
forever hearing, 'This is the judgement of God.' But actually the Bible would teach us that the judgement of God is
far subtler and far more devastating than that.

Let me turn to Romans 1 for a moment. I have just
quoted from it, and I think it's very important that we understand it. Paul goes on in verse 24, 'Therefore God gave

them over in the sinful desires of their hearts to sexual impurity for the degrading of their bodies with one another.' In verse 26 he says, 'Because of this, God gave them over to shameful lusts. Even their women exchanged natural relations for unnatural ones. In the same way the men also abandoned natural relations with women and were inflamed with lust for one another. Men committed indecent acts with other men ...' In verse 28, 'Furthermore, since they did not think it worth while to retain the knowledge of God, he gave them over to a depraved mind, to do what ought not to be done.' And then he gives a list in the following verses: wickedness, evil, greed, depravity, envy, murder, strife, deceit—you can read it for yourselves.

How does God express His wrath? He lets us go our own way. He gives us over. He allows us to go to the logical conclusion of our own choices. There will come a judgement day of course, where the secrets of all mankind will be made known. But in the meantime God isn't going to open heaven and zap us. God's judgement is that if you want to go that way, He'll let you go. He gives them over. He talks about sexual impurity, He talks in particular about homosexual behaviour. 'Every kind of wickedness, evil, greed and depravity.' Romans 1 indicates, by the way, that widespread acceptance of homosexual behaviour is not going to bring the wrath of God; it is the evidence of the wrath of God. Even when, tragically, the church itself begins to discuss the legitimacy of homosexual behaviour amongst its members and leaders, God isn't going to send thunderbolts to strike their bishops' palaces. He let them go—go ahead.

It's like the situation in 1 Corinthians 5, where a man is spoken of as being in a sexual relationship with his father's wife, and he's in the church at Corinth. What does Paul say? He says in 1 Corinthians 5:5, 'Hand this man over to Satan.' It's the same language.

You can choose to sin as a Christian and God won't zap you. He'll let you go. Is there someone here this morning involved in an illegitimate relationship? God won't strike you down, He won't make your car crash on the way to your secret rendezvous. He'll let you go. Not only that, but if your conscience hurts you the first time He won't keep bugging you with it, He'll stop talking. The first time, you lie awake at night filled with fear and remorse, maybe the sky will cave in. The second time it's not so bad. The third time it gets easier. And soon you're getting away with it.

I spent some time with a man who'd got involved in all kinds of sin, although in Christian ministry. And he said to me, 'When it first happened I expected the blessing of God to be removed from my life.' He was a preacher, and people were coming to Christ. 'But,' he said, 'to my utter amazement people still were saved. And my conscience which had been violated stopped bugging me as much, and in due course immorality became a lifestyle.' That was the judgement of God. God gives us over.

This is difficult, isn't it? And it was difficult for Jeremiah to get hold of it. But it's true, as I understand what it says here, both in Jeremiah's case and in what happened to the nation. You see the wrath of God. If God *were* to zap us, if God were to discipline us in some way that drove us back, it would be so much easier. But He says, 'If that's the way you want to go, I hand you over.'

There's a major difference between the kingdom of God and the rule of the devil in your life. The kingdom of God demands submission. But the rule of the devil says, 'Do what you want! Anything you please!'

God says to Jeremiah, 'You are out of fellowship with Me. The belt has been ruined. But there's hope, there's the potter. The glorious throne with the sovereign God. He will mould you, but if you don't respond and the clay jar becomes hard, He'll hand you over and smash it.'

No wonder Jeremiah went into deep depression in the following chapter!

Deliverance: The Field at Anathoth (32:1-44)

But there is a fourth parable, and in the light of all of this it is a very wonderful one. In chapter 32, although the book doesn't follow an ordered chronology, things have moved on. Zedekiah is now on the throne, the last king before the destruction. Babylon is breaking down the door (they held an eighteen-month siege of the city and eventually starved them into submission). At that time, the events described in verses 6-15 took place.

Do you get the message there? 'Your cousin Hanamel,' says God, 'is going to come to you, Jeremiah nad say "I'm going to offer you this field, at Anathoth, your home town."'—in other words, Hanamel is cutting his losses. Babylon is breathing down their necks, breaking down the door; all is to be lost, there is no future, there is no hope. And Han-amel says, 'Let me get what I can for this piece of land. It's going to be utterly worthless when the Babylonians have overrun us and every bit of land becomes theirs. I'll try to sell it, so I'll go to Jeremiah—there's a law which says he has the first right of refusal.' When he comes to offer it, Jeremiah buys it for seventeen shekels of silver. And having bought it he puts the legal documents in a clay jar where they'll last a long time, he says. Why? Because the day is going to come when once again there'll be houses on this land, fields, and vineyards again be bought (cf 32:15).

At the end of chapter 19 there are a thousand pieces of broken clay on the floor. 'This is what I will do,' says God, 'I will smash you, I will allow you to go your own way.' But then He whispers in Jeremiah's ear, 'Jeremiah, your cousin's going to offer you a field. Buy it.'

The most exciting thing about being a Christian is that we have a God of resurrection. Against all the odds, we never exhaust the incredible mercy of God. 'I have loved you,' He told them in chapter 31, 'with an everlasting love. Yes, the due consequence of your sin is going to come to its logical conclusion. You are going to be smashed, taken out of Judah, taken off into exile, humiliated, hurt. But the day will come,' says God to Jeremiah, 'when, even then, I'll bring you back.'

In 2 Corinthians 4:7 Paul says, 'We have this treasure in

jars of clay.' Interesting, these jars of clay. He put the scroll
in a jar of clay (32:14). In chapter 19, it was a jar of clay
that he'd smashed. 'Now,' says Paul, 'we have this treasure
in jars of clay, to show this all-surpassing power is from
God and not from us. We are hard pressed on every side,
but we're not crushed.' Yes, these jars of clay are hard
pressed, they are perplexed, they are persecuted, they are
struck down. 'We always carry around in our body the
death of Jesus, so that the life of Jesus may also be revealed
in our body. For we who are alive are always being given
over to death for Jesus's sake, so that his life may be revealed in our mortal body' (verses 10-11). Paul is saying:
'Now yes, these jars of clay, they are hard pressed, they are
precious.' He's not speaking of the destruction that
Jeremiah speaks of in that parable in chapter 19, but that in
this jar of clay we have the resurrection life of Jesus.

I don't know where you are this morning. I don't know
how God the Holy Spirit has taken His word and made it
relevant and personal to you this morning, but in a crowd
such as this, there may very well be some who know that,
behind secret doors, they're living in sin. We're never sin-
less, of course. But there are some things we have chosen:
'This is my pet sin, this is the one I'm going to keep.' And
your conscience is less troubled by it with every enactment
of it. The wrath of God says you can go; and you will be
destroyed. He's not speaking of eternal destruction; but in
this life your life will become utterly useless and worthless.

But in spite of everything that has happened, God says
in chapter 32, 'Is anything too hard for Me, Jeremiah? Buy
that field.' And that's still true today.

> There's a way back to God from the dark paths of sin,
> There's a door that is open and you may go in;
> At Calvary's cross is where you begin,
> When you come as a sinner to Jesus.

I'm talking about Christians. These were the people of
God. Are you out of fellowship with Jesus Christ today? Is
the linen belt worthless? Maybe some of you here today

have a family and your children are far from God this morning; they wouldn't be here at Keswick, they're not interested. But I tell you this: against all the odds, buy the field in Anathoth. There's hope.

You may think that some things in your life have gone for ever. But it's not the end of the story; there's a field in Anathoth. 'Is there anything too hard?' says God. 'Buy the field, put the deeds in a clay jar. You may have to wait a long time, but one day there'll be houses, vineyards and crops on the fields.' The fact that God's love is inexhaustible doesn't mean we can say, 'Whew! Relax, let's take advantage of the fact that God will never leave us. We are secure eternally, so I can live as I please.' What nonsense!

Maybe this morning some of us need to come home. You know, the easiest place to backslide is in Christian work. I'm in Christian work. Over forty of us work at Capernwray. We know it's the easiest place to backslide, because you've got the whole façade in place. I've sat with folks on the mission field in tears, who've said, 'My heart is empty and I'm a mess.' You can sit in a Keswick Convention, you can be a regular visitor, and there can be a façade.

Let the Spirit of God go right through to the heart. 'Come to Me, abide in Me,' was the invitation; but you've strayed. In His kindness He'll mould you; but maybe we don't listen, the clay hardens and He has to smash it. But there's a field in Anathoth. 'They'll be back,' says God. 'You pay the down-payment.' Are there some down-payments you need to pay this morning? Repentance is just the beginning. Confession comes next; allow God to restore and rebuild and produce in you His holiness.

That's His agenda. You've been looking into a mirror this morning? You've seen yourself exposed, stripped bare before Him with whom we have to do? Maybe it's been a long time since you heard the voice of God; the conscience has been seared. But word of the Lord has come a second time, a third time. He hasn't come to condemn you. He comes to call you home. Will you come this morning, and in your own heart say, 'Lord Jesus, forgive me'?

4 : 'Leadership in Trouble'
Jeremiah 22-23

Some of us might think that 'leadership' is rather irrelevant to us. But far more of us are involved in leadership than we realise. For example, if you have children, you are involved in leadership. So I am concerned that we should not feel that this morning's study doesn't apply to us. I want to apply these chapters very generally, and especially as we look at what is said about prophets; that under the new covenant, as Paul said to the Corinthians, every one of you can prophesy. We'll talk about what that means a little later on.

You may be a Sunday School teacher or involved in other youth work. Maybe you're a deacon in your church, or an elder, or a member of the PCC. Or you may be a lay preacher, or involved in full-time ministry. You may be involved in missionary work, you may be involved in Christian committees and so on. How many of you are in positions of explicit leadership like that? Would you put your hands up? A very significant number of you, I see.

For those of you who didn't raise your hands, the very influence of your life is something that God uses to mould and impact upon others. Some of the people who had the biggest influence on my life did not occupy any formal leadership role. I was not accountable or in submission to them, but just exposed to the influence of their lives. So I trust we'll all find this study to be relevant.

Jeremiah was very much a voice in the wilderness in his day. So where were the other men and women of God in Judah at that time? Fifty times Jeremiah refers to other prophets than himself in the nation. Where were they? What were they doing? Forty-five times he refers to the priests in Judah. What were they doing, when Jeremiah stood alone as a voice in the wilderness?

That is what I want to talk about. Today's section really

begins in chapter 21, though we are only going to read from chapter 23. The word of the Lord comes through Jeremiah in chapter 21, to King Zedekiah, the last king before the Babylonian invasion. In chapter 22 he speaks particularly to the 'evil kings'. But in chapter 23, we find three categories of leaders.

Verse 1, 'Woe to the *shepherds* [AV: 'the pastors'] who are destroying and scattering the sheep of my pasture!' These are the kings, the civil leaders, those who administer the affairs of the nation.

Verse 9, 'Concerning the *prophets*: My heart is broken within me; all my bones tremble.' These were God's spokesmen, theoretically; the men who stood between God and the people and spoke on God's behalf.

Verse 11, 'Both prophet and *priest* are godless.' The priests ministered in the temple. If the prophets stood before the people on God's behalf, the priests stood before God on the people's behalf. God spoke to the people through the prophets, the people approached God through the priests, and so the priests and the prophets stood as intermediaries between God and the people and the people and God. He addresses them, and asks that legitimate question: what were they up to at such a troubled time in the nation of Judah? They didn't contribute to any solution. In fact they were a major part of the problem.

The Shepherds

Let me say a brief word about the shepherds. The essential charge against them comes in verse 1. 'You have not bestowed care on them,' says the Lord. Here is the age-old problem with civil leaders of the nation: the seduction of power. There is a totally unbiblical understanding of leadership in the world today. There probably always has been. One of my concerns is that it has infiltrated the church. We have an idea of leadership that basically leadership is power and control. People are fighting for power in marriage, in church, in society, in relationships. The idea is that I'm to lead, I am to exercise power; I am to control.

But leadership in the Bible is very different indeed. One of its most concise expressions is in the New Testament, in Luke's Gospel. 'A dispute arose among them as to which of them was considered to be greatest' (Luke 22:24). The context is that the disciples are with Jesus in the upper room. He has taken bread, broken it; Judas has already left the room. He's passed the bread and said, 'This is My body, it's for you, eat it in remembrance of Me.' He takes the cup: 'This is My blood, the blood of the new covenant, drink it in remembrance of Me.' It is one of the most solemn occasions of all Jesus's time with His disciples. And the moment that it was over, a dispute arose among them. Fighting over which of them was to be the greatest—isn't that incredible?

You can be quite sure the dispute wasn't a matter of Peter saying, 'Well, you know, I think John is probably the greatest,' and John saying, 'Thank you very much, Peter, that's very kind of you. But I think it's Thaddaeus', and Thaddaeus responding, 'Oh! that's very kind ... But I think Matthew's probably the greatest.' No. It was Peter saying, 'Did someone ask who's the greatest? What's the problem? I mean, it's obvious, isn't it? It's me.' It was James and John saying, 'Peter, we have been to ask Jesus if we can sit one on His right and one on His left in His kingdom—and even Mummy came and asked Him as well.' You remember they went, and their mother came once and asked Him the same question. Incredible—the number of times the disciples had this discussion about 'Who is the greatest?' It's recorded on several different occasions.

On this occasion Jesus (who had dealt with the same argument once before by putting a small child in front of them) said to them, 'The kings of the Gentiles lord it over them; and those who exercise authority over them call themselves Benefactors' (Luke 22:25). That's leadership and power from the world's perspective. You've got control, you can lord it over people. Of course you call yourselves benefactors: 'If it wasn't for us, you know, you wouldn't be free.' I lived in what was Rhodesia when it was ruled by the white minority. They said, 'Of course we know what's best for the African population. We are their benefactors.' Meanwhile, of course they were walking all over them, kidding themselves—'We're doing them a favour.'

'Well,' He said, 'That's what the kings of the Gentiles do. But,' verse 26, 'you are not to be like that. Instead the greatest among you should be like the youngest, and the one who rules like the one who serves.' In God's economy, whether it's the Old Testament or whether it's now, under the new covenant, leadership is servanthood.

There's a great emphasis on identifying leaders today. I think that is not only valid, it is right and necessary. The church is in desperate need of good leadership. But one of my concerns is that at some of these conferences we develop the impression that leaders are the ones who strut around and make the decisions. But leadership will be discovered when we start training people to be servants. When some years ago I joined the staff at Capernwray Hall, a colleague told me, 'If you want to find who your leaders are, give them the worst jobs. Then you'll find who your real leaders are.' I'm so grateful for that advice, because there are people of course who would like to be visible; but you know the people that God makes leaders when you discover them serving. Our job is to make servants, and God makes leaders out of servants.

In our society and even in the church, the whole idea of going into public office is dying. When Sir Alec Douglas Home died, an obituary article described him as the last leader driven by a sense of duty towards the people. It's a generalisation; I don't believe it's really true. But the implication is that now people are in leadership primarily for their own self-interest. Tony Blair has said some very encouraging words about that: 'We are here to serve.'

That, of course, is the pattern of leadership in the Bible. But these shepherds, the national leaders of Judah, instead of seeing themselves as servants saw themselves as the place where the power lay. They had not bestowed care. And,

Jeremiah says, here and elsewhere, they had simply taken advantage of the people for their own benefit. Compare that with the teaching of Ephesians 4:12, that leadership is 'to prepare God's people for works of service', not to rule but to release, teaching people to be servants.

The Prophets

But then Jeremiah talks about the prophets. We'll look at this a little longer, because I think this is crucially important and very relevant to where we are today. 'This is what the LORD Almighty says concerning the prophets: "I will make them eat bitter food and drink poisoned water, because from the prophets of Jerusalem ungodliness has spread throughout the land"' (23:15). The very people whose task and function and ministry was to declare the word of God and be the source of godliness, were instead the source of ungodliness. Incredible!

Who are these prophets? I won't read you all fifty references to them in Jeremiah but here are one or two. 'The prophets are but wind and the word is not in them .... The prophets prophesy lies, the priests rule by their own authority' (5:13, 30), 'Prophets and priests alike, all practise deceit' (6:13). There are repeated, devastating tirades against the prophets. Who are they?

They aren't prophets of Baal. To all appearances they are prophets of God. The prophetic office was established formally in the days of Samuel, we are told by Peter in Acts 3—'All the prophets from Samuel on' (3:24). One or two people were called 'prophets' before that—Enoch was described as a prophet, and Abraham and Moses—but the prophetic office was established in the days of Samuel. Let me point out one or two verses, as it's important to understand the background to the point that Jeremiah is making. Firstly, 1 Samuel 10:5, where Saul is told, 'You go down to Gibeah, and you'll meet a procession of prophets. These are men anointed by God, the Spirit of God is on them, and in fact the Spirit of God will come on you. They are

authentic and their ministry is of God. This is genuine.'
Secondly, 1 Samuel 19:18-20, where David has fled to
Samuel at Ramah and told him all that Saul has done to
him. They go together to Naioth. Word reaches Saul that
David is at Nioth and he sends men to capture him. But
when the men see a group of prophets prophesying, with
Samuel standing there as their leader, the Spirit of God
comes upon Saul's men and they prophesy too.

By the time of Elijah, Jezebel was killing off the Lord's
prophets (1 Kings 18:4). Obadiah, a believer working in the
palace, hid 100 of the Lord's prophets (two groups of fifty
in two different caves), and Jezebel and Ahab did not even
know that they were missing. There must have been hundreds of prophets, if the absence of 100 wasn't noticed.

In Elisha's day (cf 2 Kings 2) there was a company of
prophets in Bethel and a company of prophets in Jericho—
we don't know how many, but fifty of them joined Elisha,
which is a large number. By now the prophetic office was
becoming an institution. And I want to suggest to you, this
was a very dangerous development. The criterion for being
a prophet ceased to be that you had a message from God
and that the Spirit of God was upon you. It became a matter of having been to the right school, had the right training, got the right associations, obtained the right
accreditation. The prophetic office became a job, a vocation
in contemporary religion. So much so, that when you get to
the written prophets they are spoken of as corrupt. Micah
3:5, 'As for the prophets who lead my people astray, if one
feeds them, they proclaim "peace"; if he does not, they prepare to wage war against him.' Verse 11, 'Her prophets tell
fortunes for money. Yet they lean upon the LORD and say,
"Is not the LORD among us? No disaster will come upon
us."' If you paid them good money they gave you a good
prophecy. If you didn't, you got a bad one.

Then, in Zechariah 13:2, we read that it's going to become an embarrassment to be a prophet because the prophetic office has become so corrupt. And what is said in
these verses is exactly true of Amos: 'I was neither a

prophet nor a prophet's son, but I was a shepherd, and I
also took care of sycamore-fig trees. But the LORD took me
from tending the flock and said to me, "Go, prophesy to
my people Israel."' (Amos 7:14-15). When Amos says, 'I
am not a prophet,' he doesn't mean 'God hasn't called
me'—God has. He means, 'I don't have the credentials, I
don't have the qualifications. I don't have a BP (Bachelor
of Prophecy) after my name. I haven't been to the right
accredited training grounds.' It has all become corrupt.

Several years ago I was speaking in Australia and was
interviewed on local television. The lady who was going to
interview me told me beforehand, 'I'm going to be very
kind to you today. When I introduce you, I won't call you
an evangelist.'

Well, I'm not an evangelist—I don't see that as my
calling—but I was intrigued. I said, 'Why is that kind?'

She answered, 'If I said you were an evangelist, do you
know what most of my viewers would think? That you are
here for the money, that you've got a woman in every town
you visit, that you exploit the gullible and the weak.'

I said, 'You're kidding.'

She replied, 'I'm not.'

That was several years ago. Soon after, of cours,e the
media were making a huge thing of the tele-evangelist
scandals in America. The whole reputation of being an
evangelist had become tarnished.

It was very much like that for the prophets. I understand
why Samuel started his schools of the prophets. Remember
when Samuel was born. His mother Hannah had gone to
the temple to pray that God would give her a son; she was
barren, it says, and God gave her Samuel, and when he was
weaned she gave him to be brought up in the temple in
Shiloh under Eli's leadership. And we're told, 'In those
days the word of the LORD was rare; there were not many
visions' (1 Sam 3:1). In other words, you could go to the
temple and you would hear the voice of the priest but you
hardly ever heard the voice of God. When Hannah came to
Shiloh, and Eli (who began as a good man but was a weak

one) saw her at prayer and observed that 'her lips were
moving but her voice was not heard' (1:13), he said, 'How
long will you keep on getting drunk?' He saw this woman
who meant business with God—and he accused her of
being drunk. Then later when Samuel was born and put
into the priest's home in Shiloh, one night in his bed he
heard the voice of God speaking to him and calling him by
name. He went to Eli saying, 'Did you call me?' But Eli
said, 'No, go back to bed, you're dreaming.'

When the priest assumed that a woman who was praying was drunk, and a boy who heard the voice of God was
dreaming, no wonder the voice of the Lord was rare! And
Samuel, growing up in that environment as a boy and a
young man of God, resolved, I am sure, that never again
should it be said in Judah that God's voice was not heard.
So he got together the young men and he taught them to
listen to God. It was genuine, it was authentic. As we have
already read, the Spirit of God was on them.

But now, in Jeremiah's time the criterion for prophetic
ministry was not, 'Has God called you? Is the Spirit of God
on you?', but 'This is a job. Get the right qualifications and
you're equipped.' Does that ring a bell?

That is the necessary background as we read Jeremiah
23. What gives any man or woman the right to stand and
declare the word of God? The fact that they have done
business with God, and He has given them the calling and
anointing of His Holy Spirit. But: 'This is what the LORD
Almighty says: "Do not listen to what the prophets are
prophesying to you; they fill you with false hopes. They
speak visions from their own minds, not from the mouth of
the LORD. They keep saying to those who despise me,
"The LORD says: You will have peace."' (23:16-17).

Their message was very positive and up-beat, filling
their hearers with hopes—false hopes, but hopes. They are
visionaries, but their visions are from their own minds.
They are forward-looking. Their message is peace. They
talk about safety (verse 17). These are positive, attractive,
affirming messages. But they were 'delusions of their own

minds' (verse 26). They gave the people what they liked to hear. We love to hear positive, warm, upbeat visionary messages, don't we? Well, they gave them what they wanted. But they didn't equip them for godliness, they didn't equip them for righteousness, for warfare. They didn't transform the lives of those to whom they preached.

There are always people who, rather than take time to find out what God would say to them personally, want to know what God wants them to say. And there are always people around who are gullible enough to believe it when they are told, 'I have a word from God for you to go and do something ...' I had a phone call the other day from a woman in Norway. I've never met her in my life. She said, 'I read one of your books and God told me to get in touch with you. You must leave England within the next two weeks.'

I said, 'Who are you?'

'I am someone to whom God has been speaking. Go to Sierra Leone,' she said.

I said, 'There's a war on in Sierra Leone.'

She replied, 'If you stay in England more than two weeks you'll be in trouble.'

I said, 'Well—thanks for your word. 'Bye.' Next day I received an international telegram from the same lady, followed up a week later by a letter.

Once a man came to me and told me that God had told him that within seven days I would die. I went to see him after the seven days had expired. I said, 'You have created for yourself incredible power. I didn't believe you; but I could hardly sleep the night you told me that. You are creating incredible power. And it's evil.'

These people leaped on the opportunity to take advantage and to exploit. What's the antidote? Jeremiah has spoken a lot about the negative side, but now in verses 18-22 he turns to the positive side. If these are men and women whom God has called to the prophetic ministry, what if they had only stood in the council of God and listened?

At this point it would be as well to define what we mean

by 'prophecy'. I once heard F. F. Bruce talk about what he called the Law of First Mention. 'It doesn't always work,' he said, 'but it's a good rule of thumb. If you want to know what a biblical term means, find out where it first occurs in the Bible.' For very often in the first occurrence of a word you find its meaning. For example, the word 'worship'. Do you know where it first occurs? In Genesis 22, where Abraham leaves his servants at the base of Mount Moriah and takes his son Isaac of whom God has said, 'Go and offer him on Mount Moriah.' He tells them, 'I and the boy …. will worship' (22:5). What's he going to do on the mountain? What did Isaac say? He said, 'We've got the fire, we've got the wood, where's the lamb?' He didn't say, 'We've got the guitar, we've got the drums, where's the piano?' Worship was defined there as total unquestioning obedience.

The first time the word occurs in the New Testament is in Matthew 2. The wise men came: 'They worshipped him. Then they opened their treasures and presented him with gifts.' Interesting definition of worship: giving your treasures.

The first time the word 'prophet' ever occurs is in Exodus 7:1, which I think is a definition. 'The LORD said to Moses, "See, I have made you like God to Pharaoh, and your brother Aaron will be your prophet."'

Now what does he mean? 'You are like God and Aaron will be your prophet?' Go back to 4:14-16. 'Then the LORD's anger burned against Moses and he said, "What about your brother, Aaron the Levite? I know he can speak well. He is already on his way to meet you, and his heart will be glad when he sees you. You shall speak to him and put words in his mouth; I will help both of you speak and will teach you what to do. He will speak to the people for you, and it will be as if he were your mouth and as if you were God to him …".'

What is a prophet? A prophet is the mouth of God. One of the current debates about prophecy is whether it is 'fore-telling' or 'forth-telling'. Actually neither defines prophecy,

because it's not the content of the message that defines it
but the origin: 'This is from God'. That is why I believe it's
important to acknowledge that in every New Testament
list of spiritual gifts, such as Romans 12, 1 Corinthians 12
and 14, and 1 Peter 2, the list always includes prophecy.
And you also find that when the Holy Spirit came at the
Day of Pentecost, Peter stood up and quoted from the book
of Joel, and said: 'This is the fulfilment of that prophecy'
(cf Acts 2:15). One of the things that Joel's prophecy says is,
'I will pour out my Spirit in those days, and they will
prophesy' (verse 18). Every one of us may be a mouth of
God; we may speak what is the word of God to people.

We saw the other morning that Jeremiah himself knew
that it wasn't the effect of his message that made it important, but its origin and source. God had said, 'I will put my
words in your mouth.' And if you know where the word
has come from, you don't have to know where the word is
going to. That's God's business. As He said in Isaiah, 'My
word that goes out from my mouth ... will not return to
me empty, but will accomplish what I desire and achieve
the purpose for which I sent it' (Isa. 55:11). If in Jeremiah's
case it was to be after his death, so be it: 'But My word will
not return void. If it's My word, it's going to penetrate and
have its effect'.

But if the prophet is the mouth of God, then the discipline of the prophet of God is to listen to God. That's what
Jeremiah says in verses 18 and 22. 'Which of them had
stood in My council and listened?'

That raises the question, how does God speak? I want
to suggest three ways in which God speaks.

First (and this won't be the one you're expecting first,
but I believe it's crucial), *God speaks by His Son*. 'In the past
God spoke to our forefathers through the prophets at many
times and in various ways, but in these last days he has
spoken to us by his Son' (Heb. 1:1). The last days are the
period from Pentecost onwards in Scripture. We are in the
last days, and have been for 2,000 years. The term as used
in Hebrews means this era. God has spoken in His Son.

Jesus is, as John writes in his gospel, 'the Word', the *logos*. He is the truth, as He declared: 'I just don't preach it, I am the truth.' Everything that Jesus preached was an exposition of Himself: who He is, what He was doing.

The ultimate litmus test of truth is Christ. How do you know something's true? All kinds of new spiritual movements come along, and they are exciting and dramatic, and we ask, 'Is it from God, or isn't it from God? How do I know what is from God?' If our theological grasp can be summed up as 'God can do anything He wants to do, whenever He wants to do it,' then that's true, of course, and anything goes—though if that's the sum total of your theology, how do you measure anything? But here's the crucial question. Is it true of Christ?

What is the goal of the gospel? What is God's business in us? To conform us into the image of Christ. So if somebody tells us, 'The Holy Spirit is causing us to make noises like steam engines and we have smoke coming out of our ears'—can the Holy Spirit do that? He can do anything, of course. But did Jesus have steam coming out of His ears? The goal is to make us like Christ.

Now, there are things that were not true of Christ that are not wrong. But we ought not to preach things that are inessential. We oughtn't to preach opinions from the pulpit. We have to declare what is eternally true. There should be no message preached from this pulpit today that wasn't preached 120 years ago when Keswick began—and of course, 2,000 years ago. The message is Christ. I don't think we can stress that enough. He is the truth. And so all that God is going to produce in you that is true will conform to Christ. In these last days God has spoken to us, and He has said, 'Jesus.' That is His word.

Secondly, where do you find the Son? You find Him in His word. There is no reliable understanding of Christ apart from the Bible, which embodies all the truth that God has for us to know. This book is God-breathed. That's why the only legitimate foundation of true preaching is that it is exposition of this book. And that means we have to study it and understand it.

Jeremiah speaks of the people who have not listened to the law of God. There are too many references to list them here. They rediscovered the revelation that God gave that was available to them at that point in history; Josiah rediscovered the book of Deuteronomy, or part of it, when he cleaned the temple. They had parts of the Pentateuch. But in Jeremiah 6, God says, 'Hear, O earth: I am bringing disaster on this people, the fruit of their schemes, because they have not listened to my words and have rejected my law' (6:19). And in Jeremiah 8, 'How can you say, "We are wise, for we have the law of the LORD," when actually the lying pen of the scribes has handled it falsely?"' (8:8). They choose to know the false handling of the law of God. Jeremiah 9—'The LORD said, "It is because they have forsaken my law which I set before them; they have not obeyed me or followed my law."' (9:12). In 16:11, '"It is because your fathers forsook me," declares the Lord, "and followed other gods and served and worshipped them ... and did not keep my law." In 26:4,6, 'This is what the Lord says: If you do not listen to me and follow my law ... then I will make this house like Shiloh and this city an object of cursing.' And in 31:33 (we will look at this tomorrow): '"This is the covenant that I will make with the house of Israel after that time," declares the Lord. "I will put my law in their minds."'

Again and again and again through this book he talks about the law, the revealed word of God as they had it, the truth of God. He says, 'You have not listened to it, you have not read it, you have not preached it. Therefore you are heading for disaster.'

One of the great tragedies is that even many of us who are Christians have lost confidence in what God has to say in His book. Even some preachers have lost confidence in it. We want a quick, trendy message. We live in a *Sesame Street* culture—'If you can't give it me in a couple of minutes then I don't want it.' We live in a fast-food age. I stood in a queue behind someone who was told that he would have to wait for his special order. He asked how long, and was told fifty seconds. He agreed. 'Provided it's no longer.' That is our culture. So what do we do? In our preaching and our teaching, if God has given us influence; whether it's a Sunday School class, whether it's working with young people—every time, this book needs to be opened, this truth needs to be declared. We need to read and study it, we need to place our life under its teaching.

About fifteen years ago, people began to say it was 'legalistic' to have a 'quiet time'. It used to be quite standard practice for Christians. How many of you have one who are over forty? It's probably been a habit of your life. But if I ask how many of you under forty do, probably the proportion will be less. Anything can be legalistic, of course, but this book is God speaking. We cannot emphasise that sufficiently. And if I am going to stand in the council of the Lord, I stand in the council of the Lord with an open Bible.

Yes, we need to be relevant. But don't try to get too sophisticated about the people to whom you are ministering. The modern 1997 British woman is no different to the woman of Samaria. What Jesus offered her we can offer today. Let's cut through all this façade of sophistication, and get to the heart, where people are broken because they are alienated from God. This word tells us how.

Thirdly, if God speaks through His Son, and God speaks by His Son, speaks in His Word, God speaks through His Spirit. It's the Holy Spirit's task, among other things, to guide us into all truth. That's what Jesus said of Him in John 16: 'He'll guide you into all truth.' It's the Holy Spirit's task to reveal to us, and enforce, what God wants us to know and understand.

I preach in many different places. I used to ask God to give me sermons. Often He didn't co-operate. Now I ask God to give me a burden. I say, 'Lord, lay on my heart a burden for these people.' Do you know, it's remarkable how again and again, many of you will have experienced this: God will do that.

That applies in personal conversation. You're off to

meet somebody—'Lord, I don't know how I can solve that problem, give me a burden as we speak.' Again and again they'll say, 'It's as though you know me.' Many of you will have experienced that, too. That's what the Holy Spirit does.

We need to keep the three together. If we detach Christ from the Word of God, we'll end up with mysticism. There have been many mystical Christs. If we detach the Word of God from the Spirit of God, we end up with legalism. The Pharisees of course are a prime case of those who took the law of God very seriously, but detached it from the life of God and it became bondage. But as our focus is on the Lord Jesus Christ, He is the object of our devotion. And through the written Word we search for the living Word, and we seek to understand Him. But we do so in dependence on the Spirit of God. God will speak!

I pray regularly when I go to preach, as I am sure you do if you are involved in preaching at all; I pray my preaching will be prophetic. I don't mean that half-way through I'll start predicting what will happen in 1999 or the new millennium. I pray that as I preach, there'll be those sitting there who will sense, 'God is speaking to me. This is about me!' And they'll forget the voice of the speaker and do dealings with God Himself. That is my prayer this week; that the crowds and the individuals will hear God speak. It's the Holy Spirit who speaks and reveals truth.

What happens when the Word of God is understood and conveyed, and is the subject of our ministry to one another?

Look, as we close, at 23:28-29. 'Let the prophet who has a dream tell his dream,'—in other words, be honest; it's a dream—'but let the one who has my word speak it faithfully. For what has straw [the dreaming] to do with grain [the word]? ... Is not my word like fire ... and like a hammer that breaks a rock in pieces?'

There are three images of the word here: grain, fire and a hammer. You can plant grain seed. Often there's nothing to show for a number of months. You can plant time bombs in people's lives, when you put the Word of God in their hearts. When the circumstances change, the seed germinates and comes to life. It's like grain: you are planting seed, you see no response at first, there's no germination. And that's why long after some of you have left the Keswick Convention this year, something you heard in this place will come back to you, as the Spirit brings it back. And that seed will germinate.

But it's like fire as well, He says. Fire warms us, encourages and comforts us, and so does the Word of God. At the same time fire can destroy; and there's a destructive work that the Word of God would do in our lives. It purifies, it gives light, it reveals, it exposes. All these things are ministries of the Word of God. As we sit together, for some of you your heart will be warmed, and for others you will feel the purifying force of the fire of the Word of God. It's not comfortable. Same word, same fire, but having a different function.

Then He says, 'Is not my word like a hammer that breaks a rock in pieces?' How do you break a rock with a hammer? Do you just strike one blow and say, 'That didn't work'? No. You have to go Bang! Bang! Bang! Bang!, as close to the same spot as you can; and suddenly the rock will split. That's why you should never be embarrassed about saying the same things to the same person. It's the hammer hitting the same spot; Jesus said a lot of the same things again and again. If you're smart you vary the wording, but you come back to the same thing.

You see, the scope of our message as we declare it to the world is actually not a very big message. It's big in its ramifications, but the actual message comes to the same spot. You are alienated from God, separated from God. You're dead in your sin, you need the life of God to re-indwell you and regenerate you.

These prophets had long since stopped standing in the presence of God. They still had a job, they still had their congregations, they still gathered people together. They still warmed the people's hearts with their good messages

of hope and buoyancy and vision. But the bubble, every
time, would eventually burst. Because it wasn't the Word
of God, that is centred in the Son of God, and is empow-
ered by the Spirit of God.

We don't have time after all to speak about the priests—
but listen. Some of you are sitting here saying, 'Well, this is
relevant for people in the pulpit, but not for me.' It does
have particular relevance for those in the pulpit, that's true.
But Paul says to the church in Corinth, you can all prophesy. You can all be the voice, the mouth of God to people.
As we go about our normal life, working, living in our
neighbourhood, dealing with folks in our church, living in
our families, we need that spirit of prophecy that drives us
back again and again to God Himself, to His Word, to His
Truth; so that we say, 'Lord, like Samuel, let no word of
mine fall to the ground'—for that is what was said of Samuel. 'Even in the chance few words with the lady at the
check-out at the local supermarket when I'm buying a tin
of beans, help me to say something that makes her glad I
passed her way.'

Paul said, 'You are epistles read by all men.' I heard
someone say once that God has three testaments with
which He reveals Himself: the Old Testament, the New
Testament and the You Testament. You are epistles. And
long before anybody reads the New Testament, and especially the Old Testament, they read the You Testament.
Because the look in your eyes, the smile on your face, the
words and the way in which you say it from your lips, en-
ables God to get a foothold in somebody's life. We are all in
the business of being prophets.

5 : 'Messages of Hope'
Jeremiah 29-31

I am very grateful to the Keswick Council for inviting me to undertake these mornings with you in the book of Jeremiah. There has been a very real receptivity that has made it so easy to speak, and it's been wonderful to feel it.

In this last morning we will be looking at chapters 29, 30 and particularly 31. I've called it 'Messages of hope'. Of course there is much in this book we haven't had time to begin to look at. Somebody said to me yesterday, 'I'm surprised you can get so much out of so little.' I think he meant the reverse! We have taken five snapshots, and I think that anybody else doing these Bible Readings this week would have given us five completely different messages, because there is so much here.

But I don't think we can leave Jeremiah without looking at these messages of hope that come towards the end of the book. Chapter 29 is a message to the people in exile; it is, in the main, the text of a letter that Jeremiah wrote to the surviving elders, priests, prophets and other exiles after Nebuchadnezzar had taken the people into captivity. The essential message is this: 'Settle down in Babylon, build houses, plant gardens, get married, have children, seek the peace and prosperity of Babylon. Because although you are in exile and it is the expression of God's wrath on you, He's not abandoned you. After seventy years He's going to bring you back home.' It is here we find that oft-quoted verse: '"For I know the plans I have for you," declares the LORD, "plans to prosper you and not to harm you, plans to give you hope and a future."' (29:11). He's saying, 'It's seventy years before you'll come back; two generations' time—most of you will have passed away, and it is your grandchildren who will come back.' But God says, 'I've not forgotten you, even in this time of exile.'

Chapter 30 is the message about the restoration of the

people to the land. Verses 2-3: "'Write in a book all the
words I have spoken to you. The days are coming," declares the LORD, "when I will bring my people Israel and
Judah back from captivity and restore them to the land I
gave to their forefathers to possess," says the LORD.' All the
blessing God had promised their forefathers tied into their
occupation of the land. The right people in the wrong
place would not fulfil the promise. The right people had to
be brought back into the right place, and from there the
promise would find its fulfilment.

Chapter 31 is the message about the restoration of the
people to God. He calls them 'My people' (31:1). That
term is used of the intimacy of the union that God will
once again enjoy with His people. And that comes to a climax in verses 31-34, which will be our text for this morning. This passage speaks of the new covenant, the great
climax of the book of Jeremiah. To understand Jeremiah's
message we have to understand this new covenant, made to
replace the one God's people had broken.

A covenant is an agreement made between at least two
parties who are not necessarily (and certainly are not, in
the case of the covenants God made with His people)
equal parties. God had made two primary covenants with
Israel. He made a covenant with Abraham when He called
him after leading him from Ur of the Chaldees. 'I will es-
tablish my covenant as an everlasting covenant between me
and you and your decendants after you for the generations
to come, to be your God and the God of your decendants
after you' (Gen. 17:7). That's the covenant He made with
Abraham which lies at the base of the whole identity of the
people.

The second covenant He made was the covenant with
Moses on Mount Sinai, based on an agreement to keep the
law that God gave there. 'Then he took the Book of the
Covenant and read it to the people. They responded, "We
will do everything the LORD has said; we will obey."'
(Exod. 24:7). The covenant was renewed at various times,
as for example at the end of the book of Joshua; and in

Deuteronomy 4:13 we read, 'He declared to you his covenant, the ten commandments, which he commanded you
to follow and then wrote them on two stone tablets.' Israel
agreed to observe the law that God had given to them, the
ten commandments in particular.

But, as God says here in Jeremiah 31:32, 'They broke
my covenant.' Now as a consequence, says God, there
would be no repetition of the old cycle: the promise to God
to live according to His law—the violation of it—the punishment from God—God drawing them back—the people's re-affirmation of the covenant—and then the whole
process starting all over again. In the book of Judges the
cycle recurs six or seven times, and it goes on, right through
the people's history, and the exile is just the latest example
of the punishment phase.

'No,' says God. 'I am going to make a new covenant.'
This new covenant has a crucially important distinctive. It
is all about what God does for the people. 'I will put my
law in their minds and write it on their hearts' … 'I will be
their God' … 'I will forgive their wickedness.' You and I, as
believers in the Lord Jesus, participate in the new covenant.
It's important that we understand this. That is why I want
to talk about it this morning.

It divides quite naturally into three sections. There's *a
new righteousness*—'I will put my law in their minds and
write it on their hearts.' There's *a new relationship*—'I will
be their God and they will be my people. No longer will a
man teach his neighbour, or a man his brother, saying,
"Know the LORD," because they will all know me …' And
there's *a new redemption*—'I will forgive their wickedness
and remember their sins no more.'

A new righteousness

'I will put my law in their minds and write it on their
hearts.' A hunger and thirst for righteousness lies at the
heart of the ambition of every genuine Christian. Jeremiah
tells us that this righteousness involves the law of God,

previously written in stone, being written on their minds and hearts. The big question is: what does this mean?

There are eleven references to the law in the book of Jeremiah, all negative except for this one in 31:33. They are negative because the people of God were completely unable to keep the law of God that was given to them on Mount Sinai. If you want to write one word across the whole history of the Old Testament, it could be the word 'failure'. The historical books record the details of their failure, the poetic books weep and mourn for their failure, the prophetic books preach about their failure. Since Sinai, that one word in every generation sums up the people's ability to fulfil what God required of them; 'failure'.

That, of course, raises a very important question. Why did God give the law in the first place? He knew that it was a law that no-one could keep, and that is true for every one of us in the tent here this morning. Without knowing anything else about you, I'd be quite prepared to look you in the eye as a complete stranger and say, 'You have broken the law of God.' You wouldn't get angry; you'd look me back in the eye and say, 'So have you.' Because you know, and I know, that nobody is able to keep the law of God. So why did God make a law that no-one is able to keep? It doesn't sound very fair.

The Purpose of the Law

The central principle in good rule-making is that a rule people can't keep is a bad rule. Yet God, in the ten commandments, gave a set of laws that are so high, so demanding—humanly speaking, so unreasonable—that no man, woman, boy or girl has ever kept them. Why then did God give the law? What was the criterion, if I may put it that way, that determined what the law should be? Were the commandments simply pulled out of a hat as a set of arbitrary guidelines? Or is there some more fundamental criterion that determined the substance of the law?

Well, I believe there is. Why did God give the law? It is a very important question, and I make no apology for repeating here some things I have said elsewhere in print under that title. To discover the criterion that determines what the law should be, I want to point out to you two verses in the New Testament, both of which define what all sin is. The first is 1 John 3:4. The word 'sin' means, literally, 'missing the mark'. I am told it was originally used in archery: if you fired an arrow and missed the target it was called 'sin'. If you missed by half an inch it was called 'sin', if you missed by a foot it was called 'sin', if you missed by half a yard, half a mile or if you shot in the opposite direction it was called 'sin'. Why? Because sin is not a measurement of how bad we are but a measurement of how good we are not. If you've missed a bus by a minute you've missed it; if you've missed it by an hour, you've missed it. You don't congratulate yourself on missing it only by a minute.

You see, there is a sense in which God is not actually particularly concerned with how bad we are. He is concerned with how good we're not. We've missed the mark.

If 'sin' means to miss the mark, sin isn't absolute. But what is absolute is the mark that we've missed. 1 John 3:4 tells us, 'Every one who sins breaks the law; in fact, sin is lawlessness.' John says that any time anyone sins, no matter what the nature of the sin is, we know what they have done. They have broken the law of God—because the law represents the target that we miss every time we sin.

Now, keep that verse in mind and compare it with Romans 3:23, 'For all have sinned and fall short of the glory of God.' Paul says that every time a person sins, no matter what the nature of the sin is, no matter what they have done, they have come short of 'the glory of God'; whatever that is, and we'll come to that in a moment.

Put those two verses together. If John says that the target we miss is the law of God, and Paul says that the target we miss is the glory of God, then that tells us that the law of God and the glory of God are equal, the same thing.

So to answer the question, 'What is the law of God?' we have to ask another question, 'What is the glory of God?'

Now the word 'glory' occurs with slight variations of meaning depending on its context in Scripture, but essentially the glory of God is the character of God. W. E. Vine in his *Expository Dictionary of New Testament Words* says that the glory of God is the character of God, 'what He essentially is and does'.[1] It's God's moral character, the kind of thing John had in mind when he wrote, 'The Word became flesh and made his dwelling among us. We have seen his glory, the glory of the One and Only, who came from the Father, full of grace and truth' (John 1:14).

What did John mean? He *didn't* mean that we saw a bright light suspended six inches above his head in the shape of a Polo mint, as artists sometimes portray. He is saying that we saw in Jesus Christ what God is like. 'So those of us who kicked a ball up and down the road as a boy, who went hunting in the hills with Him or hiding in the woods—in the way He acted and the way He reacted, we saw what God was like. When He began to work in His father's carpenter's shop, then, in the way He went about His business, in the way He paid His bills on time, in the way He invoiced accurately for the work He had done, in the way he put somebody's roof on in the morning that had blown off the night before—then we saw what God was like. When He began His public ministry, we saw what God was like in the way He crossed the road to talk to a dirty woman, with whom everybody else was embarrassed to be seen. When the leper came down the road ringing his bell, saying, "Unclean! Don't come near me—I have this dreaded contagious disease of leprosy," we saw Jesus cross the road, touch the man (nobody ever touched a leper!) and say: "Put your bell away, go home, you're clean, hug your wife. There's nothing for her to catch. Wrestle with your kids. You're safe."'

'We saw,' says John, 'what God was like.' Because the glory of God is the character of God.

If that was true for Jesus, it was also intended to be true

---

1. W. E. Vine, *Expository Dictionary of New Testament Words* (Oliphants, 1939), ii, 153.

for every human being. When God created man He created man in His image. Whatever else that involves (and there's debate as to exactly what it does involve) it involves His moral image. If you and I had been flies on the wall in the Garden of Eden, we would have seen in Adam's behaviour, the way he treated Eve, exactly what God is like in His behaviour. He would have been very loving, very kind. You would have seen what God is like in the way Eve treated Adam, the way they handled the animals, patted the dog and stroked the cat. To be in His image means that when you look at the image, it reminds you of the real thing.

But of course man sinned and came short of the glory of God, and he no longer showed you what God was like.

So if the law equals the glory of God, the law was given in the first instance to show what God is like, in order for human beings to understand what they are to be like, having been created in God's image. So when in the law God said 'You shall not steal,' it wasn't because stealing isn't nice (though of course it isn't), but there's a much more important reason, it's because God is not a thief; human beings were made to be in His image; so do not steal. When He said, 'You shall not commit adultery,' it's because God is totally faithful. Humanity was made to be in His image, so don't ever commit adultery. You are created to be in His image. When He said 'You shall not covet,' it's because God is not greedy and man was made to be in His image—so do not covet. When He said 'You shall not bear false witness,' it's because God never tells lies, and man was made to be in His image—so do not bear false witness.

When He said, 'Six days shall you labour and on the seventh do no work,' we are told why; it's because God rested on the seventh day. It's not because He was tired. That's not the reason for the Sabbath. God rested, not because He was tired, but because the work was finished. And we are to rest in the utter sufficiency of God, which is why for Adam the first day was the day of rest. It was a great day to have been created, a Friday afternoon—what's happening tomorrow? A day off. Why? Because he's tired?

No. Because he's to rest in the fact that he's never indispensable to God, but God is always indispensable to him as a human being.

'Children, honour your parents.' Why? In the Trinity the Son says, 'I always do those things that please the Father' (cf John 5:30). Man was made to be in God's image, so children—honour your parents.

You see, the law is not just an arbitrary set of rules. It's far more profound than that. The law is a revelation of what God is like, because you and I were created to be what God is like in our moral character; created to be in His image. And so the purpose of the law is to reveal the character of God.

The Effect of the Law

But if that is true, and if it's important that we understand it, then it's important to understand the new covenant, as we shall see.

If the purpose of the law is to reveal the character of God, the effect of the law is to reveal the failure of man. When Moses came down the mountain after forty days, he carried the tablets of stone in his hands. The first commandment said, 'You shall have no other gods before me', for one simple reason: there are no other gods. The second commandment said, 'You shall not make yourself any graven image and bow down and worship it.' And having come down the mountain, Moses discovered to his shock that the Israelites had pooled their gold; they had melted it down and built a golden calf, around which they were having some kind of orgy. When Moses saw them worshipping the golden calf, he was so shocked that he smashed the tablets of stone on the ground and had to go back up the mountain to get some more.

Moses was shocked: God wasn't. God had not learned something new about man, but man learned something new about himself; that by himself he was incapable of being what God created him to be. Romans 7:7—'I would not have known what sin was except through the law.' I could be up to my neck in sin with a clear conscience, says Paul, enjoying every bit of it—and then the law came. The law doesn't make me sin. It just exposes me as a sinner, as a failure.

Romans 3:20 says, 'Through the law we become conscious of sin.' And right through the history of Israel, from the moment Moses stepped down from Mount Sinai, all the law ever did for the nation was to expose their failure. That is why across almost every page of the Old Testament, as I've already said, you can write 'failure'—'failure'—'failure', as far as man's ability is concerned to be what God is telling him to be. And of course that is the function of the law. That is why we must preach the law. Because sin is not just an arbitrary notion with bad consequences. Sin is that which violates the character of God.

One of the things sin has to do in our lives is to make us aware of our inability, before we discover what the new covenant is really about; because the new covenant is about the same law, but in a different location.

It's a big jump from Exodus to Jeremiah 31:33, but it was necessary to give that background, as I shall explain in a moment. '"This is the covenant that I will make with the house of Israel after that time," declares the LORD. "I will put my law in their minds and write it on their hearts."' The new covenant is not going to involve a revising of the law in any way. It's going to involve the relocating of the law. Up until now it's been kept on tablets of stone in the Ark of the Covenant, in the Holy of Holies in the temple in Jerusalem. 'Now,' says God, 'I'm going to take that same law, that same requirement—because the character of God is absolute—and I am going to put that law,' He says, 'in your hearts, in your minds.'

What does that mean? How is the law of God going to be placed within our hearts, or (to change the language without changing the meaning) how is the glory of God going to be restored into our experience? We have sinned and come short of the glory of God, and the law of God and the glory of God equal the same thing. So how is the

glory of God going to be restored into our experience?
How is the law of God going to be put into our hearts?

Let me read you two verses from other parts of Scripture
and then come back to this. Paul says in Colossians,

> I have become its servant by the commission
> God gave me to present to you the word of God
> in its fullness—the mystery that has been kept
> hidden for ages and generations, but is now dis-
> closed to the saints.

Let me pause there a moment. He says that this is a full
gospel with nothing left out, and it involves what he calls a
'mystery'. Up until now, he says, there's been a mystery in
the revelation from God. A prophet would prophesy, get
back home, sit down and scratch his head saying, 'Something's missing, there's a mystery here.' But now, Paul says,
the mystery's been made known.

> To them God has chosen to make known among
> the Gentiles the glorious riches of this mystery,
> which is Christ in you, the hope of [what?—]
> glory. (Col. 1:25-27)

That doesn't mean heaven, by the way. In evangelical
slang, 'glory' has come to mean 'heaven', people 'die and
go to glory'. But that isn't the biblical use of the word.
Glory is what we have come short of, it is the character of
God, 'all have sinned and come short of the glory of God'.
Now, says Paul, this is what the full gospel is—'Christ in
you' is your hope of hitting the target; your hope of the
character of God being restored into your life once again.

Let me read you the second passage before we return to
Jeremiah. It's in the book of Ezekiel 36:27, where God
speaks to Ezekiel about the new covenant He's going to
make with Israel. He doesn't use that term, but we know
that he's speaking of the same thing. In 36:27 God says, 'I
will put my Spirit in you.' That, by the way, is going to be
something new. Jesus said to the disciples in John 14:17
about the Spirit, 'He lives with you and will be in you.'

That's the difference Pentecost was going to make. Now, looking ahead to that he says,

> I will put my Spirit in you and move you to fol-
> low my decrees and be careful to keep my laws.
> (Ezek. 36:27)

In other words, 'I'll put my Spirit in you, and what the law demands I will enable you to fulfil.'

Those two passages, I think, illustrate what God is saying to Jeremiah when He says, 'I'll put My law—that which reveals My character—in your heart, in your mind; I will be your God.'

The new covenant involves a new righteousness

The fundamental difference between the old covenant and the new is that the old covenant put the onus of responsibility on us. 'You shall not steal, you shall not commit adultery, you shall not covet, etc., etc.' The new covenant puts the onus of responsibility on God. It's by His grace. 'I will put My law in your minds. I will be your God. I will forgive their wickedness.' And that means that what was a command under the old covenant becomes a promise under the new covenant.

You probably need an illustration by now! I heard the true story of a man converted to Christ while in prison for theft in the North of England. A Christian had come to visit him in prison, had witnessed to him and in the course of time had led him to Christ. On his release, one of the first things he wanted to do was visit a church. The first Sunday of his release came. He didn't know what church to go to so he picked a church at random. He went in, sat down at the back, looked up to the front and there on the wall in the front of the church were written the ten commandments: five down one side, five down the other. He thought to himself, 'That is the last thing I want to see. I know my weakness, I know my failure, I know my history. The last thing I want to do is to read those laws that only condemn me.' But as the service went on, he began to read them. And suddenly he realised he was reading them very differently. When he had read them previously they been commands: You SHALL NOT STEAL. But *this* morning when he read them, they said, 'YOU shall not steal.' It was a promise. And all the other commandments likewise were once commands but were now promises, because Christ in you now is your hope, hitting the target; 'I have put My law in your heart, in your mind, I am your God'; 'It is God who works in you to will and to act according to his good purpose' (Phil. 2:13).

The very things that were once commands that only ever condemned, have liberally become promises. Isn't that fantastic? It's the gospel. That's why you can go to any man, woman, boy or girl, from any background and any history who is in the grip of any sin; and as God by the Holy Spirit works in their hearts and awakens them, and as Jesus Christ by His Holy Spirit comes to live in them, you can say, 'You can live the Christian life.' Because it's not a matter of you trying to live for God. It is a matter of allowing God by His Holy Spirit to live in you. And what was a command has become a promise.

Vaughan last night[1] stressed the point that righteousness is the fruit of the Spirit. And the fruit has its origin in life. As Paul said to the Philippians: I am praying, he says, that you'll be 'filled with the fruit of righteousness that comes through Jesus Christ—to the glory and praise of God' (Phil. 1:11). God says that under the old covenant, you see, the commands were absolutely true because they expressed the character of God. 'But you broke my covenant. Actually you have no capability to do anything else, for there is no-one righteous, not even one. No-one desires righteousness' (cf Rom. 3). But now, He says, under the new covenant, that same law and those same commands are in your heart. What was a command on a tablet of stone is now a promise written by the Spirit in your heart.

---

1. Rev. Vaughan Roberts had spoken at the Convention Meeting the previous evening on 'Blessed are Those who Hunger and Thirst for Righteousness'. This address can be found on p.242.

For example, is anybody here this morning with a problem of stealing? If you are a Christian, and Jesus Christ by His Holy Spirit lives in you, I've got a promise for you. You'll find it in Exodus 20. It used to be a command written on tablets of stone, but now it's a promise written by the Spirit in your heart. It says, 'YOU shall not steal.'

Is anybody here facing sexual temptations you can hardly cope with? I've got a promise for you; 'YOU shall not commit adultery.' No-one living by the Spirit of God ever commits adultery—because He's your life, He's your strength: 'I will put my law in your hearts.'

Is somebody here greedy? I've got a promise for you. 'YOU shall not covet.' Does anybody here find things become too important, and dominate your life, so that you find yourself being pushed and shoved around all the time? Here's a promise for you; 'YOU shall have no other gods before me.'

What is exciting is that the new covenant is not a revision of God's law made because, to His acute embarrassment, He was too high for the people. It is a relocating of the same law by the Spirit of God in your heart. And what is marvellous is that it's the Spirit of God who works in us both to will (that is, to give the appetite) and to do, the enabling of His good pleasure. We heard that last night. Hunger and thirst is not a choice, it's a spontaneous consequence of something else, of life within you. And as the Spirit of God comes to live within, no longer is it 'out there', a command—'Oh dear, I'm trying.' Inside, there's a hunger, there's a thirst, there's a longing for godliness, that the character of God be restored and expressed within us.

It doesn't mean, of course, that you become perfect, just in case anybody thinks that follows from what I'm saying; 2 Corinthians 3:18 is important. 'We, who with unveiled faces all reflect the Lord's glory, are being transformed into his likeness with ever-increasing glory, which comes from the Lord, who is the Spirit.' Notice the tense there: with unveiled faces (nothing between ourselves and the Lord

Jesus), we reflect His glory. He says we are being transformed (that's the present continuous tense) into His likeness. It's not in the past tense ('we have been transformed')
or even the future ('we will be'). It's the present tense. We
are being transformed. Of course, that means that the mark
of true spiritual growth is not that we know more of the
Bible than we used to know—though that's important. It's
not that we engage in more service than we used to—
though that's important too. The mark of true spiritual
growth is that there's more evidence of the character of
Jesus Christ than there used to be.

The way that I, as a husband, treat my wife should more
quickly remind you of Christ than it used to. The way as
parents we treat our kids, giving them the right in a con-
fusing dirty world to come home, close the door, look into
the face of Mum and Dad and say, 'That's what's real.' The
way we talk to our neighbours—probably more signifi-
cantly, the way we talk about them when they are not listening—the way we drive our cars down the road—the
way we spend our money—increasingly gives evidence of
the character of Christ as we grow spiritually. Until one
day we will be what the Bible calls 'glorified'. To be glorified is to be fully restored into His image, and that day will
come; but not until we are in heaven.

The new covenant involves a new relationship

'I will be their God, and they will be my people. No longer
will a man teach his neighbour, or a man his brother, saying, "Know the LORD," because they will all know me,
from the least of them to the greatest' (Jer. 31:33-34).

How is this new righteousness going to be evidenced
within us? By the fact of the new relationship. It is in our
knowledge of God that everything else has its source. Peter,
writing his second letter, says, 'Grace and peace be yours in
abundance through the knowledge of God and of Jesus our
Lord' (2 Pet. 1:2). His divine power has given us everything we need for life and godliness through our knowledge of God, who called us by His own glory and

goodness. Peter says that everything we need is available to us. How? By our knowledge of God.

But that knowledge of God is qualified very importantly in Jeremiah 31. 'They will all know me from the least of them to the greatest' (31:34). Notice the progression there; the knowledge of God is not on the basis of intellectual capacity, it's on the basis of a spiritual disposition. Knowledge of God is not obtained but received—from the least, characterised by humility and dependency; that's when we get to know God—to the greatest. And spiritual truth is revealed. Revelation grows in response to that disposition of humility and child-like dependency.

On Monday morning we read chapter 9 verses 23-34. Don't boast of your wisdom or your strength, we're warned there. Those are not the avenues by which you know God. They can become the stumbling blocks to knowing Him, because although you can be too strong, too wise and too rich, you can never be too simple, too poor or too weak. And out of weakness and our poverty—we have been thinking about poverty in spirit in our series on the Beatitudes at this Convention[1]—out of that disposition we have something to boast about. We know God! And as a result His law, His character is written into our hearts, and we begin to behave in a way that expresses Him.

The new covenant involves a new redemption

If that new righteousness has its source in a new relationship, that new relationship has its source in a new redemption. For He goes on to say: '"They will all know me, from the least of them to the greatest," declares the Lord. "For I will forgive their wickedness and will remember their sins no more."' (31:34).

Did you know, that was something new? 'I will remember their sins no more.' Under the old covenant, we are

---

1. These addresses were given at the evening Convention meeting on each night of the Holiday Convention Week. Two are included in the present book (p.231, p.242).

told, sin was never removed, only covered. Hebrews 10:11
tells us, 'Day after day every priest stands and performs his
religious duties; again and again he offers the same sacrifices, which can never take away sins.' The blood of bulls,
goats, rams and lambs could cover sin but not remove it.
What's the difference? I see it as rather like a post-dated
cheque. 'If I post-date my cheque till the end of the month
when I've got some money, will you let me have the
goods?' If the vendor agrees to that, and you give him the
post-dated cheque, the debt is covered. But it's not removed.

The blood of bulls and goats in the Old Testament
wasn't a fruitless exercise. It was the writing of post-dated
cheques, post-dated 'Calvary'. When Jesus cried on the
cross, 'It is finished!', we are told (in a verse that I don't
fully understand) that 'he went and preached to the spirits
in prison' (1 Pet. 3:19). What did he preach? 'There's cash
in the bank, the precious blood of Christ, the only currency
that removes sin.' Under the old covenant, it was covered.

He says next that this new redemption involves such a
dealing with sin that 'I will remember their sins no more.'
And when the writer to the Hebrews laments the fact that
the priest stands day after day and sin is not taken away,
not removed, he goes on to say in answer to this dilemma,
'The Holy Spirit also testifies to us about this ...' and he
quotes this new covenant from Jeremiah: '"This is the
covenant I will make with them ... their sins and lawless
acts I will remember no more."' (Heb. 10:15-17).

This is a marvellous thing. None of us deserves it, of
course. But we come to the Lord Jesus Christ, and not only
does He forgive us but He removes our sin to the extent
that we are no longer accountable. There is no condemnation to those who are in Christ Jesus, as we were remem-
bering on Sunday night under the title 'Blessed are the
pure in heart'.

The whole saving work of the Lord Jesus Christ is en-
compassed here in the new covenant. We come first to the
cross so that we might be forgiven and our sin removed.

There is no reason, in this tent on this morning, for any man or woman to live with a sense of outstanding sin and guilt. You can come in repentance. Then having come to the cross and found forgiveness and cleansing, we then come to the resurrection of the Lord Jesus Christ. You see, our cleansing is that we might know Him, risen, alive.

But then we go beyond the resurrection to Pentecost, where the Holy Spirit writes the law of God into our hearts. Many of you know that in the inter-testamental period, the celebration of Pentecost became a commemoration of the giving of the law to Moses on Mount Sinai. Whether historically those two can be tied together I don't know, but certainly theologically they should be. Because the law given on Mount Sinai was simply in written form what the Holy Spirit would come to do in action at Pentecost, to restore to us the very character and holiness of God.

Well, time has gone. One last thing, very quickly. Do you remember the upper room, where the Lord Jesus met with His disciples? He took bread, we are told, and He gave thanks and broke it. He gave thanks, He said, 'Take eat, this is My body.' Then He took the cup. And then He did something which must have shocked those with Him in the upper room. He said, 'This is My blood, this is My blood of the new covenant, drink it.'

Why were they shocked? Because no Jew ever drank blood; it was forbidden. Why? Is there something unhealthy about drinking blood? People in many parts of Britain eat blood in black puddings; it never seems to harm them. When in my late teens I lived on a farm in Africa, when we used to kill some of the old animals the people would catch the blood in buckets and take it home. Cow's blood was a real treat. It was rich in iron and other qualities. There's nothing intrinsically unhealthy about blood.

Why did God forbid eating of it? Deuteronomy 12:23 tells us. 'Be sure you do not eat the blood, because the blood is the life, and you must not eat the life with the meat.' Why? Because under the old covenant there was no provision for life in the ceremonial law. 'Well now,' says

Jesus, 'this is My blood, it's the blood of the new covenant, that which Jeremiah talked about'—because 'new covenant' is the term from his book. 'And at last,' He says, 'you can drink the blood.' You can receive the very life of God within you. We call it regeneration.

The gospel is not simply a way of getting people to change their minds. Our natural condition is that we are dead. The gospel involves the supernatural work of resurrection from the dead in order that the life of God might be implanted within the human soul. We are partakers, says Peter, of the very divine nature (cf 2 Pet. 1:4).

This is the substance of the new covenant. You come to the cross: 'I will forgive your sins and remember them no more.' You come to the risen Christ who's now alive, and you know Him, and you enjoy union with Him and communion with Him. That's why the disciples were never called followers of Christ after Pentecost. We don't follow Him any more in the way they were told to before Pentecost. As they followed Him, they only ever failed, but now we are in union with Christ—that's the description now; we are 'in Him' and He is in us, we are 'in union' with Him, 'in fellowship' with Him, we 'know' Him.

And the result of knowing Him is that you come to Pentecost, where the Spirit of God is poured out in order that He might live the life of Jesus Christ in us, and that living in us He might be our hope of glory—the very thing we've come short of. So you can go back to your home, to your place of work, to your family and to your church with a new capacity—as you live in utter dependency upon the Spirit of God—to live lives that are godly and Christ-like. As Vaughan told us last night, it doesn't mean become zombies. We are to live disciplined lives, that God works in you to will; He creates the whole appetite, and the enabling, as we obey Him, to be godly.

Aren't you glad you're a Christian? Isn't it exciting? Because everything God commands, God Himself makes possible. 'He who calls you is faithful, He will do it.'

What a wonderful gospel!

'Like a Refiner's Fire'
by Rev. Mark Ashton
(From the Malachi Series, First Week)

Malachi 2:17-3:5

Here in the book of Malachi we've been overhearing an argument between God and His recalcitrant people. It's become rather one-sided as it's developed, and that's not surprising. As someone who's spent a good deal too much of his life arguing, I have learned that in an argument you want to pick your opponent carefully. Don't argue with an expert about his own subject! So it's not surprising that the people of Israel, arguing with God, found themselves just a little out of their depth; after all, He is the expert on everything. They'd bitten off rather more than they could chew. It was one of those times when you find yourself talking to the wrong person about the wrong subject at the wrong time.

A student in the college chapel looked at the Order of Service for morning worship and groaned aloud. The middle-aged lady next to him asked what was the matter. The student replied, 'It's the preacher. It's going to be Professor Russell. He's a medieval historian, and he's my director of studies. I have to go to his lectures, and he's the dullest man alive; he's the most boring old toad, not just in medieval history but in all history.'

'Oh,' said the woman. 'Do you know who I am?'

The student looked at her for the first time. 'No.'

'I am Mrs Mary Russell.'

'Whoa,' said the student. 'Do you know who I am?'

'No,' said the professor's wife.

'Hallelujah,' said the student ….

We're not surprised to find that the Israelites have silenced their objections in chapter 2. They too sense they are talking to the wrong person about the wrong thing. Though I'm afraid to say it won't be long before they start up again, as we'll discover in the last verse of the chapter.

Those who argue with God frequently find themselves at a loss for words. Until now it's largely been God who has been speaking in Malachi. But in 2:10 the prophet begins to say a little on his own account, to drive home to God's people the truth of their situation. 'Have we not all one Father? Did not one God create us? Why do we profane the covenant of our fathers by breaking faith with one another?' Breaking faith: that's going to be the key idea in the next seven verses. It comes in verse 10, again in verse 11, again in verse 14 and in verse 15, and in verse 16 it ends this little section.

Why is this so important for God's people? Well, all relationships are based on trust, and depend keeping our word. We have a relationship with God, because we can depend on Him to keep His word to us. One of the most important things the Bible teaches us about God is that He is a promise-making and a promise-keeping God. He's beyond our understanding, but He tells us about Himself. We can relate to Him on the basis of what He tells us, because He does not break His word. The book of Malachi began with God's declaration of love for His people: '"I have loved you," says the LORD' (1:2). That's the basis of our relationship with Him, the promise of His love for us.

Personal relationships become impossible when one party can't be trusted. David Niven once said of Errol Flynn, 'You can always rely on Errol. He will always let you down.' That might have been neither fair nor true, but it illustrates this truth. With such people relationships become almost impossible, but with God the reverse is true: He is utterly dependable. He is the covenant God—that's what a covenant is; a promise-making. It's closely mirrored in human marriage. In the Anglican marriage service there comes a moment when the minister asks the bridegroom,

'Peter' (or whatever his name is), 'will you take Mary to be your wife? Will you love her, comfort her, honour and protect her?' and so on. The groom replies, 'I will.' That's not usually a moment of high suspense and uncertainty in the service, is it? And when God is asked the question, 'Will You take mankind back to Yourself?' His reply has echoed down the centuries, with all the force of the cross behind it: 'I will.' There is an open offer on His side, backed by His eternally unbroken word.

The US postal service once delivered a letter bearing simply the addressee's name, the block he lived in and the city. The postal authorities had written on it, 'What—no number, no Zip Code? Are we good, or are we good?' Well—is God loving, or is God loving? Can God be trusted, or can God be trusted? He certainly can, He most certainly can.

Verse 10 again, 'Have we not all one Father? Did not one God create us? Why do we profane the covenant of our fathers by breaking faith with one another?' In the context of this book, Malachi isn't talking about a universal fatherhood of all mankind. That 'Father' at the beginning of the verse may be a reference to Abraham; it may have a small 'f' rather than a capital. He is talking to us; not the whole human race, but God's own people brought into existence by His will and purpose, by His faithful covenant with them, 'the covenant of our fathers'. It's you and me. But then we notice that God's faithfulness, His promise-keeping, is to be reciprocated by their faithfulness, both to Him and to one another. So in the next two verses, their faithfulness is examined and illustrated by the issue of mixed marriage; and then in verses 13-16 their faithfulness to each other is examined and illustrated by the issue of divorce.

Breaking faith with God by mixed marriage (verses 11-12)

Judah has desecrated the sanctuary. This is probably not so

much a reference to the temple as a reference to God's chosen people, whom He loves. They have been desecrated by marrying the daughter of a foreign god. You will notice that the text says not 'a woman of a foreign race', but 'the daughter of a foreign god'. It's not mixed race that's the problem but the spiritual significance of marrying a worshipper of a different god.

I imagine that everybody knows the Christian teaching that a Christian should not marry a non-Christian. It's a clear and important Christian teaching. But perhaps we shouldn't be talking about a non-Christian in that context. You see, people who do not worship Christ do not worship *nothing*. They too are worshippers, however little they may care to acknowledge the fact. Every human bows down at some altar or other. Everybody sacrifices to some god or other. The more disreputable the god, the more hidden it will be. We are appalled sometimes when we read of the Old Testament gods like Molech who demanded child sacrifice; but the powerful invisible gods of our culture surround us with their worshippers. For example, those who bow down at the shrine of personal freedom and individual choice—'my right to make up my own mind and do what I like with my life and my body'—is that not a god strong in our day? A god that calls for abortion on demand as every woman's right; a god as hungry for child sacrifice as Chemosh or Molech, the abominations of Moab (cf eg 1 Kings 11:7). More human lives have been sacrificed at that altar than were ever sacrificed in ancient Canaan.

To marry the daughter of a foreign god or a son of a foreign god is to break faith with God. When a Christian knowingly enters a marriage with a non-Christian, he or she is saying to God, 'You are not the only God.' I know this is difficult. We are strongly tempted to say, 'I can't totally trust you, God, to make me happy. I must have marriage. I can't face the loneliness without it, even if it's going to put my faith at risk.' But that is saying to God that He really doesn't matter as much as someone else. It's saying we don't believe God when He says that He loves us and wants the very, very best for us. Instead, we are determined to secure our own happiness in our own way. Marriage is not the only cause of such rebellion, but it's the focus of this verse: 'by marrying the daughter of a foreign god'.

So, Malachi continues, 'As for the man who does this, whoever he may be, may the LORD cut him off from the tents of Jacob—even though he brings offerings to the LORD Almighty' (verse 12). That sanction was appropriate in Malachi's day, but the situation is different for us today. The New Testament treats mixed marriages differently, because they are unavoidable for some who get converted after marriage. Indeed, the more successful evangelism is, the more it will create that very situation. And the New Testament does not encourage Christians to divorce unbelieving partners. It encourages them to win them.

Roy Clements comments, 'If you are involved in a mixed marriage, that must be your unceasing hope and prayer. Do not treat your marriage as some kind of spiritual handicap that condemns you forever to God's second best. It is not so. By the presence of the Holy Spirit in your life you bring a sanctifying influence into your family which can only be for their good.' I quote that for the comfort of those who are in that situation tonight. But mixed marriage still represents a great spiritual danger. It doesn't imperil the future of the church in the way that it imperilled the future of God's people in Malachi's day, but it does put the individual at risk. God is interested in whom we marry and how we conduct our marriages.

For some single people this will be a hard message. Perhaps you are thinking, 'If only I had married that person all those years ago! If only I hadn't heeded this advice, what loneliness I might have escaped.' I would encourage you not to believe that voice, but to pray that God will bless you and strengthen you tonight in your loneliness. He does not break His word. He will not break His word to you. Maybe others look back and wish that they *had* heeded this word at some time in the past. If so, be comforted by what Roy Clements said. And there may be others for whom this lies in the future, for whom a time of deep, deep testing will come as to whether you can trust God with your marriage. Tonight I plead with you: trust Him, trust Him.

It's no coincidence that marriage is such a frequent biblical image of our relationship with God. It's clear, from the end of verse 10, that how we treat each other expresses our relationship to God. 'Why do we profane the covenant of our fathers by breaking faith with one another?' The little paragraph, verses 13-14, makes an even clearer link between our marital relationship and our prayer life. The health of my spiritual life and the health of my marriage are inseparable.

Now a word to the married. Peter wrote in his first letter, 'Husbands, in the same way be considerate as you live with your wives, and treat them with respect as the weaker partner and as heirs with you of the gracious gift of life, so that nothing will hinder your prayers' (1 Pet. 3:7). There is no surer hindrance to our prayers than marital conflict. Woe betide me if I try to write a sermon while I'm in the middle of a row with my wife Fiona. Imagine, if you will, a conversation in a pastor's study. 'Pastor, I'm a bit stuck in my Christian life at the moment. I'm finding Bible reading very dry and boring. I never seem to get round to telling anybody else that I'm a Christian nowadays, my evangelism's stopped really. My prayer life's drying up.' There's a pause. Then the pastor says, 'How's your marriage, Mark?'

He says, 'Hang on, I don't think you've understood what I'm saying.'

'No, tell me about your marriage.'

Some of you here have come to Keswick hungry and eager for the deep things of God. God has them for us, but first we may need to attend to our marriages. I think I'll let you apply that in your own way, as we continue to look at marriage for a little bit longer.

Breaking faith with one another by divorce (2:14-16)

The Hebrew of verses 15 and 16 is quite difficult, and you

will see alternative translations in the margins of your Bibles. But the main thrust is quite clear. God is at the centre of the marriage bond. He is the witness to marriage vows (verse 14), and He hates divorce (verse 16).

God is witness (2:14)

We make our vows to one another in marriage. But we also make them before God as Christian people. It's a promise to Him as well as to our spouse.

In one of his many helpful books, James Dobson quotes the words that his father wrote to his mother before their wedding. 'The idea of estrangement from you through divorce for any reason at all, although God allows one, infidelity, will never at any time be permitted to enter into my thinking .... I have loved you dearly as a sweetheart and will continue to love you as my wife. But over and above that I love you with a Christian love that demands that I never react in any way towards you that would jeopardise our prospects of entering heaven, which is the supreme objective of both of our lives.' You see what James Dobson Sr was saying to his wife? She was to understand that her husband was making a commitment to God as well as to her, so that if she through mental illness or physical disfigurement became an entirely different person from the person she was on their wedding day, it would not alter his commitment at all. You see, marriage is about theology; God and our relationship with Him. It's about the atonement, more than about ethics or behaviour. Dr Martin Lloyd-Jones put it very strikingly when he said,

> How many of us have realised that we are always to think of the marriage state in terms of the doctrine of the atonement? Is that our customary way of thinking about marriage? Where do we find what the books have to say about marriage, under what section? Under ethics. But it doesn't belong there. We must consider marriage in terms of the doctrine of atonement.

Well, that is the powerful theology of marriage.

Just notice in passing that word 'partner', 'companion', towards the end of verse 14. Only here in the Bible is it used of a wife, and it presents a lovely hint of what this marriage relationship is to become.

God hates divorce (2:16)

We can't move on without facing those three chilling words at the beginning of verse 16: 'I hate divorce.' And it would be wrong for me to say anything tonight to lessen that impact, particularly in a society that is moving away from monogamy (only one marriage partner for life) to serial polygamy (only one marriage partner at a time in life). Nevertheless, it has to be said that divorce is not impossible. The Bible does make provision for it in a certain circumstance. There may be one party more innocent than the other in a divorce, and it is not an unforgivable sin— God has a way of repairing lives shattered by divorce.

You notice that the section ends with another reminder of where this battle is fought: 'So guard yourself in your spirit, and do not break faith.' Faith in marriage is a spiritual matter. If you haven't got that one yet, you never will; and Malachi and I will have totally failed. So let's move on, because now the prophet moves his case on.

Face to face with God (2:17-3:5)

The people have not just broken faith with God and with each other, they have justified their faithless behaviour by their faithless words. They are back to their old argumentative ways again. Look at verse 17:

> You have wearied the LORD with your words.
> 'How have we wearied him?' you ask. By saying,
> 'All who do evil are good in the eyes of the
> LORD, and he is pleased with them' or 'Where is
> the God of justice?'

Israel had adopted the position of what we might call the

functional atheist—not denying the existence of God, but destroying the link between the Almighty and good and evil. 'Where is the God of justice? The one who'll put all things right? There's no sign of Him, no sign that God stands behind this world order at all. We look out on a world where evil seems to triumph.'

The answer to that question is unexpected. Where is the God of justice? He's coming. '"See, I will send my messenger, who will prepare the way before me. Then suddenly the Lord you are seeking will come to his temple; the messenger of the covenant, whom you desire, will come," says the Lord Almighty.' The one you are asking for is on His way. The God of justice.

Once again, like that history student, God's people hadn't realised quite who it was to whom they were talking. Verse 2, 'But who can endure the day of his coming? Who can stand when he appears? For he will be like a refiner's fire or a launderer's soap.' C. S. Lewis once wrote, 'Some people talk as if staring into the face of absolute goodness is going to be fun. They need to think again.' You see, it is the face before which heaven and earth will flee away. There'll be nothing cosy about an eyeball-to-eyeball encounter with the God of justice.

Two things will be clear at that moment. The first is that you and I will not have a leg to stand on.

We have no hold over God

'Who can endure the day of his coming? Who can stand when he appears?' We have no hold over God. We long to have a little handle on Him, don't we? Some leverage to get Him to act as we would want Him to. A small boy was writing one of those Christmas letters that children write pleading for particular Christmas presents. 'Please may I have a mountain bike,' he wrote. 'I've been good for six months now.' After a moment's reflection he crossed out 'six months' and wrote 'three months'. After another pause he crossed that out and put 'two weeks'. There was another pause, then he sighed and crossed that out. He got up from the table where he was writing, and wandered across the room to where the Christmas tree stood in the corner, with a little crib scene underneath with figures of Mary and Joseph. He picked up the figure of Mary and went back to his letter thoughtfully. Then he put the figure down in front of him on the table and started again. 'If you ever want to see your mother again ...'

We don't have any hold on God at all. There is nothing with which you and I can coerce Him, or can cause Him to act in a particular way. We are those who have broken faith with Him. And when the messenger of that covenant appears, the God of justice, we won't have a leg to stand on.

He comes not to judge but to refine

But the second thing that will become clear is that He has come, not to judge, but to refine His people.

Verses 2-5 of chapter 3 do not present a comfortable picture, but it is a hopeful one. See in verse 3, where the process will begin. God begins with His own, and He concentrates on them as a silversmith pores over the metal he is refining, skimming off the impurities brought to the surface by the intense heat, and looking to see His own reflection in the molten metal. It's a lovely picture. We usually picture fire as trials and tribulations, and God certainly does use our sufferings to refine us. But not all of us will be suffering; we won't all be in that furnace of affliction. I am sure there are some who will be, but I suspect the majority of us will not. That's not the picture here.

What is the fire? Please answer that yourselves from verse 2 (incidentally, there wasn't any soap in the ancient world. This would be fuller's alkali, a far fiercer cleansing agent). It is the presence of God Himself that will be the fire that will refine. How do you and I encounter that God? Here and now, through His word. It is Bible teaching that does this work. Here at Keswick we come to the word, and in it we encounter God and the heat starts to intensify. Things start to bubble to the surface of your consciousness and mine, as we bring ourselves to God's word together and find the heat of His presence beginning to burn in our lives. Has that been happening to you this week?

Habits and attitudes, maybe things that have characterised the whole of your lives to this day, have maybe just begun to bubble up to the surface and you think, 'Hang on, I'm not sure God isn't dealing with that thing. I'm not sure God isn't putting His finger on it, and starting to try to take it out of my life.' But we love these things so much, don't we? We know they mar us, these acts of selfishness, these attitudes that just put 'me first' in one way or another; they just cling on to our own comfort and self-esteem, our own control over our life. But I wonder if the heat's been growing this week, as the word of God brings the presence of God to bear on your life?

Some of us may have set our hearts on marriage at any price, even to the daughter or son of a foreign god: 'Lord, anything—but don't stop me marrying.' Or, 'Don't stop me having children.' Or, 'Don't let one of my children die.' Or, 'Don't touch my position, my career, my life. Don't call me to full-time service.' Perhaps it's the way we've begun to break faith in our marriages. Oh, not perhaps adultery, yet. But neglect, coldness, indifference, other interests squeezing that central relationship. Or perhaps it's the way we weary God by doubting that His justice will prevail, that this is His earth and that He is in control of it.

His justice will prevail. He will deal with, has dealt with evil. Malachi didn't have the cross before his eyes—but you and I do. We know that God has dealt with evil once and for all. And that is His word to us; that He will one day complete that work and wipe the tear from every eye and deal with all the consequences of sin once and for all. But He wants to deal with it in you and me now, as your refiner. For Christ's sake, let Him have His way. May we trust ourselves to Him. He died for us, and you and I can trust this refiner. As the heat increases, let Him do His work. He loved us, He wants us, He refines us.

'Prelude to Revival?'
by Rev. Clive Calver
(From the Malachi Series, First Week)

Malachi 3:6-18

I remember preaching about revival twenty years ago when very few people were saying anything about it at all. Today it has become an 'in' word. We were told that revival would come on May 17th, and it didn't. We were told it was expected in June, and nothing happened. I'm not trying to mock those who are anticipating an imminent move of God. I just wish we'd get our language sorted out, because we seem to confuse three manifestations of the Spirit of God and call them all 'revival'; and I desperately want us to distinguish between them.

You see, there is such a thing as an 'awakening'. When the Spirit of God comes upon a nation and turns that nation upside down, inside out and back to front; when society is changed by the word of God, revealed through Scripture and proclaimed by His servants—as with Wesley and Whitefield at the end of the eighteenth century in the Great Evangelical Awakening—there is such a thing as an awakening, and we often call it revival.

Then of course there are moments when thousands of people turn, in faith, in repentance to Jesus Christ. Moments like that which was associated in part with this Convention, that which happened in Wales at the start of this century; when it was said that even the pit ponies stopped functioning because they couldn't understand the language being used towards them now that blasphemies were no longer attached; God changed people's lives and they were converted in their thousands, and that is called revival.

But there are moments when God moves on His people, and He touches His people's lives and He turns us round. And we call that revival too.

(I'm excluding those usages I encounter in the United States when I am told that the next 'revival' will be on Thursday at 7.30 p.m: the word then merely means a type of meeting.)

To get our semantics straight tonight: I believe that when God moves among His people that's 'renewal'; that when God works through His converting power towards thousands, that's 'revival'; and that when God changes the destiny of a nation, that's an 'awakening'.

There's never been an awakening or a revival in history that hasn't started with renewal. But there have been many times when God's people have gone into renewal and have been satisfied. And there have been many times when there's been a revival, and people have been converted, and they've been satisfied with that. But I believe there is a need for some holy dissatisfaction among the people of God in this nation. For twenty years we have been seeing something happen, and when I talk tomorrow about the state of the church in this nation,[1] I'll give you the statistics and I'll point to the fact that we have seen the number of evangelical Christians in the UK more than treble in the last twenty years. God is doing something among us, there is a change in the way that we live and the way that we pray among many of us. But I don't believe we are in a revival yet. And I don't believe that we should be predicting when that revival will or will not come. I believe we should be praying for it, we should be hungry for it, and we should be learning the lesson of Malachi, because the lesson of Malachi is very straightforward: it is that when God wants to work, He's not after words, He's after actions. And Malachi 3 is

---

1. Mr Calver is referring to the second of two Keswick Lectures he gave at the 1997 Convention, entitled 'The State of the Nation' and 'The State of the Church'. Though the lectures are not included in the present volume, see p.255 for details of video and tapes available.

about what we do, not what we say.

I love the lines that Eliza Doolittle sings in *My Fair Lady*: 'Words, words, words, I'm so sick of words ... Sing me no song, read me no rhyme, don't waste my time. Show me.' I believe this nation is waiting to *see* something in the lives of the people of God. And I believe that God is waiting to see something in the lives of His people that will be the harbinger of all that He wants to do among us. Let me take you to Malachi 3:6-7, where we find the first of three actions that God requires from His people.

Return to God (3:6-7)

Now that principle of return is linked with the Greek word *metanoia* (repentance) in the New Testament. But *metanoia* means a change of mind that leads to a change of heart and a change of direction. In the Hebrew of the Old Testament, the word used means a simple change of direction, a physical change.

So why should we change? The answer is there in verse 6: because God doesn't change. In a changing world He remains the changeless word. He's the one secure point in a shifting universe, He's the one on whom you can always depend, He's the one you can trust, He's the one you can rely on, He's the one who you know will never let you down. He'll never fail you, He'll never leave you, He'll never forsake you. 'Because I the LORD do not change.' He's a rock on which we can build. And we read here that God loved Jacob; so that means that a changeless God loves his descendants, even though their own consistency only lay in the way that they continually deserted Him. God has not changed in the past, so we can be confident that He won't change in the present or in the future.

The affirmation of these verses is the same as we looked at the other night in chapter 1:2—because God loves us, He doesn't destroy us and He goes on caring for us. But when He says, 'Return to me, and I will return to you,' He is laying out the principle of covenant. In the ancient Near

East, the covenant was the treaty that said, 'If you do, then I will do.' It's a two-way relationship. 'Return to me, and I will return to you.'

You see, we have a problem. God is a holy God and we are a sinful people. And holiness and sin do not coexist together. If the lights were to fail here and this tent were to be plunged into darkness, when the back-up generator was brought out the darkness would be gone. Light and darkness can't coexist, and neither can holiness and sin. So by returning to God we make it possible for Him to return to us. We need to turn back from what we have been, and in coming back in repentance we can receive His forgiveness and live in the love and life that He brings us. It is the most wonderful fact of human history that it took crucified love to bring you and me and the living God together. Because of Calvary and the cross we can know Him, love Him and live with Him now. And His love to us doesn't change. 'Return to me, and I will return to you.'

It's a bit like a young boy sitting in a pigsty, wondering how he's going to survive and thinking how the servants of his father are living in comfort back home. And he says, 'I will set out and go back to my father and say to him: Father, I have sinned against heaven and against you. I am no longer worthy to be called your son; make me like one of your hired men' (Luke 15:18-19). And even as he gets over the horizon on his return home, the father is looking for the son and he welcomes the prodigal home. That's the kind of changeless God we've got. We come back to a love that's compassionate and committed to us. But the message is straightforward and clear, for Israel then and for us now—'Return to me, come back.'

As evangelical Christians, there are things we need to come back to. We need to come back to a passion for God's word. We need to come back to a passion for God's love. We need to come back to a passion for knowing Him, not just knowing about Him. We need to come back to a passion for loving, and for being committed and involved in this world in which we live today. We need to come back to a demonstration of that love in our daily lives; we need to keep on coming back, that we might know more and more of His goodness and grace worked out in us. 'Return to me, and I will return to you.'

I have an older friend, Alex Buchanan. I was sitting in a prayer retreat with him last year, as part of a group of half a dozen who have come together to pray for a couple of days, three times a year, for around nineteen years now. Alex looked at me straight in the eyes and said this. 'Nowadays it is hard to find Christian leaders who are deeply in love with the Lord Jesus.' He said it in a private meeting, not said to cause a stir, just said as a fatherly word to five guys younger than he was. What did he mean? Did he mean there are always hypocrites ministering to you? No. What he meant was this: that it's possible to love the work of the Lord more than we love the Lord of the work. It's possible for our love to flow more to God's people than to the Lord of those people. It's possible for our love to be more involved in the patterns and habits we've got used to, of how God works and has worked in the past among us. And I want to tell you that while God doesn't change, our love can; and that's why we need to keep on coming back, coming back and coming back. It's not enough to live on an experience of twenty or thirty years ago. We need to keep coming back to the arms of a God who loves us.

The story is told of a West Countryman named Seth who married a lady named Mary. He said to her, 'Mary, I want to tell thee that I love thee. I hope though rememberest it, because I won't be bothered to tell thee again.' You'll have gathered this is a nineteenth-century illustration. I'm not sure if we know any better in this century. If I expected my wife Ruth to live on protestations of devotion from many years ago, I would get told in quite forcible terms that that is not sufficient for today or tomorrow. We need to love God and go on loving God. Return to God, go on returning to God. Give Him our devotion, give Him our hearts, give Him our lives and then watch what He'll do. 'Return to me, and I will return to you.'

I had the great joy at the end of last year of taking my oldest son Chris with me on a trip to North Florida. We went to a place called Pensacola, which is a naval base. I went because I'd got an appointment to see an evangelist there. I wanted to see him because there were reports of 125,000 being converted in twenty-two months at the church he was ministering at. Now this is a little unusual, so I went to have a look. When we got into Pensacola we couldn't find the church, and I stopped outside a supermarket and asked a local citizen. I said, 'I'm sorry, it's an unusual request—I'm looking for a church.' He said, 'Don't worry! I know exactly where you want. Even though you'll pass five churches on the way, you need to go down that street, go five blocks down, turn right and you'll see the cars.' The first thing we saw were the crowds. It was an hour and a half before the meeting was due to start, and there were 1,000 people queueing. We jumped the queue and got in to meet the evangelist and interview him. Then we went into the meeting.

I don't know how many of you come from Pentecostal churches, Elim or Assemblies of God, Apostolic, or New Testament Church of God, but you'd have felt very at home there: it's an Assemblies of God Church, and it was a very typical Pentecostal service. There was nothing particularly unusual about it. The gospel was preached right down the line, very firmly, with lots of emphasis on morality, lots of emphasis on Scripture, lots of emphasis on prayer and lots and lots and *lots* of emphasis on repentance. Good solid Pentecostal stuff; it was all right, but humanly speaking, it wasn't brilliant.

But God was there. And at the end, after about four hours, when the appeal was made I was rather bemused to see men running to the front to commit their lives to Christ. I asked what usually happened. 'Well, last week the Sheriff came,' I was told. 'So we sent him to the youth meeting. And when he got there, he was a bit surprised by the skip.' (That's a large rubbish container, just like over here.)

'What was the skip there for?' I asked.

'It was full of condoms, needles, pornographic magazines, weapons, bottles and so on. Because when the kids come to Christ, they repent. And their actions match it.'

The Sheriff (who is roughly equivalent to a chief constable in England) had said, 'Until now I thought the major evidence of what was going on here in this church was the size of the traffic jams. Now I'm beginning to think it might have other contributions to make.' And he added, 'I do notice that the Pensacola crime rate has dropped to a low unheard of in this century.'

When we return to God and He comes to us, something happens. The something that happens is accompanied by actions. We do not want a nice, smooth, trendy move of God that just suits our own agendas. We want to see God move and change people's lives. We want to see Him move and change people's directions; we want to see God coming and moving among us in power.

For that, we have to come back first. Let me give you that from Scripture. Psalm 51:17, 'The sacrifices of God are a broken spirit; a broken and contrite heart, O God, you will not despise.' Isaiah 66:2, '"Has not my hand made all these things, and so they came into being?" declares the LORD. "This is the one I esteem: he who is humble and contrite in spirit, and trembles at my word."' Joel 2:13, 'Rend your heart and not your garments. Return to the LORD your God, for he is gracious and compassionate, slow to anger and abounding in love.'

Are we robbing God? (3:8-12)

The question in verse 8 is almost rhetorical, presupposing the answer 'No.' God's answer is blunt—'Yet you rob me.' And we can only ask, 'How do we rob You, Lord?'

An Australian friend, John Mallison, tells of a retreat at which they had a guided Bible study on the Good Samaritan. The leader asked them to spend some time adopting the character of one of the people or groups in the story and then to report on how they felt. One came back and said, 'I feel like the priest, I've walked by on the other side too often.' Another said, 'I feel like the Levite, I've looked at situations and ignored them.' A third said, 'I feel a bit like the guy who fell among the thieves. I've had my nose rubbed in the dirt so often.' A fourth said, 'I'm a bit like the Good Samaritan, I do try to meet people's needs.' Someone even suggested that they were like the inn keeper, because their house was where needy people came. John said, 'I feel like the robbers. I've robbed my wife and I've robbed my family. I've been so busy for God in working for His people, I've forgotten to be busy for God in loving those He's given me most specially.' He said, 'So I took my time writing to them, and saying that I'm sorry for the times I've robbed them of myself.'

It is possible to rob God. For Israel the answer didn't lie there. It lay in their tithes and their offerings. The practice of giving 10% was established by Abraham and Melchizedek (Gen. 14:20). It's seen in Jacob at Bethel (Gen. 28:22), and it was part of God's law when 10% was to be holy to the Lord (Lev. 27:30). This money was to support those who were being used in God's service, the Levites, and they in turn were to give 10% for the priests. The instructions are given in Numbers 18, but Deuteronomy tells us that the poor, the widow and the orphan and the stranger would also benefit from this practice.

Once the tithe had been given, the good news: now you could give your offerings—your wheat offering, your meal offering, your gift offering, your thank offering, that came next. Tithe is the tax, offerings come after. It's a little worrying, isn't it! We are not always that good at giving. God made the clouds, and they give. God made the trees, and they give. God made the rain, and it gives. God made the sun, and it gives. God made the flowers, and they give. God made the ground, and it gives. God made the moon, and it gives. God made human kind, man and woman—and we have a bit of problem sometimes, when it comes to giving.

It was twenty years ago, they met at the university of

York. They fell madly in love and so they asked the Lord's permission and got married. She graduated in maths, he in German, and they got jobs as teachers in the West Midlands. They had a lovely house, beautiful furniture, lovely wedding presents and everything was going wonderfully. Until one day, God came and messed it all up. Have you ever noticed that the Lord has the capacity to do that? He does comfort the disturbed, but my goodness, does He disturb the comfortable. They were comfortable, and God disturbed them. I should say that Kevin was not one of God's natural enthusiasts. He was a true Christian Englishman, one of God's frozen chosen.

Then God said to them very clearly, 'I want you to go on a journey for Me, and it's for life. I want you to go to West Africa with Wycliffe Bible Translators, and use your linguistic gift to translate My word.'

Being a very practical guy, Kevin said, 'Lord, what do we do with the house, the furniture and the wedding presents?' The Lord said, 'That's easy, offer them to both sets of your parents. Honour your father and mother! They'll both say no—and then you'll meet a young evangelist and his wife whom you don't know. You'll offer them your house, your furniture and your wedding presents. They'll accept and you can go free of that and serve Me.' So Kevin said, 'Thank you, Lord.'

It happened exactly as God had said. They went to London Bible College to complete their training. When they got to LBC there was no accommodation left for married students, and they were going to have to live separately.

But God never owes you anything. Scripture says in verse 10, '"Test me in this," says the LORD Almighty.' They were testing God in this. They weren't robbing Him, they'd given everything. So three days before term started, the Lord gave them a little country cottage with its own tennis court and swimming pool for £8 a week. They had one great problem in life, they couldn't have children; so while they were in Niger translating the Scriptures into the

Kanuri tongue the Lord gave them two boys of their own—He suspended the laws of human nature twice and honoured them, because they had honoured Him.

After seventeen years translating the Scriptures the Lord said, 'Now go home to Wycliffe and teach others how to do what you have done.' And so they came back but they didn't have a house, furniture or wedding presents. So the Lord gave them a house opposite the Stokenchurch Centre of Wycliffe and He gave them furniture and wedding presents and they were happy.

You may say, 'I hear those kinds of stories so often, how do you know it's true?' I know it's true because I was the young evangelist. Ruth and I were given the house, the furniture and the wedding presents all those years ago.

How we need to avoid robbing God! Everything we have is His. You say, 'I haven't got much.' Well that's probably because God can't trust you with much. So make sure you look after your little properly. You may say, 'Well, I've got a lot.' God's trusted you with it; live up to the trust. You may say, 'But it hurts to give it.' That's the idea, folks! It wasn't meant to be easy. Giving to the work of God is not easy. But it's to support the work of God. We have a chance to do that in a few minutes—I hope we're going to give hilariously. I hope we're really going to enjoy giving. It will help mitigate the pain that we feel afterwards when we realise how much we've given! Don't rob God. Honour Him and give where He tells you to and give under instructions.

The curse (verse 9) that comes from failure is, then, an absence of blessing. God wants to provide for us. Our actions so often prevent us from receiving what He wants to give. And that curse also means that there's a drought. In the time of drought, locusts' eggs would multiply so that when the rain came the problems of the pests were bigger. That's what Malachi is referring to in verse 11. We are called to test God by trusting Him, by giving to Him, by going out on a limb for Him. I would love to see a restoration of risky Christian living, and the kind of Christian living that means we go out in total abandon, giving what we have and are to the Lord Jesus, letting Him take us and lead us wherever He wants us to go, to make us whatever He wants us to be.

My daughter Vicki who's now twenty-one—she's just finished reading theology at Durham University—is going out to India to teach theology and work with street kids— what a combination! If you said to Vicki, 'What's your Dad's favourite Scripture?', she'd say: 'That's easy, it's the one he's always written in my theology books: John 2:5, where the mother of Jesus says at the wedding feast of Cana, in Galilee, "Do whatever he tells you."'

Risk it with God. Don't rob Him, of your time, of your money, of your resources, of your experience. Some of you may be feeling, 'What could I do?' The answer is, you can do a fantastic amount. Early retirement is a glorious release for experience to come into the kingdom. We've got lots of young people coming forward, we need some older ones. Some of us are desperate for some older people with experience and gifts, prepared to go out on a limb, to risk it with God because God tells them to, and not rob Him of their lives and experience, but actually trust Him.

You may say, 'Well I'm too old.' Don't you believe it. Moses was eighty. God's been using you right through, you've got no evidence He's going to stop now. You may say, 'At least I'm young enough not to worry.' Jeremiah was a youth (Jer. 1:6). And the disciples were in their teens and early twenties. If John was in Patmos in around AD 90 he wasn't that old when Jesus called him by Galilee. You're never too young for God to use, you're never too old for God to use—but you're young enough to rob Him and you're old enough to rob Him. And how much we've got to go out on a limb, giving ourselves, risking it, trusting Him.

You may say, 'The problem with you preachers is, you always talk about us and never about yourselves.' I want to risk something among you tonight. I want to say that in December last year I knew that it was time to leave the Evangelical Alliance. I knew I had to go; I'd been there for fourteen wonderful years, but I had twelve more years to retirement. I'd have ended up doing twenty six-years; and I had preached so much about younger, emerging leaders. I would be the cork in the bottle. I knew I had to go. I had to practise what I preached.

What I never dreamed of for a moment was that God would say, 'Yes, go; and go to America'; because I'm British. When the call came to head up the World Relief Corporation in the States, to head a staff of over 500, to work releasing funds from the richest nation in history, to actually transform the refugee situation in the States and to work in the two-thirds world in twenty-four countries— what a wonderful challenge!

And God added, 'It will mean leaving your sons behind you. It will mean losing a daughter, and just taking a daughter with you.' That's when Ruth started to cry and my heart started to break. A friend said, 'You'll fail in the USA. We all believe it's right for you to go, but you're still going to fail.' I said, 'Why?' He said, 'Because everything you've always done, you've done through and with your friends. And you're leaving us behind.' Sometimes when God comes and says, 'Go,' it is without human reason.

That's when the opposition started to stop us going, not from here but from overseas. And the pressures built and built. And we were boxed in by the will of God. Everything that came against us was removed point by point. It almost got hilarious. Everything that was going to happen was going to go wrong. Even last week the visas fell through, and were restored forty-eight hours later. It's happened time and again. You dare not rob God, however many years you've been involved. You dare not duck away from the will of God.

When I arrived in the States they said, 'Why have you come?' And I said, 'I haven't wanted to. I don't want to leave my country, I don't want to leave what God's doing, I don't want to leave what I've seen through the years, I don't want to leave my friends, I don't want to leave my kids, and I don't want to leave my home. But God said come, so here I am and you are lumbered.'

Remember Him (3:13-18)

Malachi reminds God's people, '"You have said harsh things against me," says the LORD.' Your conversation betrays you. There are some of you who have probably got a good religious façade, but when you talk about the Lord, it's with criticism and complaint about His people. That reveals where your heart is.

Some of you talk about the Lord with excitement and enthusiasm about Him and His people. Verse 16, 'Then those who feared the LORD talked with each other, and the LORD listened and heard.' Our conversation betrays us. It betrays the kind of people we are. And we need to consistently remember God, because He remembers us.

Verse 16 speaks of a book of remembrance. In the ancient Near East there were two of these. They had a history book, and they also had a book of remembrance where the king registered those who'd been particularly helpful in service, just as the king registered Mordecai in Esther 2:23, and when there was real trouble the king could send for the book to be examined and remembrance came of what Mordecai had done. We need to remember God. He remembers us.

In verse 17 there's this lovely phrase, '"They will be mine," says the LORD Almighty, "in the day when I make up my treasured possession."' He speaks of the distinction He will make between the righteous and the wicked—between those who serve God, and those who don't. There is no such thing for a Christian as anything other than 'full-time Christian service'. That's one of the most stupid phrases ever invented. You can't be a Christian and *not* be in full-time Christian service. If you've given your life to Jesus, you belong to Him. You might say, 'But I'm in my nineties'—so what? Don't you pray, live and love Jesus? You're a servant of His, and you can teach the youngsters an awful lot. You may say, 'But I'm not a preacher.' Look,

God wants full-time Christian bank clerks, factory workers, businessmen, students, housewives; and those He can't find anything else for He makes full-time Christian preachers. I'm joking, but I'm trying to get us to understand that we are all special to Him. We are all meant to be involved, we are all His servants.

Think even about where you live. If you live in the suburbs, has God called you to be there? Then you are there as His servants. By the way, if He hasn't called you to live in the suburbs, try the villages or the cities; they need a bit of reinforcement. But if God's called you to the suburbs, stay there and work from there, that's where He's called you to be.

Is the job you are doing what God's called you to do? Are you doing it in His service, is it His job and you His vehicle in it? Is the money you have His money? You are just the steward of it, are you ready for Him to take it from you? Is the car His car? Not your car, it belongs to Him. And that's the love He wants from us. It's the life He wants from us. That's what God is after from us, a people all called to mission. There is a world out there waiting for Jesus, there's a nation out there ready to be won for Him and there's a world ready to be won for Him. And He's called us all.

And I want to challenge you tonight. Before that day of distinction when God calls the line between those who serve and those who do not, are we ready to go where He tells us to go, be what He tells us to be, do what He tells us to do? Are you ready to move house if God wants you to? Are you ready to change job if God wants you to? Are you ready to retire if God wants you to, and take up a new service? Are you ready to actually volunteer to go and serve God in other parts of the world? Come and be another missionary to America. They don't like that, by the way— very understandable. But God loves us, He has got a role for us. Let's get back to Him, let's not rob Him of us, and let's always remember His love for us and give Him everything of ourselves.

I want to end by telling you an African fable told me by a good African friend. There's a special kind of African eagle, which, at around the age of seven, flies up into the mountains until it finds a high peak. It settles there and begins to strip out all its feathers one by one. When it has stripped its wings, it strips its body. When it has stripped its body, it uses its beak to extract its talons one by one, and then crushes its beak against the rocks until its beak is broken, and the eagle is now totally empty, broken and useless. Then other eagles bring it food. They feed it through the weeks until its plumage starts to grow again. But this time it grows richer, more lustrous and stronger; its talons grow again and its beak grows again, until the day that it flies and lives another ninety years.

True or false, the illustration is apposite. We've lived too long in our strength, in what we are, in the security of our possessions. Sometimes the time comes to listen when God says, 'Return to Me, don't rob Me. Remember Me, let Me strip you of what you're confident in, let Me strip you of what you are.'

I'm cautious about using the personal illustration. But imagine what it's like as a preacher, finding you are in a country where no-one knows you can preach. When you find it difficult to walk along the road without somebody stopping you and saying 'Hi,' and now you find yourself in a country where no-one knows you. When you are so used to being in people's homes and being given hospitality, and you are living in a motel for two-and-a-half months and you see no-one except the staff. Sometimes God strips you, so you start again.

Tonight is starting again time. Some of us are going to pray as others start again. Some of us are going to start again ourselves, into a new chapter of our lives. We are going to enter it stronger, fitter and better as God strips us and gets us ready for a new beginning. Others of us, as we return to Him, are going to stop robbing Him and remember Him for whatever it means. But brothers and sisters, there's a world that needs Jesus. We are a people who love

Him. This year at the Keswick Convention, let's let Him
strip us down, build us up, take us out, because folks, you
can trust Him and He'll take you through it.

'Healing in its Wings'
by Rev. Liam Goligher
(From the Malachi Series, First Week)

Malachi 4:1-6

Tonight, following Clive Calver's exposition last night, I'm going to go back a little to show the relationship of the last few verses of chapter 3 to chapter 4.

I'm one of those sentimental people who loves a happy ending, where boy meets girl, boy falls in love with girl, girl falls in love with boy, and they go off into the sunset holding hands with the assumption that they live happily ever after. I know it's unrealistic; in the real world it doesn't happen very often. The Old Testament doesn't have a very happy ending either, in fact so depressing is the end of Malachi that the Masorete scholars, who gave us most of our Hebrew versions of the Old Testament, rearranged the text to avoid the last word of Malachi being 'curse' (4:6). But I'm afraid we can't juggle it to make it sound better. Malachi ends badly.

Jesus was probably familiar with the Greek version of the Old Testament. It ended with Malachi and finished on this note of a curse. If you look at the final verses of chapter 4, you'll find two things stand out. In verse 4 we are told that the people of God have been given the Bible; therefore they must heed it. Right at the end of the Old Testament we are told what the Old Testament is. It is law. It is about the decrees and the laws that God gave for all Israel; a legal document, full of requirements. But more; God has given them messengers. Many of the Old Testament prophets were God's messengers, and they came saying, 'Thus says the Lord.' Elijah, John the Baptist, and many other messengers came and their task was to call the people back to God, to turn the hearts of the fathers to their children, to bridge the generation gap if you will, by bringing both parents and children to repentance. They have the Bible; they have the messengers. They need to hear the Bible, they need to hear the messengers, if they are going to avoid the curse that God predicts will fall upon them.

Let's go back to chapter 3. We have found that these people are a very recalcitrant people, who have a controversy with God.

Verse 14: 'It is futile to serve God,' they were saying. 'It is worth nothing, it's empty, unreal, there is no advantage to it.' They were saying there was no profit in serving God: 'What did we gain?' they were saying. 'Where is the net worth of being an obedient follower of God? Where is the material prosperity, political influence and the like? Where's our cut?' They'd gone up to the front at the altar call, reconsecrated their lives and rededicated themselves over and over again. They'd brought their sacrifices, but no matter what they did, it seemed, there was no advantage. God didn't seem to be doing anything spectacular for them. There was no evidence that God was going to intervene in their history or in their nation.

There was no advantage in mourning repentance.

Their particular complaint was that God apparently wasn't going to distinguish between the evildoers and the godly. When was He going to act to separate them? When was He going to act to justify those who loved and served Him, and vindicate Himself in judgement against those who didn't?

Malachi writes that there is a day coming, the 'great and dreadful day of the LORD' (4:5); the day of the revelation of God's judgement, the day when God comes down into the situation, the day when the one who operates the whole universe will, as it were, appear to the universe and say, 'Time, gentlemen, please.'

The second coming of Christ to which he points in those words, will, says C. S. Lewis, be an intolerably frus-

trating thing. Perhaps you were going to get married next
month, or were going to get a rise, or were on the verge of
some great scientific discovery. You may be maturing some
great social and political reforms. And now of all moments,
God intervenes and Jesus returns. Malachi says a day is
coming when evil and good will be separated, when there
will be that distinction of which Clive spoke, between the
righteous and the wicked, those who serve God and those
who do not. He warns the people, 'You don't want that day
to come quickly or suddenly.' Because on that day God is
going to deal with evil; not just the mega-evil of society but
the micro-evil of your heart and mine. On that day He is
going to do a decisive judgement work. One of the most
solemn messages of the Bible is that judgement is coming.
We need to trumpet it to the society in which we live today:
'He has set a day when he will judge the world with justice
by the man he has appointed' (Acts 17:31)—Jesus Christ
the righteous one. Judgement is coming.

But in the midst of his message of judgement, Malachi
speaks of a group of people who are going to avoid judgement.

Who are the people that God blesses?

They are the people *who feared the LORD* (3:16). To fear
God means simply to take God seriously, to give God your
allegiance and the love, affection and trust of your heart.
To fear God means that I am afraid to hurt Him, that I am
afraid to break His heart and therefore to break His law. It
means that I want Him to have absolute pre-eminence in
my life. Those who fear God, trust Him and have committed their lives to Him; those who've come to the conclusion that frankly it's better to get right with God and be not
right with everybody else, because He is the most significant being in the universe and I need to be right with
Him—the people whom God blesses are people who fear
the Lord.

They are the people *who valued the Lord*. Verse 16:

'feared the LORD and honoured his name'. The Hebrew word translated 'honour' means 'think on something and put a value on it'. It means to take an inventory, or to use Paul's word in Philippians 4:8, to think on these things.

The people that God blesses are people who have weighed things up and looked at God and His name—at who God is and at all that God has done—and have come to the conclusion that God is their wealth, their prosperity, their greatest asset. 'Where your treasure is, there your heart will be also,' said Jesus (Matt. 6:21). 'As someone thinks in their heart, so are they', said Solomon (cf Prov. 27:19). And these people value the Lord. 'As the deer pants for the water, so my soul longs after you,' says the Psalmist (Ps. 42:1). 'All I once held dear, built my life upon, I've counted it loss … Only You, Jesus.' Can you say that this evening? Are you people who value the Lord?

God's promise is given to those, thirdly, *who share the Lord*. 'Those who feared the Lord talked with one another.' God never intended us to live solitary lives. You need the fellowship of God's people, and not just those superficial Christian acquaintances with whom you can socialise and have good times. You need people with whom you can speak about the things of God. The Puritans used to say, 'You need one good spiritual friend—a brother, a partner, someone with whom you can share in the things of God— or else you won't grow in the things of God.' Can I urge you to think seriously about Christian friendship? In our churches we have a lot of social friendship, but we know very little about Christian friendship. The redeemed of the Lord, those who feared the Lord, talked with one another.

The writer to the Hebrews said, 'Let us not give up meeting together, as some are in the habit of doing, but let us encourage one another'—and here's the context for Malachi—'and all the more as you see the Day approaching' (Heb. 10:25). Let's build up friendships in which we speak of the things of God.

What is the promise that God makes?

Again there are three things.

First, *He will hear and heed*. 'The Lord listened and heard,' verse 16. You know what the Lord said through the angel, to the father of John the Baptist? 'The Lord has heard your cry' (cf Luke 1:13). Do you know what God did to Simeon and Anna, those godly folk who were waiting for the redemption of Israel? The Lord heeded and heard.

Second, *He will record and remember*. Abraham believed God, and in so doing, the Bible says, he was accounted righteous. 'A scroll of remembrance was written in his presence concerning those who feared the Lord and honoured His name' (verse 16). Do you remember the great picture of the Day of Judgement in the Book of Revelation? 'Another book was opened, which is the Book of Life' (Rev. 20:12). But have you ever wondered what's in the first load of books? There are suggestions in the Bible that in them were inscribed all the prayers of God's people. Earlier in Revelation, we see all the prayers of God's people ascending, and they accumulated in a great bowl, until there came a moment in the economy of God when the fire of God was thrown into that bowl; and the prayers of the people of God and the fire of God, together mingled, were flung upon the earth to accomplish God's purposes. Don't give up praying! For if you are people who fear the Lord, a day is coming when the prayers of the saints and the fire of God together will accomplish God's purpose in our land and in our world.

The Psalmist says that all of your tears are listed in His scroll. God has written them down. All those nights you have cried and prayed for your loved ones, for your children, your parents, your spouse, your family members—all of those tears are recorded in His scroll. All those tears of loneliness because you are the only Christian in your family, or an abused spouse—they are all recorded in God's book. Brothers and sisters, nothing that you suffer is overlooked by your heavenly Father. It is all recorded in His book of remembrance.

And *He will choose and cherish*. '"They will be mine,"
says the LORD Almighty, "in the day when I make up my
treasured possession"' (verse 17). 'Mine' is emphatic in the
Hebrew. This has always been God's way. I think it was
Malcolm Muggeridge who said, 'I have never wanted a god
or feared a god or felt under any necessity to invent a god.
Unfortunately I am driven to the conclusion that God
wants me.'

'Mine,' says the Lord. He came to Israel and He said,
'My son' (cf Hos. 11:1). He comes for you and me and He
chooses us in Christ, before the foundation of the world (cf
Eph. 1:4); He redeems us by the blood of His Son, adopts
us into His family, seals us by His Holy Spirit, and sends
His Spirit into our hearts, enabling us to cry out, 'Abba,
Father' (cf Rom. 8:15). Isn't it great! 'Mine,' says the Lord.
'He called you to this through our gospel, that you might
share in the glory of our Lord Jesus Christ,' says Paul to the
Thessalonians (2 Thess. 2:14). Jesus gave us to redeem a
people for Himself, eager to do what is good. 'But you are a
chosen people, a royal priesthood, a holy nation, a people
belonging to God' (1 Pet. 2:9). 'Mine,' says the Lord.
That's what God says about you as a child of God this evening. He puts a circle of grace around you, and says, 'You
are Mine.'

And when the final day of judgement comes, Malachi
says, believers will be remembered and cared for. God will
spare them the judgement that's coming on the earth, and
the universe will see for itself the difference between the
righteous and the wicked, between the one who serves God
and the one who does not. Verse 17 indicates the righteous
will be spared on that day. In other words, ultimate judgement turns on a person's relationship to God. It is dependent on our returning to God (3:7). 'How great is the love
the Father has lavished on us, that we should be called
children of God! And that is what we are!' (1 John 3:1).

Where is the provision that God makes?

One of the problems in interpreting the Old Testament is
that when the Old Testament prophets describe the future,
they are simply describing what they see, almost in a flat
pictorial way.

We could look in a certain direction from this tent and
see two very strangely shaped hills. I might say, 'Look at
those funny hills!' From a purely pictorial point of view,
they look fairly close to one another. But if you try to walk
from one to the other, it takes quite a long time.

The prophets are describing what they see. They talk
about the first coming of Jesus and His second coming—
and they run it all together. They simply describe what's
going to happen. There's going to be judgement and
there's going to be mercy. There's going to be a kingly
reign and there's going to be a baby boy. There's going to
be one who will ride in triumph and there's going to be one
who'll be the suffering servant of the Lord. There's going
to be one who will tread all His enemies under His feet,
and there's going to be one who's going to be afflicted, de-
spised, and killed.

That's what they saw. And only the unfolding of history
has put what they saw into perspective. The Day of
Judgement is coming. But before that, there's another day
coming: the first coming of Jesus. Where is the provision
God makes for His people? It is to be found in a person
who in 4:2 is described as the sun.

He comes as the sun of righteousness

It's an image that goes back to Balaam the false prophet,
who called Him the star that would come out of Jacob
(Num. 24:17). It's picked up by Isaiah, who calls Him a
light to lighten the Gentiles (cf Isa. 42:6). You're familiar
with many references in Isaiah: 'The people walking in
darkness have seen a great light' (9:2), or Isaiah 60:1,
'Arise, shine, for your light has come, and the glory of the
LORD rises upon you'—The sun of righteousness.

Zechariah, the father of John the Baptist, cradling the

baby Christ, called him the rising sun from heaven (Luke 1:78). At His birth, Simeon called the Lord Jesus a light of revelation for the Gentiles and the glory of His people Israel (cf Luke 2:32). Jesus said, 'I am the light of the world' (John 8:12). The writer to the Hebrews says Jesus is 'the radiance of God's glory' (Heb. 1:3). And in the language of the Revelation of John, we are told that he saw Jesus glorified in heaven and His face shone like the sun in its strength (Rev. 1:16).

What is the provision that God makes for His people who fear, value and talk about Him? It is the provision of a person. It is the provision of Jesus. He is going to break into the world. Judgement is suspended until this one arrives. That day of dreadful reckoning is held back until this one comes—the sun bringing His warmth, light, understanding and life into the world. He is the sun, He is the sun of righteousness.

In Jeremiah 23:6 He is called 'the Lord our righteousness'. In Him righteousness is personified. What Malachi has been giving is an exposé of Israel, and this week we have discovered that Israel was unrighteous. But we have also seen that we are unrighteous. We can't stand back from this story and point the finger at the Jews of Malachi's day, saying how bad they are; we have seen ourselves here. Have you seen yourself here? Your boredom with the things of God? Your grasping attitude towards money, time and talents that you've held back from giving to God? Did you sit through last night with a sigh of relief that God hadn't spoken to you to commit your life in dedication to His work and service? As we have studied Malachi, we have discovered that it wasn't just the Jews of Malachi's day who were unrighteous.

But Jesus, the sun of righteousness, was going to please God entirely. There was not going to be one flaw in His character, not one twist in His temperament, not one defect in His personality, not one moment of conscious or unconscious disobedience. There was never going to be one iota of the law of God that He was not going to fulfil perfectly and with enthusiasm. In Jesus we see the shape and the substance of moral and social righteousness. We see it in His relationships, in His compassion to the hurting and the disadvantaged, in His indignation at hypocrisy, especially religious hypocrisy. We see it in His challenge to His accusers—'Which of you convicts me of sin?' We see it in the reaction of His executioner—'Surely this was a righteous man.' We hear it in the verdict of His judge—'I find no basis for a charge against him.' We hear it in the testimony of His friends—'He committed no sin and no deceit was found in his mouth.' We hear it in the Father's response to Him—'This is my beloved son with whom I am well pleased.'

Now, brothers and sisters, we need to stand back and look at the absolute perfection of righteousness that we find in our Lord Jesus. And we need to worship that. In Him there is an absolute credit of righteousness; in us there is a deficit of righteousness. Is that demoralising? But get this! We evangelicals are very good at preaching the cross, and that's good. The cross is all about what God has done for us in terms of the penalty for our having broken the law: the penalty, the wage of sin is death. Jesus died to bear our penalty. Theologians call that His passive righteousness, in that He was put to death. He suffered death, your death and mine, on the cross for you and for me, His blood shed for His people.

But there is an active righteousness of Jesus. He did that for us. He came to act on our behalf, and to be righteous on our behalf. He came to take our place, not only to bear our penalty but also to live our life. For the Bible says, 'For Christ died for sins once for all, the righteous for the unrighteous, to bring you to God' (1 Pet. 3:18). Now here's the deal. You give to Him your boredom with worship, your lack of enthusiasm for the things of God, and what does He give you? He gives to you the zeal of the Lord of Hosts that consumes Him as He goes into the temple. You give to Him your harshness; He gives to you His gentleness. He gives His truth, for your deception. He gives His forgiving spirit, for your critical spirit. He gives His purity, for your lust. His contentment, for your covetousness. The ministry of the Holy Spirit in this age is to convict the world of sin, and righteousness and judgement, and it points to Jesus. The Spirit of God points always to Jesus as the source of our righteousness. I want us as God's people this evening to find the Lord Jesus giving, not only His life to secure our freedom from the penalty, but His whole life and His whole obedience to us, to wrap us round in God's sight with the righteousness that is His; so that we become the righteousness of God in Him, so that God, looking at your life and mine, sees the absolute perfection and loveliness of our Lord Jesus Christ.

It isn't just that He died for me; He lived for me. It isn't just that He delivers me from the penalty of sin so that I don't go to hell; He prepares me to be clothed with those wonderful garments that will enable me to live in heaven. When you and I get to heaven we're going to be wrapped in those robes of righteousness, the wedding garment that will enable us to sit down at that great feast and enjoy that great party.

He comes to bring healing

Healing—don't be scared of the word. One of the great features of Jesus's life was that wherever He went He rolled back the frontiers of sickness and death. One scholar says that for that three-year period of His ministry, sickness was almost banished within Palestine. Wherever He went, the Gospels tell us, crowds and crowds of people were delivered mightily by His healing touch.

What is He doing? He is declaring His law on all the effects of sin. By expelling demons, by healing the sick, He is saying 'I have come to invade Satan's territory, to invade this world that is absolutely torn apart by sin. I've come to do something radical and new.' Of course His healing ministry went further than that. He healed relationships that were broken, He healed hearts that were broken. He healed the relationship between men and God as well as between man and his brother. He came to heal. He comes to heal your guilty conscience, to heal that relationship with a brother or sister with whom you have fallen out in your local church back there, with whom you'd find it very hard to be sitting, here in Keswick under this banner, 'All one in Christ Jesus'. He comes to give you the peace of God that passes all human understanding. Even now, from time to time, in His providence He heals both physically and spiritually, in order that the world may know that His ultimate purpose is one day to step back into this world and to heal us all, absolutely and finally and completely. He will raise us from the dead, give us resurrection bodies, and make all, altogether, at the same time, perfectly well for ever in a new heaven and a new earth where there will be healing for the nations. He comes with healing in His wings. And there's no doubt that if you allow the word of God to have its effect in your life this week, God will heal, restore, bring health back into your Christian life, if you'll let Him.

Where is the provision that God makes? It is to be found in a person who is the sun of righteousness, with healing in His wings. The whole point of this chapter is to point us to Jesus. It's to leave us looking open-mouthed at Him, to leave us nudging one another and saying, 'Is this what we have in Him? Is this the provision that God makes for us? Has God made provision, not only that I might not go to hell, but that right now, whatever I may be—whatever faults I may have, however many failings I may have, however much I may struggle with obedience— I am clothed with the righteousness of the Lord Jesus Christ, faultless to stand before the throne?'

No wonder then that when He comes, 'You will go out and leap like calves released from the stall.' I've seen it myself on a farm; the calves came out, they tripped one another up, their feet were clambering all over the place and it was as if they were drunk. And eventually they found their feet and their hind legs went up and they were absolutely exuberant with joy. That's the picture. When you come to know the sun of righteousness, when you know that God has dealt with your sin, what does it lead to? It leads to exuberant joy. Praise the Lord! To know that your sin is forgiven, that God regards you as being as righteous as His own Son, that there is therefore now no condemnation to those who are in Christ Jesus. To know that nothing can ever separate you from the love of God that is in Him. To know that death is not the end but it means going to be with the Lord, which is by far the best. To know that if you fall or fail tomorrow, it isn't the end of the story for you, that there is a way back to God from the dark paths of sin, there is a door that is open and you may go in. To know that there is daily pardon, there is power to resist temptation. To know that we are no longer bound to cave into Satan's attack, that one day we are going to share with Jesus, and the God of peace is shortly going to crush Satan under our feet.

To know that—doesn't it make you exuberant with joy?

We saw at the beginning that this book ends with a reference to the law and the curse. It's interesting that in the economy of God, that is where the Old Testament stops. Paul picks up the theme; by the works of the Lord shall no flesh be justified. Then comes Jesus, not to abolish the law but to fulfil it. He obeys it to the letter. On the cross He experiences—what? The curse: 'Cursed is everyone who is hung on a tree' (Gal. 3:13). 'All who rely on observing the law are under a curse, for it is written: "Cursed is everyone who does not continue to do everything written in the Book of the Law." Clearly no-one is justified before God by the law, because, "The righteous will live by faith"' (Gal. 3:10-11).

The Old Testament ends with the law that you can't keep, and a curse that you can't avoid. The New Testament proclaims the sun of righteousness who has kept the law and endured the curse. Have you come to Him? I tell you there is still a curse for those who are still outside of Christ Jesus. There is still a day of judgement that is going to come upon the world, for those who do not know God.

When Jesus comes to be admired by those who believe, He comes also in burning fire to consume all the enemies of God in that dreadful day of judgement. There is still a curse.

But the New Testament does not end on the note of a curse. It ends on the note of grace. 'The grace of our Lord Jesus Christ be with God's people' (Rev. 22:21). Can I say this evening to you: there is grace only for sinners. There is no grace for the righteous among us, for those who feel this word is for someone else, for those who smugly think in their self-satisfaction that all the hard words we've heard this week were for other people and not for them. There is no grace unless you yourself, within your own heart, are crying out to God for mercy. Where there is a humble heart, where there is a fear of the Lord, where there are those who value the Lord, where we speak about the Lord, there is great grace for us.

The New Testament ends not on a curse, but on grace, grace that is greater than all my sin. 'There is therefore now no condemnation to those who are in Christ Jesus.' Will you find your way there this evening with me? Let's pray together.

'Blessed are Those Who Mourn'
by Rev. Stephen Gaukroger
(From the Beatitudes series, Second Week)

Matthew 5:4

I am so grateful to God for the opportunity to be here at the Keswick Convention and to have the opportunity tonight to preach on this very moving, very profound verse in Matthew chapter 5. Our focus will be in a very narrow area—just one simple verse, which we'll quarry away at until we get to some of its profundity. If you have your Bible open as we go, that will be a great help.

Some years ago I was researching the Beatitudes, indeed the whole Sermon on the Mount, in the course of writing a commentary. I discovered that this Beatitude is different from the others in one particular way: that all the others are easy to understand, but hard to do or to be. We can work out what 'Blessed are the meek' or 'Blessed are the poor' mean; understanding them is not too difficult. But actually living like that, in the new kingdom lifestyle Jesus obviously had in mind, is another matter.

This Beatitude stands out in the list as different. It is hard to understand and hard to do, because everything is wrapped up in the meaning of the words 'mourn' and 'comfort'. And even in those simple words, there are all sorts of pitfalls for the unwary. However, in the complexity of some of this, it's my prayer tonight that many hundreds of us in this tent will go from this place newly comforted by God; and that wherever we are, whatever position we are in now, we will leave in a different state because we've engaged with this Beatitude.

The Sermon on the Mount (Matt. 5, 6 and 7) is, as

Jonathan Lamb told us on the opening night, a Christian manifesto—the manifesto of Jesus. Centuries before, the Jews had watched another man go up a hillside. Moses came down with the ten commandments from God. Here thousands of years later, another man who fulfilled those commandments completely is on another mountainside, bringing another message; the radical manifesto of what it is to live in His kingdom, to stand counter-culturally against the values and standards of the day, and to live out a lifestyle quite different from His contemporaries.

All of the Beatitudes stand strongly against the received wisdom of the day. J. B. Phillips, author of a famous Bible paraphrase, attempted to summarise how the Beatitudes would read if they were written in the twentieth century. He came up with this: 'Blessed are the pushers, for they get on in the world. Blessed are they who complain, for they get their way in the end. Blessed are the blasé, for they never worry over their own sins. Blessed are the slave-drivers, for they get results. Blessed are the knowledgeable, for they know their way around. Blessed are the trouble-makers, for they make people notice them.'

All the Beatitudes of Jesus stand strongly, confrontation-ally against where our culture is today. And this Beatitude is particularly contradictory; not just contradictory to the culture in which we find ourselves, but contradictory inter-nally. It seems to make the least sense at first reading. To make you aware of how sharp that contrast is, if 'blessed' means 'happy' then this Beatitude seems to say, 'Happy are the unhappy, happy are the sad, happy are those who mourn, for they will be comforted.'

The struggle with interpreting this verse is precisely that the great riches of the other Beatitudes call us into radical Christian living, hungering and thirsting after God, and meekness when everybody else is shoving and pushing to get their way. They address grand, profound themes. At first sight Jesus simply seems to be slipping in a word of very gentle pastoral concern—a good word, but seemingly out of place. Is He really saying, 'Blessed are all those who've endured a recent bereavement, because they will know the comfort of God'? That's a wonderful thing, but it seems out of keeping with the profundity of this whole passage. I think that what we will find as we unpack this particular verse is three strands being woven together. And Jesus's use of the word 'mourning', understood in these rich dimensions by first-century Jews listening to this sermon, will emerge for us with greater and greater clarity as we consider them now.

Blessed are those who mourn ...

There are nine words in the New Testament for 'mourn'. The word here is the strongest, the most in-your-face, the most confrontational of them all. It means 'to weep, to be in desperation'. But behind the word and the idea of mourning lies this rich tapestry that the word itself will obscure—unless we look at it carefully.

Words are strange things. What I say, you may not hear. What you think I said, I may not have said. Or I may have said it, but I didn't mean it. Or at least I didn't mean what I think I thought you heard I said. Some of you will leave this tent with completely different ideas of what tonight was about. Whatever is said, you will receive something different, perhaps.

A very affluent, swanky family in America paid a genealogist to research their family tree. But the genealogist came across a problem. 'It's Uncle George,' he told them. 'He was a murderer. He was executed in the electric chair. It's not going to look very good on your family tree. But don't worry,' he reassured them. 'I can sort it out. I'll write this: "Uncle George occupied a chair of applied electronics, at an important government institution. He was attached to his position by the strongest ties and his death came as a real shock."'

Words are strange things. They can obscure truth and reveal it. And in this deeply moving Beatitude, the words in English —'mourn' and 'comfort'—can, if we are not care-

ful, lead us into far narrower, more limited revelation than
they need. It seems to me that what we are faced here with
is a threefold strand of teaching in the ministry of Jesus. He
is saying, 'Blessed are those who mourn'. And they mourn
in three ways: for themselves, for their sins, and for society.
In those three ways this Beatitude calls the believer (and
believers in the plural, as the church) to the mourning that
is not mere therapeutic self-pity.

Mourning for ourselves

The widow of Nain (Luke 7) was a woman in mourning
for herself—fearful, sad, distraught at the loss of her loved
one. This is the classic meaning of the word 'to mourn':
bereavement, the loss of someone that we love. The Bible is
replete with stories of people who have lost a loved one.
For example, David and Absalom: a classic father-son example of desperation and loss, despite the horrors of the
son's behaviour. Blessed are those who mourn in this way.
And although it is probably the least significant of the
meanings of Jesus in this particular Beatitude, it is founda-
tional, because it is right to mourn. When we mourn for
ourselves we are not engaging in self-indulgence. This
verse is pastorally potent, long before psychiatrists started to
say that mourning and bereavement was a good healthy
thing to do psychologically.

It *is* a good and healthy thing psychologically. Many
Christians have failed to grieve over the physical death of a
loved one, because somehow we believed that if we grieved
(and particularly grieved openly), we were letting God
down; that our tears somehow denied the veracity of our
faith, as if somehow to express grief, anger and brokenness
was to say that God hadn't met me where I was supposed
to be. Far too many people believe that if we claim to be
filled with the Spirit, we cannot have space in our lives for
genuine mourning and grief. Do not believe it.

There are many people here tonight. I have prayed that
hundreds of you will come to a new place where your
mourning for yourself is turned into dancing (Jer. 31:13).

You may be experiencing the agony of the loss of a loved one, or it may be some other agony such as the anguish of a broken and severed relationship. On top of your mourning tonight, you may also be feeling guilt. Many of you are owed an apology by the church that has condemned your activity as wrong. Perhaps you've been involved in a divorce of some kind, and it may have been wrong, but they have failed to show you the love and compassion of Jesus in your pain. Blessed are those who mourn for themselves, because the great embodiment of the kingdom, Jesus Himself, will be your comfort.

I preached recently on the victory of Jesus over death, and the comfort that He brings. At the end of the service a lady put a piece of paper into my hand, on which was written, 'As someone living with terminal cancer, tonight's message filled my heart with joy. I do not want to die, but I can now approach God's throne boldly secure, in God's love, that I will be comforted by Him now and in eternity.'

This is not a God who leaves us alone. Jesus was talking about ordinary mourning, ordinary suffering, the loss of a loved one in bereavement, the pain and anguish of abuse in our lives of whatever kind it has been; the utter rejection some of us have felt by those whom we love. Jesus is not some distant God on a foreign planet. The incarnation demonstrates that the one who preached the Sermon on the Mount lives among us. The chief of police has walked the beat, the captain has been in the engine room. God was made man for us. And the certainty of the incarnation means that this Beatitude is no mere pompous, pious platitude—'Cheer up, you bereaved people, it'll all be all right.' Far from it, brothers and sisters.

Today is a crucial anniversary in the history of the world. On this day, 21 July at 3.56 a.m. British Standard Time, a man called Neil Armstrong got out of a space craft in 1969 and walked on the moon. Yet there's something even more important to celebrate tonight: God has walked on earth. And He is here in His comforting power tonight, not some theoretical abstraction, not some gospel of theory or philosophical reality alone; not a virtual reality, but real reality; God's healing touch on those who mourn.

Mourning for our sins

Secondly, Jesus is calling us to a mourning for our sins. The Jews would be familiar with this concept. The word 'mourning' used here would invoke for them all sorts of breast-beating at the actual physical demonstration. Some of you have seen pictures of the wailing wall in Jerusalem. Or you may have seen people in the Middle-Eastern countries—for example Iraqis or Iranians—beating their chests in frustration and pain and wailing over the loss of a leader, or some such event.

This Beatitude seems self-consciously to echo Psalm 51, where David in abject misery over his murder of Uriah and adultery with Bathsheba cries to God, 'Against you, you only, have I sinned.' The old saints writing years ago used a little Latin phrase, *Mea culpa*: 'I am guilty.' One of the reasons that much of our spiritual life is insipid and superficial is that we've never been truly sorry for our sin. We've wanted Pentecost, without the cost of the cross. And much superficiality and spiritual flabbiness in church life is because this Beatitude has not been grasped by the late-twentieth-century church that desperately needs afresh an abject mourning for the sinfulness in the human soul. We trivialise sin at our peril. When we do not mourn for it, God is mocked. When we mourn for ourselves, the call is to know His comfort; but only when we mourn for our sins and are truly aware of the horrors of what we are, does the flooding-in of forgiveness become a possibility. The church of Jesus for too long has wanted forgiveness without repentance. It's not on offer. There has to be deep-seated mourning.

My grandfather, who's now with the Lord, belonged to a particularly strict group of believers in the north of England. I won't mention the name of the denomination, because both the people who are left may be here tonight. But it was very strict. My grandfather made a spiritual gift out of misery. When we were growing up, it was nothing to hear him say a grace that would last almost twenty minutes. I'm not exaggerating; I wish I were. The grace would start often with this phrase, quoting Scripture: 'Dear Lord, I am a worm and no man.' And it would go downhill from there.

I don't want to go back to that constant, enveloping misery. I don't think it's appropriate. But the more I look back, I realise that my grandfather actually possessed—though I still think, inappropriately applied—a dimension that I sometimes lack. He was quite clear about his relationship with the Almighty God. He did know how sinful sin was. He mourned for his own sinfulness.

Brothers and sisters, we rob ourselves of spiritual power when we trivialise our own sinfulness. We will only be released into all that God has for us when we recognise it for what it is.

Mourning for our society

It is interesting that one the great prophetic statements, Isaiah 61:1-2 from which the manifesto of Jesus Himself emerges—'The Spirit of the Lord is upon me, to preach good news to the poor'—goes on to say, 'and the mourning will be comforted'. Those who have this desperate bleeding passionate heart for society, those who care for the needs of the world, those who see a culture in chaos, a world in crisis falling apart at the seams, those who agonise for their world—those people will ultimately be comforted.

Brothers and sisters, we are called to mourn for ourselves and to mourn for our sins. But the Bible is full of another kind of mourning of which Jesus was absolutely well aware; and that mourning was going to take Him with His kingdom manifesto to the cross itself. Societies, communities, everything in the world around Him needed to be addressed with this manifesto. And when the world in all its dishonour was compared with the manifesto, mourning was the result.

Nobody here, I guess, could fail to be moved by a young

teenager's struggles to know what to do when she discovers that she's pregnant. Sometimes abortion is the result, and we may believe that girl made the wrong decision. But who can fail to feel her pain? Or we may not understand the struggles of a young man grappling with his sexuality, not knowing whether he can give voice to inner feelings he doesn't seem able to control. We may not approve of his choices; but who here has been involved in pastoral care and can fail to anguish with people like him?

Take society as a whole, let alone our pastoral care for those who struggle. I want a world where my children can walk the streets of their towns and villages in safety. I want a world where casual abortion is not a feature of society. I don't want to live in a world where there's pressure to administer euthanasia to the elderly; where we hurry the young prematurely out of the womb to their death, and hurry the old prematurely to the tomb. I know that God hates what's happening in our world. He's angry at the swollen distended bellies of the hungry children, the homelessness, the poverty, the desperation, the taking of innocent life at every level.

That fact should cause us to live out the reality of this Beatitude, mourning for our society and the sick and tragic state in which it finds itself. But most of us as believers have become immune to the horrors of our society. Somehow we have become desensitised. Isn't that what television, the press and other media are doing—desensitising us to the horrors of the world? I want to be in a church that is so radically aware of this manifesto that it knows how to mourn for the sins of the community around it.

Jesus says, 'What you see is not normal, it's abnormal. I want to bring My normality.' I want to be part of a church—don't you?—as this millennium comes to a close, that believes, lives and dies by these principles, and stands against the world in all its sinfulness and, with horror and pain, mourns for a world fallen far from God's grace, desperate to engage His truth. Don't you want to be part of that world? The hellish suffering in Cambodia is but one example of a world gone wrong. Jesus calls the church to mourn for ourselves, for our sins, and for our society, in order to fully understand what it is to be comforted. Until we mourn like that, how can we know His comfort?

... For they will be comforted

Now, what does it mean to be comforted? What's the converse of mourning? The word 'comfort' is from a Latin word. It means simply 'with strength'. The original word is slightly more subtle than that. It means 'to crawl alongside to help'. It's translated in John's Gospel, for example, sometimes as 'comforter', and sometimes as 'counsellor'.

But there is a subtle nuance that we miss if we're not very careful. 'Mourning' could well be translated 'brokenness'. Let me translate this verse for you. 'Blessed are those who are broken in pieces—by their selves, their sins or their society—for they will be made complete, stuck back together again.'

Many who mourn the loss of a loved one feel incomplete. Their loved one is not there. It's like losing a limb; something's missing. The glorious truth of the gospel is that the day is coming when all brokenness will be mended and every wrong thing will be put right and made totally complete. That's the song of the universe. We hear it in our most faithful moments. We just know it's true. God will put all those wrong things right, because somehow He's making it complete and giving His comfort.

Let me try to illustrate that. Completeness is something we hear with our ear. [*At this point Rev. Gaukroger sat down at a piano.*] These chords I'm playing are in C major. Chords and harmonies are the basis of music. You all know it innately, the musical ones know it in theory ... That's the base note of the C major chord ... that's the third above it ... that's the fifth above it ... and that's the octave completed. Almost all choruses and songs end with something called a perfect cadence, or with a plagal cadence [*playing examples of cadences*].

Years ago, Wolfgang Amadeus Mozart at the age of eight or nine understood things in the musical realm that many of us are never going to aspire to. His father could never get him out of bed in the morning. So he used to play chords like these on the piano [*playing a series of chords that maddeningly never quite reach a resolution*]. Well, you all know that's got to go somewhere! So he kept on playing them until little Wolfgang Amadeus came belting down the stairs and … [*strikes a resounding chord that satisfyingly brings the sequence to a conclusion*].

We *hear* the sound of completeness. Those technical terms don't really make one wit of difference. What matters is that to all of us, musical or not, completion happens. If we just leave it hanging in the air it is enormously frustrating, just as it was to the young Mozart.

Tragically, much of life is enormously frustrating to the believer at those three levels of mourning. We anguish over loss: 'God, I feel incomplete, it's hopeless.' We mourn for our sins: 'When am I ever going to behave in a way that pleases God?' We mourn for our society: 'When will this world ever get back to God's values and standards?' And it's as if God points us at all these things and His kingdom's future dimension—they will be comforted. One day it will all be complete. It will be put right, we will be comforted. The emphasis of modern society is this: 'Party now, don't worry about the future.' The emphasis of Scripture is this: 'Mourn now, and party for ever.' That's the gospel.

To paraphrase D. L. Moody: one day you will hear that Stephen Gaukroger has died. Do not believe it. I will be more alive on that day than I have ever been. We are not going from the land of the living to the land of the dead, we are going from the land of the dead to the land of the living. That's why we can say, 'Blessed are those who mourn, for they shall be comforted.' They shall be completed. They shall be drawn alongside, by Jesus Christ.

So those who mourn for the anguish of a circumstance that seems to have wrecked their life beyond repair; who mourn for our own rebellion, who agonise over the brokenness of society—all of that mourning will one day, on that great day, be wrapped up in His glorious completeness, some of which we will experience now. This future is both now and not yet.

We will be comforted now, but totally comforted on that great day when, according to Scripture, there'll be no more tears, death or pain. Because Jesus, the one who instituted the kingdom manifesto, has broken through all the mourning and is alive for ever: out of death itself, because of the resurrection. This manifesto would have been rotting away somewhere, or gathering dust, had it not been for the resurrection. But the resurrection fills the manifesto with reality. Jesus didn't just teach this, He rose from the dead in order to give us power to experience it.

Tonight I, in all my weakness, can know something of the comfort of God. Not the full comfort, for that complete comfort will only be known on that great day. But the day is coming when there will be a wonderful, glorious, absolute completeness for all of us. It may be that tonight God is calling some to know healing from their mourning for themselves. He's calling others of us to know what it means to treat our sins seriously in order that we can have the remedy. And He's certainly calling the whole church of Jesus in the world to take seriously the rebellion of the planet against Him. Because as long as they stay rebellious and not mourning for their sins, they'll be depriving themselves of the eternal comfort He can bring. How we long, in all our pain, to receive the comfort of the One who said to me and to you and all of us, 'Come unto me all those of you who labour and are heavy laden, and I will give you rest.' What a wonderful gospel we have; not a denial of pain, but the presence of His wonderful victory.

'Blessed are Those who Hunger and Thirst For Righteousness'
by Rev. Vaughan Roberts
(From the Beatitudes Series, Second Week)
Matthew 5:6

It's a beautiful sunny day and a packed house at Lord's Cricket Ground. They're are all on their feet cheering the batsman back to that famous pavilion. He's just scored a debut century, saving England from an appalling situation. The selectors are grinning smugly at the Press box, for the Press has pilloried them for selecting an unknown Oxford clergyman who has never played first-class cricket before in his life —certainly not a Test Match.

I have to say that's only going to happen in my dreams. I'm a lousy cricketer. But what's your great ambition? When your mind switches into neutral and you begin to dream dreams, what do you want Jim to fix for you? Perhaps a meeting with a celebrity—the Queen, or Posh Spice? (She's a singer, by the way, if I can flatter her with that title). Perhaps yours, like mine, is a sporting ambition. Maybe it's something to do with your work or family. Whatever it is, there's nothing wrong with the things I've mentioned. But none of them represents God's great longing for your life and for mine. His passionate ambition for us is that we should be holy, and He wants us to share that longing. In the words of Jesus, He wants us to be those who hunger and thirst for righteousness. It's one of His most emphatic Beatitudes: 'Blessed are those who hunger and thirst for righteousness, for they will be filled.'

Very few, if any of us, have ever really known what it is to be hungry or thirsty. Ours is a society of plenty. A supermarket recently advertised 103 types of cheese from thirteen countries. With all that food around, it's hardly surprising that we don't really know what hunger is. We might have missed the odd meal now and then, but that's as far as it's gone.

And yet even in this society of plenty I think we can begin to understand what Jesus means by hunger and thirst. To hunger and thirst means to have an urgent desire; to crave for something like a starving beggar pleading for bread; like a weary traveller in the desert longing for water.

By 'righteousness' Jesus means a way of life that pleases God and reflects His standards. He's not using the word here in the Pauline sense of 'justification', of being in the right with God. He's referring to a longing to be holy. Those who hunger and thirst for righteousness, have, in Jim Packer's famous phrase, 'a passion for holiness'. They long to see it, both in their own lives and the world at large. And, I'm afraid, I have to confess that in my life—and I guess it's the same with you—desire to be like Christ does not dominate me, at least not for very much of the time.

This longing for holiness is unfashionable in the Christian world. Make a list of Christian books published this year; you'll find Christian cookery books, Christian joke books, even Christian slimming books. But I think you'll find very few on the subject of holiness. We have to admit that we don't often have that passionate longing to be like Jesus. Our lives are dominated by other ambitions. That's why this Beatitud comes as a powerful challenge to our complacency and self-righteousness.

We are going to spend the rest of our time in Galatians 5:16-26. These verses are not an exposition of our Beatitude, but they are closely related to our theme of righteousness. From what Paul says, I want to consider three steps that are necessary if we are to grow in righteousness and become more like Jesus. First,

A recognition of our sin

If you are familiar with Paul's letter to the Galatians, you'll know that for much of it Paul has been stressing that we have been freed from the bondage to the law. We don't have to try desperately to live up to God's perfect standards. And that's a huge relief, because as long as we have to live up to those standards before we can get right with God, we're in bondage. We can never live up to that standard.

But Paul comes with wonderful good news, good news that many of us know (and which some may not yet have accepted for themselves). Jesus Christ did it all! We don't have to do anything ultimately, except to receive what He did for us, dying in our place on the cross. It's a wonderful message of justification by faith; getting in the right with God not through what we do, but through what Jesus Christ has done.

But whenever that message is preached, there's always a danger it will be misunderstood. Some might say, 'If it all depends on what Jesus Christ has done, it doesn't really matter how I live. I can just accept His death on my behalf as an insurance policy for the life to come, and then carry on living the good life, doing whatever I want.' So in the last chapters of the letter, Paul deals with that kind of thinking. He makes it very clear that as Christians who are justified by faith, it still matters very much how we live. We are to live godly lives.

We need to understand that won't be easy for us. We are being called to live in a way that is profoundly unnatural for us as sinful human beings. That's very clear in verses 19-21, where he is not just describing the non-Christian. He's speaking about 'the desires of the sinful nature' (more literally 'the desires of the flesh'). He's speaking about the natural 'us', what we're like before God intervenes in our lives. We are all like this and we continue to be like this by nature after coming to Christ, although He's changing us wonderfully. The natural us without God at work in our lives is a sinful us, a sinful nature. That's what we are like. And yet so often as Christians we forget it.

One of the reasons we don't hunger and thirst for righteousness is that we are quite satisfied with ourselves as we are. You don't go round looking for a meal if you feel full. And so often we are smug and self-satisfied, though in our more humble moments we would admit we are not perfect. But we don't do anything really bad. We are good people. We are righteous people. Sometimes you hear people give testimonies that give the impression that before their conversion they were dreadful, they did all sorts of wicked things; but now—well, it's all wonderful! 'Once I was so sinful, now I am so smug.' But do we recognise the truth? 'Once I was so sinful, now I am so sinful.' It's time to stop believing the lie and face reality. We are very sinful.

A little boy, playing spacemen, looked for a space helmet and found a vase that was just right. He he put it on his head and had a great time playing in it. At the end of the game he tried to take it off. It wouldn't come. He went to his mum, but she couldn't get it off. She panicked and rang her husband at his office. 'Shall I break it?' He said, 'Don't you dare! I had it valued last week, it's priceless. Take him to Casualty, they'll sort him out.' She was about to get the car out when she realised it was being serviced. She was going to have to go by public transport. She didn't like the idea at all; but then she had a brainwave. She told the boy to put on his school blazer; at once it made him look respectable. And before they went out of the door, she grabbed his school cap and placed it on his head.

That's a picture of how we are with our human nature. There is something badly wrong, and if we only had eyes to see it, it would be very obvious. Yet we try to hide it with our little cap of respectability and religion. We go to church, we come to Keswick, we are nice people, we are good people. And so often we fool other people. You look around, and I look at you, and you look very nice. I'm fooled. Sometimes, we even fool ourselves. We begin to believe the lie; we think, 'Maybe I am quite respectable and quite nice.' But God isn't fooled. He doesn't just look at that blazer and the cap, He sees right through to our hearts. He sees us when no-one else is looking, He knows what we are like, and it's time to stop pushing those skeletons to the back of the cupboard and to face up to them, acknowledging the truth. We are sinful people.

There's a gruesome list in verses 19-21 of the kind of behaviour that flows from our sinful nature. Remember, it is still with us; sadly, we didn't leave it behind when we came to Christ. We are not meant to understand that, left to ourselves, we'll exhibit all of these sins; but these are the kinds of actions and attitudes that a sinful nature produces in us.

Paul begins (verse 19), 'The acts of the sinful nature are obvious.' He begins with warped sexual behaviour, 'sexual immorality, impurity and debauchery'. Which of us here this evening can honestly say we are blameless in this area? In a group of this size, there will be some who are engaged in immoral sexual activity. And even if we are not actually committing adultery, what books, what films, what magazines do we read and watch and enjoy? What jokes do we enjoy and laugh at? What's going on in our thought lives?

In verse 20 there's false religion: 'idolatry and witchcraft'. Perhaps before turning to Christ you were involved in other religion, or occult practices. It can be a big problem for those working in other cultures, as young converts are tempted back into their old ways. But of course idolatry is broader than that. It's any religion that's not based on God's revelation of Himself in His word and through Jesus Christ. We're tempted to say, 'I know the Bible says that, but I really don't like it. I know that's what God's like, but I wish He weren't.' We begin to drift towards idolatry.

Then, fractured relationships; a long list. 'Hatred, discord, jealousy, fits of rage, selfish ambition, dissensions, factions and envy'. Which of us can say we are not guilty of some of these? By sinful nature, we are very competitive. We long to get our own way. That's what selfish ambition is all about. We join with those who want the same as us. Factions are, sadly, very much a feature of church life. Of course we justify them. We are fighting together in a noble cause. But so often our discord and dissension stems simply from our pride; we want to come out on top. And when we don't, and others prevail, we are full of jealousy, envy, even fits of rage. Can we really say there's no hint of these things in our relationships at home or at church or in the work place or in the neighbourhood?

We are too easily satisfied with ourselves because we don't reckon these to be really bad sins. We've got a sort of system. The really bad sins tend to be things we don't do. I don't know what you don't do, but whatever it is, it's at the top of the list. 'Oh, dreadful! Those people who do x, y, z.' And the sins that don't really matter tend to be the sins that we do. How many of us would say that these are particularly serious sins? And yet they are. God takes them very seriously, because He's passionately concerned with the quality of our relationships; yet for us it's neither here nor there.

Verse 21 mentions riotous excess; 'drunkenness, orgies'. I work among students, and sadly I hear often of Christian students who get drunk or get involved with drugs. There's the kind of life-style that our natural selves, our sinful natures, engage in. In some people the effects are very obvious and outrageous. Others of us are outwardly respectable. We've got the blazer on, we've got the cap on our heads—but let's not fool ourselves. There's something badly wrong with us. The seeds of all these sins lie embedded deep within us, and we've allowed some of them to grow.

There's a very solemn warning in verse 21. Remember, Paul is speaking to Christians. 'I warn you, as I did before, that those who live like this will not inherit the kingdom of God.' It matters how you live, says Paul. If you follow the sinful nature, it shows that you've never really put your trust in Christ, and you face the judgement that comes on the unbeliever. Strong words; we can't go on applying them to other people, they are written to us and our sinful nature. We need to recognise our sin. It's the first step in growing in righteousness and longing to be like Christ. If we don't, we won't think we need help and we won't hunger and thirst for this change.

A dependence on God's Spirit

Once we accept the truth that left to ourselves, our natural bias is always to oppose God and disobey His standards, we'll see how utterly dependent we are on supernatural help if we are to change and grow in holiness.

That is not a popular message today. We are forever being told that we can do it all, that the power lies within. Norman Vincent Peale's *The Power of Positive Thinking*, has sold over 15,000,000 copies. It begins with these words: 'Believe in yourself, have faith in your abilities.' Gudrun Kretschmann writes in the same vein in *Ten Keys to Prosperity*: 'We have the power to build and shape our lives in the way we choose and desire.' We can do it, that's the message. We've got the power, as a recent song puts it.

It isn't true. On our own we are helpless. If we want to become like Christ, it's not just a question of pulling up our spiritual socks and saying, 'Well I'm going to be a nicer person from now on.' It's not even good enough for God to say, 'Right, I've justified you, you've put your faith in Christ, now you're okay with Me. Over there you'll see My law written up. Just get on and obey it, would you.' It's not enough, because I don't have the power within me, even as a forgiven sinner, to obey those standards and the law.

The very good news, which Paul makes clear in this letter, is that once we've come to Christ, God doesn't simply point to letters of stone on the wall and say, 'Now get on with it.' He sends us His Spirit to live within our hearts. He is mentioned seven times in these verses. There's a great contrast—and in that contrast lies the gospel—between verses 19-21, the acts of the sinful nature, and verses 22-23, the fruit of the Spirit. That word 'fruit' makes its own point. If we begin to see these qualities at work in our lives, we can't congratulate ourselves. They're the fruit of the Spirit. They are the result of His working in our lives, and they are wonderful qualities: love, joy, peace, patience, kindness, goodness, faithfulness, gentleness, self-control.

Notice that these qualities are mainly concerned with our relationships, both with God and with other people.

That's the great longing of the Holy Spirit, to see us relating well to God and to one another. So much of modern Christianity is self-obsessed. We expect the Holy Spirit to give us great experiences, to make us feel good about ourselves. We go to Christian meetings to see what we can get out of them. But that's not the main concern of the Spirit. He is far more concerned with the quality of our relationships than with the quality of our experiences. Paul's is a marvellous list of characteristics, it's the kind of life that Jesus lived when He was on earth.

Paul comments (verse 23), 'Against such things there is no law.' As one commentator has put it, a vine doesn't produce grapes by Act of Parliament; they are the fruit of the vine's own life. Similarly these qualities can't be produced simply by the demand of some law—even God's law. They are the fruit of the divine nature that has been planted in our lives by the Spirit.

On our own we are helpless. But we are not on our own. God has sent us His Spirit, and if we want to grow in Christ-likeness we need to be dependent on Him, because He can change us utterly.

Not long after the war, a family of hill-billies was crossing America, heading for the West. They hadn't been to a big city before and were very excited when they ended up in one. Dad was very keen to go to a posh modern hotel, so they parked their car outside, and he and his son went inside. They were amazed as they looked around at the huge impressive opulence. They noticed a little cubicle. They'd never seen a lift before so they stared at it, quite unable to work out what it was for. An old lady hobbled towards the lift and went inside. The door closed. About a minute later, the door opened and out came a stunningly good-looking young woman. The man couldn't stop staring. Without turning his head he patted his son's arm and said, 'Go get your mother, son.'

It's as if God pats us on the shoulder and says, 'Go get your sinful nature, and bring it to the wonder-working God who can bring about amazing transformation.' We might feel spiritually very grimy, dirty and ugly. But God can make us beautiful by the work of His Holy Spirit in our lives. Are you finding it hard to live up to God's standards as a Christian? We all do. As we look around each other at Keswick, it can be very discouraging. You look at the person next to you and you think they look so solid. 'They've got it sussed in the Christian life. There's no way that they could ever experience some of the battles that I go through.' Don't believe it. We all face these battles. Some here tonight are very conscious, at this very moment, of the battle against sin. Maybe it's one particular sin you've been struggling against for years. You don't seem to be getting anywhere, you are tempted to give up. You say to yourself, 'What's the point?' Don't despair, there is hope.

Others of you have begun to be aware how much needs to be changed in your life. Maybe God, through the teaching this week, has drawn to your attention particular things; and you think, 'I don't know why I even bother to try. My sins are so massive, and I am so weak. I can't do it.' You're absolutely right; you can't. But you are not alone. Don't despair! God has given us His Spirit, the mighty, powerful presence of God. He can do all things. He can produce His fruit even in the most unpromising soil.

Have we begun to recognise the truth about ourselves, how sinful we are, how much we need to change? If so, we'll know something of that hunger and thirst for righteousness of which Jesus speaks. Remember that Jesus has good news for those who are hungry and thirsty. He says, 'They will be filled.' We'll only see that perfectly in heaven, but even in this sinful world we can expect that promise partially to be fulfilled. We don't have to go on being defeated by temptation again, and again, and again—a constant catalogue of despair and defeat. We can expect change in our lives. Not because we are special—we are not; not because we've got power—we haven't; but because God the Spirit has massive power, and He is in our lives. Let's recognise our own sin. But then let's turn away from ourselves and depend on God's Spirit. He can change us.

A determination to work at it

So finally, if we want to see change in our lives, if we want to grow more into the likeness of Jesus Christ, we will need determination to work at it.

If I just stopped after my second point, there'd be a great danger that some of you would have gone away and misunderstood me totally. You'd have reckoned, 'I don't have to do anything, really. God the Spirit is with me, He'll do it. If I need to change I'll just let Him do the work.' The old saying was, 'Let go and let God' (or as it was once awfully put, 'Don't wrestle, only nestle'). Sit back, leave it to the Spirit, without engaging in the battle ourselves.

That is a serious misunderstanding. Paul in these verses insists that you and I have an important role. That's why he pleads with us in verse 16: 'So I say, live by the Spirit.' You've got something to do. You're not to sit back and wait for God the Holy Spirit, like some cosmic superman, to zoom down and do it all for us while we sit back and watch, like Lois Lane, from the sidelines. We are involved.

If we choose to go the way of the Spirit, there's great encouragement. 'You will not gratify the desires of the sinful nature.' You will be able to resist temptation. But first we must make that decision to go the Spirit's way, and often that is very hard. It's not automatic. There's an urgency about Paul's appeal in verse 16, because verse 17 tells us we are in a battle. 'For the sinful nature desires what is contrary to the Spirit, and the Spirit what is contrary to the sinful nature. They are in conflict with other, so that you do not do what you want.'

Struggle, says Paul, is part and parcel of the Christian life. It's as if we've got two natures. We've got the old sinful one that sadly doesn't miraculously disappear when we come to Christ, and is still very much there; as each of us, if we're honest, will accept. But that's not all there is to us. God has filled us with His Holy Spirit. There's a tug-of-war going on all the time between our natural self without God (the sinful nature), and our new nature implanted by the Spirit of God.

How are we going to go the way of the Spirit? By conscious effort. We need to make the choice. Every time a temptation comes, I am aware of those two voices; the voice of the sinful nature saying, 'Go on, everyone does it! You really haven't lived until you've done x, y, z. Treat yourself! Anyway, Jesus Christ died for you, He'll understand. He's forgiven you anyway. It doesn't matter if you sin just this once.' And the voice goes on and on. Then there's another quiet voice that says, 'No. Go God's way. You know what's right. Jesus Christ died for you, He loves you—live for Him.' And I've got a choice; I can go either way each time. It takes effort to say, 'I am going to go the Spirit's way, I'm determined to do it.'

So once again Paul appeals to us. Having considered the fruit of the Spirit in verses 22-23, he now explains something about ourselves: 'Those who belong to Christ Jesus have crucified the sinful nature with its passions and desires' (verse 24). 'Have'. It's the past tense. He's talking about our conversion. When you and I became Christians, we made a decision to submit to Christ as Lord, to go His way through life, the Spirit's way, not the way of our sinful nature. In effect, we pick up that sinful nature, nail it to a cross and say, 'That's finished, I don't want anything more to do with it, it's dead, I've done with it.'

Have you ever done that? If you haven't, you are not—dare I say it—a Christian. It might have happened over a period of time, but a Christian is someone who has both believed and repented. Repentance means saying, 'I don't want to go the way of the sinful nature any more. I've done with it. From now on I want to go God's way.' Of course that's what you've done. Those who belong to Christ Jesus have crucified the sinful nature.

Having made such a clear renunciation of sin, how can we go back to it? Of course, we all do so day after day. We go back to that cross where our sinful nature is hanging and we nurse it, we stroke it. We almost take it down again, we indulge it. Paul would say, 'No, you've finished with that, you crucified it.'

He goes on (verse 25), 'Since we live by the Spirit'. He's talking about us now. We are those who as Christians live by the Spirit of God. Our spiritual life exists because God the Holy Spirit lives within us. We are new people, we have been born again. Since we live by the Spirit we have a responsibility. He doesn't say, therefore, we can just sit back and let the Spirit do it all. Since we live by the Spirit, let us keep in step with the Spirit. That is our responsibility. It's hard work.

Think of the temptation you are battling with at the moment. I don't know what it is, it'll be different for each one of us. You've been failing, you've fallen again and again. Don't expect a miracle; at least, not this kind of miracle. Don't expect God to zoom in and remove it. He doesn't, always. Some people battle with the same temptation all their lives and will do so till the day they die. Don't expect that if you simply sit back, God will help you to defeat it without any struggle on your part. It won't happen that way. We are to keep in step with the Spirit. That means that we move as the Spirit moves. You've got that sin down; and you want to take the axe to kill it.; don't expect God to do it all for you. It's as we pick up the axe that we find God's Spirit giving us the power to wield it.

A German wood-carver was a brilliant craftsman. He was one of the best. But he was near the end of his life and some of the old skills had disappeared. He'd retired, and was living with his son who was also a wood-carver. He carried on working at wood day after day. But it wasn't the same; it wasn't as good. It broke the son's heart to see the old man past his prime. So every night, after his father had gone to bed, the son got out his tools and finished his father's work off, smoothing off the rough edges, making it look beautiful.

It's rather like that with us. It is as we work and do our best—so often our feeble best—we find that God the Spirit works as well. As we work, God works.

Since we live by the Spirit, let's work at it. It'll take hard work. I still long to make that century for England at

Lords. In fact, if I'm honest with you I've done it many times in my dreams, I've received that standing ovation, I've had that whole crowd on its feet. I don't know what you dream about, but the challenge of the word of God from that Beatitude is that our great longing, our hunger, our thirst, should be to be like Jesus; to long to be righteous. Jesus said, 'Blessed are those who hunger and thirst for righteousness.' Much of the time, those words convict us. Let's make sure we leave this tent this evening longing to be like Christ.

As we draw to a close, I want you to think what that will mean in terms of practical action. It's not good enough to leave and completely forget what God has said. So let's be quiet for a moment and think about what we've heard from the word of God.

First we need to recognise our sin, to repent of our self-righteousness, to acknowledge before God the wickedness of our hearts. In recognising our sin, we need to depend on God's Spirit. If we belong to Christ He lives within us; let's ask Him once again to fill us, to give us His desires and His power to fulfil them. Let's acknowledge that without Him we can do nothing. Then finally we need a determination to work at it. Let's ask for forgiveness for those different areas in our lives in which we've been disobedient to God. Some of you need to make quite specific resolves. You know things are wrong. Sort it out tonight. Determine to change. We'll not be perfect this side of heaven, but with the help of God's Spirit, we can be more like Christ.

Jesus said, 'Blessed are those who hunger and thirst for righteousness, for they will be filled.' Lord God, please give us more of that hunger, more of that thirst. Please change us so that more and more, we might become like Jesus. For His name's sake.

Keswick 1997
Tapes, Videos and Books

Catalogues and price lists of audio tapes of the Keswick
Convention platform ministry, including much not
included in the present book, can be obtained from:

ICC (International Christian Communications)
Silverdale Road
Eastbourne
East Sussex BN20 7AB.

Details of videos of selected sessions can be obtained from:

Mr Dave Armstrong
STV Videos
Box 299
Bromley, Kent BR2 9XB.

Some previous annual Keswick volumes (all published by
STL/OM) are still in print, and can be ordered from:
The Keswick Convention Centre, Skiddaw Street,
Keswick, Cumbria CA12 4BY;
from your local Christian bookseller;
or direct from the publishers, OM Publishing, STL Ltd,
PO Box 300, Carlisle, Cumbria CA3 0QS, England UK.

Keswick 1998

The annual Keswick Convention takes place each July at the heart of England's beautiful Lake District. The two separate weeks of the Convention offer an unparalleled opportunity for listening to gifted Bible exposition, experiencing Christian fellowship with believers from all over the world, and enjoying something of the unspoilt grandeur of God's creation.

Each of the two weeks has a series of five morning Bible Readings, followed by other addresses throughout the rest of the day. The programme in the second week is a little less intensive, and it is often referred to as 'Holiday Week'. There are also regular meetings throughout the fortnight for young people, and a Children's Holiday Club.

The dates for the 1998 Keswick Convention are 11-18 July (Convention Week) and 18-25 July (Holiday Week). The Bible Reading speakers are Rev. Dr Chris Wright and Rev. Alistair Begg respectively. Other speakers during the fortnight include Dr Steve Brady, Mr Dick Dowsett, Mr Jonathan Lamb, Rev. Hugh Palmer and others.

For further information, write to:

The Administrator
Keswick Convention Centre
Skiddaw Street, Keswick
Cumbria CA12 4BY
Telephone: 017687 72589